LOVE YOU MADLY

MICHAEL FLEEMAN

St. Martin's Paperbacks

LOVE YOU MADLY

Copyright © 2011 by Michael Fleeman.

Cover photo of Rachelle Waterman © Brian Wallace / *Juneau Empire*. Cover photo of woman in frame © Dana Hursey / Masterfile. Background photo on cover © IndexStock / SuperStock.

For information address St. Martin's Press, 175 Fifth Avenue, New York, NY 10010.

EAN: 978-0-312-53089-1

Printed in the United States of America

St. Martin's Paperbacks edition / November 2011

St. Martin's Paperbacks are published by St. Martin's Press, 175 Fifth Avenue, New York, NY 10010.

10 9 8 7 6 5 4 3 2

"Just to let everyone know, my mother was murdered."
—Rachelle Waterman on her blog,
My Crappy Life, November 18, 2004

CHAPTER ONE

A night of frigid, blustery winds and light snow turned into a wet, gray morning, the clouds hanging low over the mountains of the glacier-carved valley. As he drove his four-wheel-drive Ford Expedition, Alaska state trooper Bob Claus kept an eye out for black-tailed deer darting onto the slick two-lane road. It was a weekend in November 2004, and the woods would be full of deer, and, Claus knew, men with high-powered rifles.

The road took Claus past familiar scenery: briny inlets, trout-filled streams, snowcapped ridges thousands of feet high and forests of spruce interrupted every few miles by the ravages of clear-cutting, the stumps standing gray like tombstones. The side of one mountain to his left was scraped clean of timber from a 1980s clear cut.

Even after a decade, the scenery never ceased to amaze Claus, an Illinois transplant, just as the scars from logging always saddened him. As one of two troopers, Bob Claus had patrolled wild and sparsely populated Prince of Wales Island for more ten years, working out of a small wood-framed building in Klawock, an ancient Indian fishing village that marks its heritage with a hilltop stand of totem poles.

Driving north out of Klawock, Claus was responding to a call that had come in to the trooper post about noon. No apparent danger loomed, just the prospect of a long cold day in the rain, but Claus had quickly learned that every venture in rural Alaska carried risks that no city policeman could imagine.

Prince of Wales Island is the largest of the islands in Alaska's southern archipelago, about the size of Delaware, but it has only 250 miles of designated road—100 miles paved, the rest compacted gravel, full of potholes and wash-outs. A routine call could keep him out of the office for hours or days; a complicated call could turn disastrous quickly. Backup—if it could be summoned—might take hours to arrive. Most locations had spotty radio and cell phone reception, and medical services were minimal. Ambulances were converted pickups. The island has one twenty-four-hour doctor-staffed clinic in Klawock. The closest hospital was in Ketchikan, and no road went there. It was reachable by medevac helicopter, floatplane, or ferry.

To prepare for anything, Claus kept the Expedition stocked with camping supplies to last two to three days in the woods, boots with spikes for walking through dense forests, a stretcher, oxygen tanks, and a first-aid kit. He had the tools of investigation and crime scene analysis: tape measure, rules, evidence bags. For protection from man or beast—bears also prowled the woods this time of year, fattening up for winter hibernation—the truck was armed with rifles, shotguns, hand-guns, and lots of ammunition. Claus wore one Kevlar vest and kept a second as a spare.

He took a second precaution this time: an Alaska Department of Fish and Game trooper who shared office space with him accompanied him in the vehicle that followed.

His route this Sunday afternoon took him twenty winding miles around Big Salt Lake until the road hit a T intersection, one of just three major intersections on the entire island. A left turn would have led to the former logging camp of Naukati, twenty-five miles away over mostly paved surfaces, until the highway turned to crushed rock and continued for a bone-jarring seventy miles of twisting gravel road to the northernmost tip of the island at Labouchere Bay on the Sumner Strait. Claus turned right and went over a curving paved road toward the hamlet of Thorne Bay on the eastern side of the island on the Clarence Strait.

After several miles, Claus looked through rain-streaked windows and found his landmark: a gravel road marked by a small sign several yards to the right of the highway reading Forest Service Road 3012. He pulled off the highway, the Expedition tires crunching on the coarse rock, and came to a stop. He got out and, in the drizzle, met a deer hunter from Thorne Bay named Scott MacDonald.

Only about two thousand people lived on Prince of Wales Island, and Bob Claus knew virtually every one of them, including MacDonald. The thirty-two-year-old hunter worked for the Forest Service, inspecting second-growth groves that sprouted after logging. Glenn Taylor, the Fish and Game trooper following Claus, pulled up to the scene, and MacDonald relayed why the authorities had been summoned.

Scott explained that he had left home at about nine a.m. with the idea of spending his Sunday hunting in the woods off the main highway. He drove to the Forest Service Road 3012 turnoff and made his way down the abandoned gravel logging road. The road went up a steep mountainside through a vast open area from clear-cut logging about ten years earlier. Streams trickled down the mountain and cut small arroyos through the old road. On the periphery stood an old-growth spruce forest, prime deer hunting ground. Scott MacDonald saw three or four other people that morning, all probably hunters, but nobody he knew.

As he drove up a steep section where it continued to switchback through the clear-cut area, Scott MacDonald saw smoke rising about a quarter mile away as if from a chimney, but as far as he knew there were no cabins in the area. Through his binoculars he saw that the smoke originated from the blackened wreckage of a large vehicle, probably a van. Scott drove closer, got out of his truck, and hiked the rest of the way. The wreckage clung to the side of the mountain, having tumbled off the road and then becoming pinned against a log. The van itself wasn't on fire; the smoke came from smoldering branches and logs beneath it.

Peering through a blown-out passenger window, Mac-Donald made a grisly discovery. He trudged back to his truck and drove down the mountain to where he could get a cell phone signal and called his mom, who worked as a business management supervisor at the Forest Service and knew the local law enforcement people. She put in the call to the trooper post in Klawock.

Claus asked MacDonald to lead him and Taylor to the scene. As he drove behind MacDonald, Claus paid close attention to their route. About one thousand miles of logging roads crisscross the island, almost none of them marked or memorialized on any maps. In rain or darkness it would be easy to become lost or disoriented even within earshot of the cars whizzing by on the main road. Claus wanted to be able to find this road again.

The first few miles took them across a relatively smooth road, and the caravan of three four-wheel-drive vehicles went along at a thirty-five-mile-per-hour clip. Along they way Claus spotted other trucks carrying hunters. The trooper stopped each one and asked if they had also seen a burning van. None had. After four miles the road branched into a Y, with Mac-Donald leading them along steeper, narrower road. Barely a lane wide, the road was of loose wet gravel, ravaged by potholes and washouts and littered with boulders and old logs. Claus noticed the road also was covered in car parts that he suspected had been dislodged from the van on its way up here. The road forked again, and MacDonald drove on a few hundred yards, stopped, and got out. Claus and Taylor parked their vehicles in a wide section of the road so they could turn around.

The men hiked through the rain over slippery rocks and branches toward the twisted, blackened heap lodged amid fallen timber logs, stumps, dirt, grass, and bushes. A blue vapor rose from beneath the wreck, steam forming off the rainwater creeping onto the smoldering undergrowth and logs in the nearly freezing temperatures. Up close, the vehicle appeared to be a minivan. The fire had scorched away most of the paint, with patches of the original purple remaining. Heat had blown out the windows all around and melted the license plate, now a glob of aluminum puddled beneath the rear bumper. Claus looked for the metal plates stamped with the vehicle identification number, normally affixed to the inside driver's-side door and on the dashboard, but found nothing but twisted metal and ash.

The trooper looked into the backseat area at what had prompted Scott MacDonald's call. Resting on the blackened remains of passenger seat was a skull beside a blackened human torso. Other charred bone fragments and a pile of ash lay nearby. The arms and legs had been burned off, as had the skin, hair and clothing. It was impossible to determine if this had been a man, woman or child. But these were definitely human remains.

Claus pondered his next step. In fifteen years as a trooper, he had handled every kind of case: burglaries, robberies, search and rescue, first aid, medical calls, drunken drivers, disorderly conduct, traffic accidents, and assaults of every stripe. This was the advantage of being only one of two troopers responsible for law and order on the 145-mile-long island. His experience also included a number of death investigations, including missing-and-presumed-dead persons, suicides, fatal accidents, and suspicious deaths that turned out to have medical causes. Every case came with its own challenges and often required improvisation. Hours could pass before a supervisor could even be reached. In past death investigations Claus would do an initial determination of the circumstances, photograph the scene, collect evidence, put the body in the truck, and call the medical examiner and "then ask for permission to do what we just did," he said.

But this case called for more caution. Of his death investigations in the course of his career, only three were homicides, and this one had all the hallmarks of a fourth. Claus could come up with no other plausible explanation for a body found burned up in the backseat of a suburban family vehicle on a desolate, barely accessible mountainside road.

Asking Taylor to stand guard against any curious hunters, Claus made his way back down the hill to the main road, where he could get a cell phone signal.

He called the dispatch center, which routed calls for all the public safety agencies on the island, and reported the discovery of a burned van containing human remains on Forestry Road 3012 off the road to Thorne Bay. Claus asked to be advised of any missing-person or missing-vehicle reports on Prince of Wales Island, the trooper assuming jurisdiction. His next call went to his supervising lieutenant in Ketchikan to say that he had a likely homicide and to request help. Claus had no idea who owned the van or who the victim was and the two-man trooper post in Klawock lacked the investigative resources to find out. He asked for a crime scene technician and a fire investigator; headquarters in Anchorage would add one more person, a homicide detective. They were expected to arrive the following morning. Taylor guarded the crime scene until morning. Wildlife troopers are the game wardens of the state but are trained in police work. He then went to his home in Craig, the largest village on the island, and waited for the phone to ring.

The call came that night at 9:45 p.m. The Craig Police Department had received a report of a missing person and a missing purple minivan. Fifteen minutes later Claus called a familiar number. The phone was answered by Carl "Doc" Waterman, a real estate broker in downtown Craig and one of the most respected citizens on the island. Since moving from Anchorage seventeen years earlier, Waterman, who owned Island Realty, had handled the sale or purchase of many of the homes, vacant and wooded lots, and businesses on all of Prince of Wales Island. Doc was also a mover and shaker in town, serving on the school board and a member of the Girl Scout council.

Doc told Claus that his wife, Lauri, was missing and so was her minivan.

This was a jolt to Claus. The Waterman and Claus families had known each other for years, going back to when the Watermans' fifteen-year-old daughter, Rachelle, and her older brother, Geoffrey, went to elementary school with Claus's two daughters. Claus's wife taught school in Craig, Doc was president of the school board, and Lauri worked as a teacher's aide. The two families saw each other at school functions and at church. Lauri and Doc occasionally visited Claus's home for social gatherings, the last one just a couple of weeks earlier. Claus's older daughter had once dated Geoffrey, who was now away at college, and the two young people had remained friends. Claus's younger daughter, Stephanie, had long been a friend of Rachelle's: the two girls most recently traveled together with Lauri to the mainland town of Haines, four hundred miles to north, for a school honor choir event. Claus's wife had tutored Rachelle in geometry.

Doc Waterman explained that he had spent that weekend in Juneau for a Girl Scout council meeting, flying home Sunday morning. Several times he called home from his cell phone to check in with his wife, but the calls went to the answering machine. Doc left messages to say he was on his way home, then boarded his flight. The plane stopped in the island town of Sitka, three hundred miles to the north, where at the small airport Doc coincidentally ran into Rachelle. A high school junior active in music and sports, Rachelle was returning from Anchorage, where she had spent the weekend competing in a state high school volleyball tournament.

From Sitka, they took the same flight to Ketchikan, where they boarded separate floatplanes for forty-five-minute flights to the hamlet of Hollis, a water-landing and ferry port on the eastern side of Prince of Wales Island. Together they drove a friend's truck west across the island to Craig, with 1,400 residents. They arrived about three thirty p.m. at their home at 604 Ocean View. The Watermans owned one of the nicest houses on the island: three bedrooms, den and living room over three levels on a packed gravel street with a spectacular view of Bucareli Bay and the spruce-choked islands of the Alaskan archipelago.

Entering the house through the garage, Doc and Rachelle noticed that Lauri's minivan was not there. Lauri would usually greet Doc or Rachelle when they came home from trips. They went upstairs to the main level, where the living room, kitchen, and Rachelle's room were located. Doc continued up to the third-floor master bedroom, unpacked, and checked the answering machine. All three messages had been left by him during this trip; none had been played before. He deleted them.

Her purse, normally kept in a small pantry between the kitchen and living room, was also gone.

Doc reasoned that Lauri must be out on an errand. She kept a busy schedule—she had told him she would be volunteering for a chamber of commerce dinner the night before—and Doc thought she may be out helping clean up. His hopes dimmed as he went into the kitchen, where he found an empty wine bottle (Doc recalled it was on the counter; Rachelle later said it was in the trash). Lauri rarely drank—at most a wine cooler while they were socializing—and Doc never knew her to imbibe at home alone.

Doc went back upstairs and inspected the master bedroom more closely. The bed was unmade, the sheets thrown back, which also was strange. Lauri and Doc "shared the habit," he later said, of making their bed first thing in the morning. On the bathroom counter, he saw that his wife's wedding ring set had been left behind. He had never known her to leave the house under any circumstances without them.

His wife and her car were gone; there was no note, no message on his cell phone.

Taciturn by nature, Doc later described himself as feeling only "a little bit concerned," and held out hope she was somewhere nearby. He drove to the building that had housed the chamber of commerce banquet the night before looking for his wife's 1998 purple Plymouth Voyager minivan with a rear-window sticker that read "Craig Panthers," the high school mascot, but it wasn't there. He tried the other logical places his wife could be: the high school on the main road just outside of town, then the Catholic church in Klawock. Still no sign of the van or his wife.

Doc returned home. He doubted his wife would have driven any farther than Klawock. When she was younger, she'd brave any of the island's treacherous winding streets, hauling Rachelle and Geoffrey and their friends to T-ball games over unpaved roads. Now, at age forty-eight, Lauri had become cautious, rarely venturing even outside of Craig. She kept to flat, paved roads, and wouldn't even drive on the newly paved highway to the ferry terminal in Hollis since the road was so winding.

Doc called his neighbors, Don and Lorraine Pierce. Lorraine was Lauri's best friend. The Pierces had two children, a daughter the same age as Geoffrey and a son a year older than Rachelle. Don, a special education teacher, told Doc that he had last spoken with Lauri the night before—Saturday—when he called to tell her that Lorraine was ill and couldn't accompany her to the chamber banquet. Don said neither he nor Lorraine had spoken to Lauri since and had no idea where she was. They had not heard anything next door, though the night had been windy and loud and could have masked any unusual noises.

With no place else to look and nobody left to talk to, Doc called Craig police, who in turned contacted the state troopers.

Claus's ties to the Waterman family put him in an awkward position. As soon as Doc spoke of his missing wife and van, the trooper knew the remains in the burned van clearly were those of a longtime friend. No other reports of a missing person or a missing van had come in. The island probably only had a few dozen minivans; pickups were the dominate means of transportation.

But since neither the identity of the remains nor the ownership of the van had been officially determined, Claus held off telling Doc anything about the burned wreckage and body on the logging road. The investigators from Anchorage still hadn't arrived, and Claus wanted to work this case by the book. The last thing Claus and his small team of lawmen needed was a bereaved husband rushing to the crime scene, tailed by half the curious population of the island.

Claus hung up, got a few hours of sleep, and returned the next morning, Monday, to the logging road and relieved Taylor. A light rain continued to fall, and in the quiet of his Expedition, Claus reflected on the case and what he knew about the Waterman family. He toyed with the possibility that a stranger murdered Lauri—somebody who had drifted onto the island looking for work or was trying to get away from another life and somehow decided to commit murder, perhaps as part of a burglary or sexual assault. But this was a quiet time on the island. The seasonal workers on the fishing boats had long since left with the last days of summer, and few outsiders had arrived. One ferry came to Hollis from Ketchikan each day, and one ferry left. A handful of tiny floatplanes shuttled a few passengers.

The more likely and unsettling possibility was that the killer was somebody known to both Lauri and people on the island.

Police work on Prince of Wales Island offered its own unusual circumstances and challenges, but Claus knew that murder was murder anywhere. First rule of thumb: ties between victim and assailant usually were close. When looking for a killer, start close and move outward. The husband, in this case Doc Waterman, would normally be the first suspect, but he had an alibi: he had been 220 miles away in Juneau when his wife was killed. The next closest people to Lauri were her children, both also gone, Geoffrey in college in Washington State, Rachelle in Anchorage playing volleyball.

That left Claus wondering who on the island would want Lauri Waterman dead. The concept defied reason. While people respected Doc, they adored Lauri. Warm, selfless, giving, she volunteered for every cause and had devoted her life to her children, coaching their sports teams, serving on school committees, leading Rachelle's Girl Scout troop.

But Claus, as a friend and trooper, knew things that others didn't, and in the quiet of his Expedition, he began plotting what would be the road map for the investigation of Lauri Waterman's death. Before it was over, the case would send shock waves through the close-knit island community, shattering illusions, confirming private suspicions, and leaving Claus disillusioned. He would retire early from the Alaska State Troopers, a job he had always enjoyed and found fulfilling. "This," he recalled later, "is the case that took all the fun out of law enforcement."

While Bob Claus stood watch at the crime scene, James Donald See began his week by working Monday morning traffic patrol at Craig High School. Stationed at the car drop-off area in the driveway, See made sure harried and distracted parents didn't collide with one another while fumbling with backpacks and heavy jackets. That Jim See was the chief of police spoke to the nature of the town and the size of its police department—three officers and a sergeant under See—and the personal touch residents could expect from their sworn officers. See's second in command, Sergeant Mark Habib, had the same duties at the nearby middle school Tuesdays through Fridays. Chief See was known around town as Jim, and Sergeant Habib as Mark. It wasn't unusual for them to give somebody a ride or chew the fat at the town hub, the post office. It also spoke to the safety and security of living in Craig. Residents kept their doors unlocked and felt safe walking after dark. After morning drop-off, See would stroll the halls, saying hello to students and staff and listening to people's concerns.

After school duty, See went to a coffee shop in Craig for a morning pick-me-up and the latest gossip. It was here, over a cup of coffee, that See first heard that a burned-out van with a body inside had been found off the road to Thorne Bay. Somebody had apparently picked up the report over a police scanner Sunday and by Monday morning word had spread across the island. Chief See had had the weekend off and nobody had told him about it.

He went to the police station, up the hill from the coffee

shop, and checked the weekend logbook, which confirmed
that his friend Bob Claus at the trooper post in Klawock had
called in that he was investigating an apparent homicide.
The logbook also reflected that Doc Waterman had reported
the disappearance of his wife and her minivan. Chief See
had known the Watermans casually for years. He'd speak to
Doc at the bank or post office and would see Lauri around
the ball field at the high school. He knew they had a high-
school-age daughter and a son in college, by all accounts
good kids who had never had a brush with the Craig Police
Department.

See called Habib at home—the sergeant normally had
Mondays off—to tell him to be prepared to come in for work.
Habib had not heard about Lauri's disappearance either. He,
too, knew the Watermans; Doc had been the seller's agent
on the house Habib and his wife purchased. Chief See
wanted to coordinate efforts with the state police as soon as
possible. It was only a matter of time before the town connected the burning van rumors with Lauri Waterman's disappearance, then the heat would be on the police department.
See wanted to know more than the customers at the coffee
shop.

At about the same time that Chief See went to the coffee
shop, a small float plane was buzzing through cloudy skies
over Prince of Wales Island, headed toward a flare sent up
by Trooper Bob Claus. Three men from Anchorage were
aboard, among them Deputy Fire Marshal John Bond, who
snapped photos of the blackened wreckage clinging to the
logging road etched into the side of the mountain. Next to
him sat crime scene technician Dale Bivens and trooper
homicide investigator Sergeant Randy McPherron.

After Bob Claus had called his supervisor for help on
Sunday, a trooper commander contacted McPherron with
orders to get to Prince of Wales Island to investigate the
suspicious circumstances surrounding the discovery of remains in a burned vehicle. McPherron paged the on-call
crime scene tech, Bivens, who was at a birthday party, and
then called Bond's supervisor. The men were told to pack

their bags for what could be a week or more in southeastern Alaska. Within hours they flew to Juneau, where they spent the night, then caught a morning flight to Ketchikan with a floatplane connection to Prince of Wales Island.

They landed forty-five minutes later in the bay of Hollis. With the weather worsening, Bond recommended they fly over the area to get photographs. From the ground Claus saw the plane pass by a couple of times and to help them locate the wreckage he sent up the flare. After Bond got his aerial photos of the scene, the plane landed off a logging and fishing town of six hundred people called Thorne Bay, sixty miles from Hollis, and they met a village public safety officer, peace officers who handle minor crimes and assist state troopers. The VPSO drove them west from Thorne Bay to Forest Service Road 3012, where Bob Claus waited. It was now ten a.m. and growing colder and wetter. The temperature had dipped to just above freezing with a light drizzle.

After the men exchanged greetings, Claus briefed them: The van with the remains inside was discovered by a hunter, and several hours later Craig resident Doc Waterman reported his wife and her van missing. The body was too badly charred to make identification, and the license plate and VIN tags also were gone.

Claus passed the leadership of the investigation to Sergeant McPherron, the ranking investigator.

Claus had never worked with McPherron but knew his reputation, which was already legendary in Alaska. Tall and built like a linebacker, McPherron was a former army infantry officer with the 82nd Airborne Division, based in North Carolina's Fort Bragg. In 1984 he moved to Alaska where he took odd jobs until entering the Trooper Academy. Like all fresh graduates, he rotated among posts: Anchorage, Kodiak, Ketchikan, Palmer, and finally Anchorage again. But rather than remain in an outpost and become a generalist like Claus, McPherron became a specialist—and a rising star—in the department. He worked his way up to a major case detective, investigating sexual assaults, sexual abuse of children, and homicides. For the last three years he supervised a unit at the Alaska Bureau of Investigation and had investigated about thirty homicides, eight of them as lead detective.

McPherron built a national reputation with his work on the case of Robert Meyer, a businessman from Juneau who told authorities in 1996 that his wife and teenage daughter had been washed overboard when their fishing boat caught on fire. McPherron found that Meyer had in fact murdered them for the insurance money and so he could be with his mistress. The case made headlines outside of Alaska and became the subject of Court TV documentary called *Fire and Ice*. People started calling McPherron the Columbo of Alaska, though any similarities ended with their shared knack for solving whodunnits. Unlike the sloppy, absentminded TV detective, McPherron operated with military precision and a calm relentlessness.

Claus drove the three men in the Expedition up the steep, bumpy gravel road to within a dozen yards of the wreckage. As they walked toward the van, Bond snapped 35mm and digital photos and crime scene tech Dale Bivens scoured the area, collecting a cigarette butt, sandwich bag, gum wrapper and paper, paint chips, Coke bottle, and car parts that had apparently been knocked off the van on the way up the mountain. Claus stood by, driving back and forth to the highway to make phone calls and would serve as liaison between the out-of-town investigators and both the local police and the villagers.

The task of processing the scene fell to Bond. With more than twenty years experience working for volunteer fire departments, he had joined the fire marshal's office five years earlier, inspecting buildings, reviewing architectural plans and investigating fires—fifty-five to this point. Bond walked around the van checking out the burn patterns. The fire had melted the tires down to their steel belts and vaporized the twenty-gallon plastic gas tank. It burned so hot that the nitrogen-filled pistons that operated the back hatch exploded.

From the tangled and blackened mass Bond could reconstruct what had happened. The blaze had started inside in the backseat area, the damage more extensive in the rear than in the front. For the most part the flames remained inside the confines of the van, with minimal charring to the log under the vehicle and the smaller shrubs on the surrounding hillside. The back hatch had been open at the time of the fire, evidenced by the back-window glass shards left on the roof of the van instead of on the ground.

After taking more photos and making additional notes, Bond looked through the blown-out window into the backseat. All that was left of the body was the thorax, the pelvic girdle, and the large leg bones—the femurs—above the knees. The smaller leg bones and the tiny bones of the feet had burned and broken apart, some scattered amid the ash. Only the large bones of the arm remained, with nothing visible below the elbows. The skull was there but appeared brittle due to the high temperature of the fire, followed by the rapid cooling from the near-freezing temperatures. Several teeth lay in the ashes.

When Bond completed his survey of the wreckage, the remains were removed and placed inside a white body bag liner. Alaska Fish and Game trooper Glenn Taylor carted the bag away on a litter and arranged for them to be shipped overnight to the coroner's office in Anchorage for autopsy. As Taylor did this, Bond caught the odor of gasoline. His nose took led him to spots on the ground, where he collected rock and soil samples to be sent to the crime lab.

As Bond inspected the truck, McPherron poked around the wreckage looking for a VIN tag. He finally found it: the tag had fallen into the engine compartment after the dashboard melted. Claus called the Craig dispatcher to run a DMV check on the number and got confirmation on the ownership of the van. It was now about one p.m., the rain getting heavier. A tow truck hauled the van to a Department of Transportation garage in Klawock while Claus called his supervisor to relay a message to Craig police chief Jim See. The van was registered to Carl and Lauri Waterman of Ocean View Road.

Chief See said he would inform Doc Waterman. "I felt

that he needed to hear it from me," See recalled later at trial. "It was all over town. I felt it was my duty to make a notification."

Sergeant Mark Habib had two tasks. The first was calming the nerves of island residents who feared a homicidal maniac was on the loose.

Habib hailed from hot and dry Texas but fell in love with Alaska and its outdoor sports when he was stationed in the state for the military. An avid fly fisherman, Habib keeps a rod in his office. He began his law enforcement career as a reserve officer in Anchorage before working full-time in Whittier, Alaska, on the Kenai Peninsula south of Anchorage, then moving to Craig in 1993 as a patrol officer. Promoted to sergeant, he supervised patrol cops, handled investigations, and oversaw the dispatch center and the jail. Gregarious like his boss Jim See, Sergeant Habib goes by his first name around town and knows virtually everybody in Craig—and knew that this morning they were on the brink of panic.

He started the day at the middle school where Lauri worked and tried to sort fact from rumor. "There was a lot of concern by teachers. They wanted some answers," he later said. "I told them at this point in time we could not confirm if the body was Lauri Waterman's. We were investigating."

Next, Habib interviewed Lauri's friends and coworkers, including those who had been with her the night before the van was found. On Saturday night Lauri arrived solo at the Craig Community Association building for the chamber of commerce dinner, telling people her husband and daughter were both out of town. She appeared as she always did, upbeat, energetic, happy to lend a hand even though she wasn't a member of the chamber. This was a big night for the chamber—there would be guest speakers, awards and speeches for distinguished citizens and volunteers, a raffle with prizes donated by local merchants—and Lauri came dressed in business casual: a colorful tropical print skirt, black sweater top, black nylons, and black shoes.

Janice Bush, who ran a contracting company operated

out of her home in Klawock, organized the event and welcomed Lauri's assistance. Janice and Lauri had long been friends; they attended the same church and both had school-age children. Lauri had called Janice earlier in the week asking if she needed help. Janice eagerly took her up on the offer.

"It wasn't something I asked her to do," said Bush. "She was home and didn't have anything else to do and helped us clean up afterwards." They spent five hours together on Friday, talking about their children as they ran around Craig picking up plates, dishes, and decorations. Janice's children also were involved in sports, and Lauri said that her daughter Rachelle was in Anchorage for a big high school volleyball tournament. Rachelle's team had lost its first game.

"We talked about how difficult it is to be away from your kids and not be able to keep in contact with them," Bush recalled. "We discussed cell phones. She said Doc was in Juneau that weekend. He was hoping to look at getting cell phones for the family so that when Rachelle was traveling she would have a cell phone so they could find out more quickly what the status of the activity was."

On Saturday, Lauri set up tables and laid out the decorations: 750 little toy bears a woman had loaned for the dinner, the theme of which was "Welcome to Bear Country." The no-host cocktail hour started at six p.m. and dinner began at seven p.m. "Lauri was able to relax at her table and just be able to visit with people at table throughout evening," said Janice.

Janice didn't see much of Lauri during the dinner, since she was scrambling to keep things running smoothly. The emcee couldn't make it because of bad weather, so they used a stand-in, "which meant I had to be at her side leading her through an unfamiliar program," Janice later said. The raffle went without a hitch, and Lauri won a fleece jacket from First Bank. A friend of Janice's took photos of the event, and several captured Lauri in her element, mingling with friends and picking up her First Bank jacket from Janice Bush.

After the banquet finished at about nine p.m., a half

dozen people stayed to take down tables put away the chairs. Among them was Lauri, who as always was one of the last to leave. By ten p.m. Janice turned off the lights and headed out with Lauri. The last thing Lauri said to Janice was to ask if she needed help the next morning. Janice said chamber volunteers already planned to return at eight a.m. Sunday to return the little bears.

"I asked her if she was going to church," recalled Janice. "She said yeah. I said I'll see you there." Church meant more volunteer work and more committees. Janice and Lauri were raising money for World Youth Day, a Catholic celebration of faith started by Pope John Paul II. Lauri's daughter had planned to travel to Germany for the event the next summer.

Janice watched Lauri drive into the night in her purple minivan. It was the last time she would ever see her.

CHAPTER TWO

For Rachelle Waterman, the morning of November 15, 2004, began like any other Monday in Craig, Alaska. Rather than stay home brooding over her missing mother, Rachelle trudged off to school, one of the hundreds filing past the chief of police on traffic patrol. Her volleyball practice and tournament travel had put her behind on her homework. She had calculus to catch up on. Rachelle had always been a busy overachiever, juggling sports, church, and extracurricular activities, all while keeping good grades.

She seemed destined to follow her brother to college. But over the last year a change had come over Rachelle, starting with her appearance. She had long been fond of loose-fitting clothes, including her brother's hand-me-downs, a result of her self-consciousness over her full figure, which developed earlier than other girls'. In recent months, however, she favored all black, including black clothes, black nail polish, and black leather collars, one of them studded. Although still friendly with the other girls, including Bob Claus's daughter Stephanie, Rachelle had spent more time over the summer with a new circle of friends, mostly guys, some of them older, who shared an interest in video games and the elaborate fantasy role-playing game Dungeons & Dragons. The computer store where she worked over the summer was a hangout for the D&D crowd.

On this Monday morning she should have been returning

to school as an object of envy. Her volleyball team had spent the weekend at the state championship tournament, and while they didn't finish well, that was beside the point. The tournament was in Anchorage, and that meant something Craig lacked: shopping. The girls hit the mall and loaded up on Hot Topic clothes and boots.

Instead, all eyes zeroed in on Rachelle as she limped through halls on an ankle sprained in volleyball practice before the tournament. The island rumor mill was in overdrive, with word already reaching the school halls that the body in the burning van found out near Thorne Bay was probably Rachelle's missing mother. Rachelle's emotions flew in all directions. For some of the day she was quiet and sullen, unwilling to talk about her mother. At another point in the day she seemed locked in denial, acting oddly glib.

"Have you seen my mother?" she casually asked her friend Amanda Vosloh, who was part of her music clique, during class. Amanda told police that Rachelle was strangely matter-of-fact, saying after class, "My mom is missing. We don't know where she is."

John Wilburn, a fourteen-year-old member of her D&D circle, heard Rachelle say she feared her mother had died in a drunk-driving accident. Rachelle told him she had returned from Anchorage to find a wine bottle in the trash and the van missing. It was the same thing she related to school counselor Sheila Beardsley.

Rachelle kept it together until the afternoon, when she broke down in tears. Amanda surmised that Rachelle had been jolted back to reality when her friends gave her a sympathy card for the loss of her mother, for by then everybody had assumed that Lauri Waterman was dead.

At two p.m. the Watermans' neighbor Don Pierce received a call from the secretary at Craig High School. "Rachelle was losing it," Pierce recalled. Don made the short drive to the high school and knocked on the door to the principal's office.

Inside, he found Rachelle crying. They hugged each other.

"We need to go home," he told her.

But Rachelle said, "I can't. I've called Jason."

Don was taken aback. Jason Arrant was one of Rachelle's new friends, a man in his midtwenties who worked as a janitor at the school in Klawock. Don knew little about Jason except that the man hung around the computer store where Rachelle worked—and that Lauri Waterman didn't like the attention he was paying her daughter.

There was a knock. Don opened the door and in walked a heavyset man with red hair who "blew right by me and went right to Rachelle." This was Jason Arrant—well over two hundred pounds. Rumor had it that he was an island washout, no college education, still living with his parents in Klawock, spending his time playing video games and hanging around a teenage girl.

Jason closed the door behind him and dominated the cramped principal's office with his bulk. He rounded the desk and embraced Rachelle. They shared quiet words, with Jason telling her that everything was going to be all right. They sat in the chairs—Jason taking the one that Don had been sitting in—and held hands with Rachelle while she continued to cry.

Another knock, and this time the principal's secretary was at the door. Don went out of the room, leaving Jason with Rachelle, and spoke to the secretary. She said that police chief Jim See had called to say that Rachelle needed to go home. The chief had to meet with her and her father.

Don went back into the principal's office and told Rachelle to gather up her things, he was driving her home. Jason objected, saying that he—Jason—would be the one to comfort and console Rachelle. The men had words. Rachelle was Don Pierce's unofficial goddaughter (the Pierces weren't Catholic) and he was taking her home so that she would be with her dad at the time that they were going to hear the news from Officer See.

As Don led Rachelle down the hall to get her coat and books from her locker, the big man followed, angrily telling him to leave Rachelle with him. Don ignored him. As a special ed teacher, Don could tune out what he called Jason's "white noise."

Don brought Rachelle to the teachers' parking lot, where they got in his truck and headed home. Along the way she rocked in her seat and said Hail Marys.

Within minutes they got to her house. Don walked her to the front door and into the living room, not wanting her to be alone while she waited for her father to emerge. When he showed up, Don realized he had parked in Lauri's space in the driveway.

"We had assumed the worst, but there was a chance that he was bringing good news, and I didn't want to have the wrath of the wooden spoon," he later said. "So I went and moved my truck to my house, which was next door."

Outside, he saw a truck pull into the spot that Don had just vacated, and in stepped Jason, who had obviously followed them. Don braced for another argument with the big man when Chief See arrived in a police truck. See told Jason to leave, but he refused, insisting that he be with Rachelle while the chief delivered whatever news he had for her.

See arched his eyebrow—like the wrestler The Rock, Don thought—and said, "And you are?"

Jason gave him his name.

"I don't have time for this now," See said. "Get in your truck."

Jason backed down and drove away while See went into the house with Don. It was a grim scene. Doc Waterman and his daughter appeared tense and agitated, bracing for the worst.

Chief See didn't mince words. He confirmed that the rumors were true: a burned-out van with a body inside had been found on a logging trail, and state troopers had confirmed the van belonged to Lauri.

Rachelle burst into tears. Doc reacted with a calm that often perplexed all but his closest friends.

"He took it like a person that had been waiting for the other foot to fall all day," recalled Don. "He was stoic about it, his shoulders slumped."

The chief of police cautioned that the body had not yet been positively identified, but he stressed that it didn't look good. Nobody else on the island had been reported missing and all signs pointed to the victim being Lauri.

After hearing the news, Doc now told See he wanted to show him something upstairs. Doc led the chief up to the bedroom. The day before he found blood on the sheets. He first thought it was menstrual blood, but he had his doubts when he saw that it was on both sides of the bed.

"I need to show you something else I found in the sheets and blankets," Doc said, taking the chief to the bathroom. On a portable mirror lay what See thought was the tip of a rubber glove and a fiber, about five inches long, that seemed to have come from a rope. Doc was about to hand the items to the chief when See warned him not to touch them.

"They've already been contaminated," said Doc, explaining that he had moved them from the bed to the bathroom.

Chief See now realized that the house was a crime scene. He told Doc to pack a change of clothes for himself and Rachelle and find a place to spend the night. Investigators would have to comb the home for evidence.

Doc looked at the chief. "Do we have a wacko here?" he asked.

Jim See had no answer for his old friend.

As Doc and Rachelle gathered their belongings, downstairs the chief quietly asked Don Pierce where Lauri Waterman went to the dentist, if it was in Craig or in Ketchikan. Pierce said she had a dentist on the island. See sent an officer to the office to pick up Lauri's X-rays to help make positive ID on the remains.

See went outside to find Jason and his truck gone. Jason's appearance at the Waterman house meant serious complications.

At 6:15 p.m., Sergeant Randy McPherron and Trooper Bob Claus arrived at the home of Don and Lorraine Pierce. The van had been hauled to a garage for further inspection, the body was being shipped to the coroner's office in Anchorage, and a search warrant had been secured for the Waterman house next door.

McPherron spoke to Doc Waterman for the first time. The Realtor repeated what he had told See previously. He told the detective of returning home from Juneau on Sunday afternoon after a weekend trip to find his wife and her van missing, followed by the discovery of the fiber, piece of rubber, and blood on the unmade bed, the wedding ring set in the bathroom, and the wine bottle in the kitchen.

Between Doc's account and that of Lauri's friend Janice Bush, investigators put the time of the murder between ten p.m. Saturday night, when Lauri left the chamber of commerce event in Craig, and nine a.m. Sunday morning, when the hunter found her body in the smoldering wreckage of her van about fifty miles away.

The rings in the bathroom and the unmade bed suggested Lauri had made it home and gone to bed. The fiber, which may have come from a rope, and the piece of rubber, likely from gloves, suggested an intruder. She may have been killed at home or she was driven off alive and murdered somewhere else and burned along with the van or, more chillingly, burned alive. McPherron was counting on the search of the house and the autopsy to fill in the gaps.

After McPherron interviewed Doc Waterman, he and Claus went into another room to speak with Rachelle. The detective introduced himself and Claus said hello.

"Before I go any further," McPherron told her, making clear this wasn't a social visit, "you understand we are police officers, right?"

"I understand that you're police officers," said Rachelle.

"And you don't have to answer anything you don't want. You can end this conversation at any time. You also have a right to have a parent present if you so desire."

"Yeah."

"I understand you want to talk to us alone."

"Yeah," said Rachelle.

McPherron then got down to business.

"We're trying to build a timeline and figure out when you last saw your mom, what was going on with you guys," he said. "I understand you left town on the Wednesday to go to the volleyball tournament, right?"

Rachelle explained that she had been in Anchorage, returning with her father about three thirty or four p.m. on Sunday. She said she had spoken with her mother while she was away, the last time about five thirty p.m. on Saturday.

"She was fine, she was happy," said Rachelle. "She was about to go the chamber of commerce dinner and I had just got done shopping."

Rachelle gave a little laugh with the word shopping.

"And I told her what we were doing," she continued, "and I told her how we've been doing, [what] our plans were for the night."

"She give you any idea of what's going on with her, other than going to the chamber of commerce dinner?" asked McPherron.

"Not really."

"Did she have any plans for Sunday?"

"No."

"Did she normally go to church?"

"Sometimes; not all the time. Usually she would go with me. She would go every once in a while by herself."

"Was she planning on meeting you guys at the house or at Hollis?"

"At the house," she said, explaining that her father had picked up a friend's car in Hollis and drove that back to Craig.

"When you left Wednesday, how were things going?" asked the detective.

"Fine," said Rachelle.

"Any problems between her and your dad?"

"Not that I know of. I mean, I heard a while ago . . . I heard rumors about my father having an affair."

Claus had heard the same rumors and passed them on to McPherron before the interview with Rachelle. The Waterman marriage had been whispered about for years on the island. They seemed a mismatched pair—the vivacious Lauri and her older, stoic husband.

"Over this summer?" asked McPherron.

"Yes," said Rachelle.

"Do you know who it was?"

"No, I don't."

"What was the gist of it?"

"I heard it from somebody," said Rachelle. "And the things that were interesting, that kind of made me go, 'Hmm,' like he'd say, 'Oh, I've got a meeting. I'll be late,' and she [Lauri] would drive by and the car wasn't there. And he'd go on long drives to watch the ocean. Just things like that. I'm not saying anything."

McPherron left the subject for now. He asked her if there was any reason for her mother to be in Thorne Bay.

"Not that I know of," said Rachelle. "I have an ex-boyfriend there, but that's about it."

"Who's that?"

"Kelly Carlson."

"Any problems at home?" the detective asked.

"I like got in trouble, like, a month ago, but other than that, fine."

"Any problems with any of your friends, any of your boyfriends?"

"I don't have any boyfriends," said Rachelle. "She doesn't like that I hang out with a couple of people."

"Who is that?"

"Jason Arrant," said Rachelle. "I worked with him over the summer. And he's older. My mom doesn't like that I talk to him sometimes."

"You go out with him?"

"We're just friends."

"Your mom doesn't like him?"

"No, she just doesn't like the fact that I'm talking to an older man. . . . We were not, like, really close, it was just, you know, casual."

"Anything else she had a problem with?"

"No."

"When you got home on Sunday, did you notice anything out of the ordinary at the house? Anything missing?"

"Nothing missing, but there was a wineglass in the sink and an empty bottle of wine in the garbage."

"Your mom drink?"

"Sometimes. . . . Every once in a while," said Rachelle. "I've never really known her to just sit around, watch a movie, and have some wine."

"Aside from the car being gone, was anything else missing."

"No, not that I know of."

"Any sign of a struggle?"

"I looked upstairs and the bedroom's fine."

"Is your mom the type of person if someone comes over that she knows, even casually, she'll still invite them in?"

"Oh, yeah," she said, but Rachelle didn't think her mother would do it late at night.

McPherron brought Rachelle up to speed with what police had determined from the short investigation, telling her, "As best we can piece together, she did go to this chamber of commerce dinner, people saw her there, she helped clean up, and that appears to be the last sighting we have of her. Who are her friends?"

Rachelle gave some names, and McPherron said, "OK, I have no more questions. I may have more later on." He told her police were getting a search warrant to go through the house. "Something may have happened in the house and that's what we'll look for."

Then McPherron asked Rachelle, "Do you have any questions for me?"

She did. "Do you think that somebody has done something to her?"

"We don't know," he said. "We found the van, we found the body in the van. The vehicle was burned. We don't know who this person is or anything yet. So that's going to take a while."

Her comments gave investigators plenty with which to work. But he didn't want to press too hard at this stage.

McPherron saw this as a preliminary interview and hoped to have another chance to talk to her alone.

Listening to Rachelle, Bob Claus was certain she wasn't telling the entire truth.

CHAPTER THREE

Investigators searched the Waterman house until late Monday night and again for much of Tuesday. Crime scene tech Dale Bivens led the search with help from Trooper Claus and the local cops. "For us, lots of times, it's a learning experience to see a professional do his work," Chief See said later in court. "I actually held the end of the tape measure. I may be the chief, but I'm always wanting to learn stuff."

Looking through the garage, it appeared that somebody had attempted to break into the house through a door that led from the garage to the downstairs family room. The striker plate for the doorknob had fresh scratches from a screwdriver or another tool. Doc Waterman said this couldn't have been the work of anyone who knew him well: he always kept a key to that door hanging nearby. For a brief moment the investigators thought they also had found evidence of a horrifying murder scene in the garage. There was dried blood on the floor beneath metal hooks on the rafters. But Doc Waterman explained he had used the hooks during hunting season to dress a deer. Later lab tests confirmed the blood wasn't human.

Upstairs, Chief See crouched on hands and knees with a flashlight, looking for more of the fibers of the type Doc had found on the bed. He found several more on the carpet, nylon strands that appeared to have come from the yellow and red ropes commonly used on boats on the island. The chief marked their locations. "We don't have those fancy crime scene things with the numbers," he recalled, "so I started ripping paper so the tech would know where."

In the closet were the clothes Lauri wore to the chamber dinner. The tropical-patterned skirt was on a hanger. The black sweater lay on the floor next to the black shoes beneath a white flannel nightgown with pink designs. A pair of black nylon hose were in the left top drawer of the dresser, lying on top of other clothing.

Doc would say it was unusual for his fastidious wife to have left the clothes so haphazardly: she never would have thrown the nightgown on the floor, for instance. Taken together, it looked like Lauri Waterman had returned home from the dinner, changed into her nightgown, and gone to bed, leaving her wedding rings in the bathroom. She was snatched from her bedroom late Saturday night or early Sunday morning, perhaps awakened by an intruder who had entered through the garage, forced her to change out of her nightgown, tied her up, and taken her down the stairs and away from the house in her own minivan. Only a tiny amount of blood had been found on the sheets, suggesting she was killed somewhere else. The kidnapper may have worn latex gloves, leaving behind that piece of rubber that Doc had found.

The one piece of evidence that didn't fit was the wine bottle in the kitchen. While Lauri may have had a drink before going to bed, Doc doubted it. "I haven't seen her have a glass of wine for probably ten years," he would say. "Her average alcohol consumption is maybe two wine coolers a year."

The wine bottle mystery only deepened when Deputy Fire Marshal John Bond inspected the van wreckage at the Department of Transportation garage in Klawock. The backseat area had a stain of melted nylon, either from pantyhose or rope, located in the same place as the body; a pair of glasses that would be connected to Lauri; and, interestingly, a piece of melted brown-green glass that appeared to have once been a wine bottle.

The rest of what Bond found was to be expected. From what little paint had not been melted away, he could see this was once a purple Plymouth Voyager that still had the key in the ignition when it was set on fire. A glob of melted brass remained in the ignition cylinder. Broken glass located on the inside the driver's door and the driver's-side passenger door meant that these windows were rolled down during the fire. The other windows were likely closed and blasted out by the heat. From the burn patterns, the fire appeared to have started inside the van and was fueled by some form of accelerant, most likely gasoline.

Bond estimated the fire burned at 1,800 degrees, the same temperature at which a body is cremated. But the fact that the body was not reduced to ash meant that the fire burned only shortly: crematoria go for four hours. The torso, small bones, and some teeth discovered in the backseat had already been removed, but some parts remained. More teeth and small bones ended up near the front seat, having probably tumbled down there when the van was hoisted by the tow truck and hauled off. Bond packaged these to send to the coroner.

In Anchorage, the autopsy was conducted by Deputy Medical Examiner Susan Klingler. She inspected the contents of a bag shipped to her from Prince of Wales Island, what forensic pathologists call "cremains": just thirty-three pounds of badly charred remains, with clothes, skin, and many bones burned away. There was enough of the jaw and teeth left to X-ray to try to identify the victim. Those X-rays were given to a forensic odontologist who compared them to Lauri Waterman's dental X-rays collected by Chief See's patrol officer. The odontologist concluded the identification of Lauri was "made to a certainty."

Otherwise, the poor state of the remains limited Klingler as to what she could determine. X-rays found no obvious signs of violence—no broken knife tips or bullets. The neck had little tissue left, so Klingler couldn't look for signs of strangulation. A test of the tissues for elevated levels of carbon dioxide—a sign Lauri was still alive and breathing at the time of the fire—was inconclusive. There was no soot in the small tubes of the lungs, but that also said little. Dying people usually don't take deep enough breaths to get the soot all the way into the lungs.

In the end, all the autopsy could say was that Lauri was badly burned either before or after death. Any clues to how or where she died, or who may have killed her, couldn't be gleaned by the examination. That would have to come from Sergeant Randy McPherron's investigation.

Trooper Bob Claus searched Rachelle's bedroom. It was a typical teenage girl's room, not unlike his daughters', with clothing on the floor, photos of friends on the walls, trophies on the shelves. Rachelle's computer was taken away for later examination at an Anchorage electronics lab, but Claus found a stack of letters apparently written in Rachelle's hand. The notes had writings about Rachelle's relationship with one of her girlfriends and about Kelly Carlson, the former boyfriend she mentioned in her interview with McPherron. Again, it was the usual teen stuff, with nothing that could be linked to her mother's murder.

One of the letters was different: it had been written on a word processor. It was from Jason Arrant, pleading with Rachelle to take him back.

Almost from the moment Doc Waterman had told him that Lauri was missing, Claus suspected that Jason had something to do with it. While sitting in his Expedition guarding the wreckage, Claus had gone through what he called "the logical progression of suspects," rejecting those closes to the victim— Doc, Lauri, and Geoffrey—as the actual killers because all were away, but thinking how any of them could have still somehow been involved.

"I knew that Rachelle and Jason had a dating relationship; I knew that Lauri didn't like that," Claus recalled later. "I knew there was tension between those two people."

Claus had briefed McPherron on this before they spoke

to Rachelle, but it turned out to be Rachelle who brought up Jason, not the investigators.

Claus had a personal tie to Jason through Jason's mother, who worked as a dispatcher for the Craig Police Department. For the rest of the case, Claus and other investigators had to proceed carefully so as not to tip off Jason, via his mother, to what they were doing. Though not close friends, Claus and Jason's mother spoke every day at work and the trooper knew about her wayward son. He had left the island at least twice since graduating from high school but returned to live with his parents.

"He was an odd kid," Claus would later recall. "I had been in the Marine Corps and he was going into the Marine Corps and had asked me advice on what do before he went. I basically told him to get in shape, to run a lot." Jason never made it out of basic training. "He was too big and did not lose the weight in time," said Claus.

Both Chief See and Sergeant Habib knew Jason, too, since his mother worked just a few feet away from them. Jason was not known as a dangerous or violent person, but he had had at least one brush with the law. When he lived in Hollis and was working as a school aide he faced complaints from a young girl. Claus investigated but never found any evidence.

When Rachelle started spending time with Jason over the summer, her mother objected, noting his age and apparent lack of direction. Lauri Waterman shared these concerns with Don and Lorraine Pierce.

"[Lauri and Rachelle] had their little squabbles, and they had their good moments too," said Lorraine at trial, repeating what she told investigators. "They shared things like going to honor choir and Lauri chaperoned, and she was very proud of her daughter. And there were times where she wished that Rachelle wouldn't act the way that she did or date the boys that she did; I know that they had little squabbles over it and major discussions. And Lauri, being the parent she was, would try to talk through and help her with her reasoning and help her make her decisions."

The Watermans discussed this at least a half dozen times. "Lauri was very concerned that Rachelle was dating, first of all, a much older man, and secondly she was concerned that Jason might not have much of a goal in life," Doc Waterman later recalled in court. "She was very concerned that her daughter would become involved to the point of marrying somebody who would not help her realize her potential."

Doc Waterman couldn't remember if he personally spoke to Rachelle about it. "Generally speaking, the day-to-day things with the children Lauri dealt with," he said. "If she wanted a heavy hitter, she asked me to come in. I was the one who would ground her, that sort of thing. I don't recall whether we talked jointly with Rachelle."

Investigators reached out to Rachelle's friends, asking if they thought she had been dating Jason or if they were casual friends. "I had heard rumors. I didn't know anything officially," her friend Amanda Vosloh recalled.

Although Rachelle never talked to Amanda about Jason, Amanda did see them together. Jason had been cast in the community theater production of *The Importance of Being Earnest* in the fall. Amanda was also involved, as was Rachelle, who was part of the lighting crew. Rachelle wasn't required to go to the rehearsals on Tuesday and Thursday because she was on the technical crew, but she would come anyway, apparently just to see Jason. "She would come in after a practice and say hi to him and give him a hug," Amanda recalled.

Stephanie Claus recalled seeing Jason with Rachelle when Rachelle worked at the T-shirt shop over the summer. "We went in once to invite Rachelle to go to the beach with us and Mr. Arrant was there," said Stephanie. "They seemed to be getting along just fine. Rachelle was behind the counter doing whatever and Arrant was just sitting in a chair." From their body language, Stephanie was aware that they were friends at least and perhaps something more, she said. "I kind of inferred that. But she had never confided in me about it."

According to Bob Claus, it was not unusual on Prince of Wales Island for a girl of fifteen to be dating an older man.

"In rural Alaska, sometimes that's all there is," he said. "There's a saying here they put on women's T-shirts: 'The odds are good, but the goods are odd.' It's not uncommon for somebody in the twenty-something crowd to not be able to break out of the orbit and just be hanging around here, scratching out a living, socializing with the usual high school kids."

Still, it would be more common to find a fifteen-year-old dating a nineteen- or twenty-year-old. "Rachelle was pushing that," he said. "It was clear she was being disciplined for that. I sympathized with Lauri and Doc."

Rachelle's friends and family said she had had at least two boyfriends before Jason, both of them older. Her first love was Kelly Carlson. She was a fourteen-year-old high school freshman and he was a junior from another school when they met at a youth leadership conference in Craig. The event was called a "lock-in," in which the kids were isolated in a building for two intense days of team-building activities. Kelly had grown up in a village called Point Baker on the northernmost tip of Prince of Wales Island. One of the most isolated communities in America, Point Baker has about three dozen residents and is accessible only by boat, the gravel roads ending miles away. At the time he met Rachelle, he had just moved to Thorne Bay.

After the conference, they kept in touch by e-mail, and when he was in Craig they'd hang out at the Voyageur Bookstore. It was Rachelle who made the first move, he told investigators, asking him out on a date after they'd known each other for about three months. They went to one of the only places on the island where young people could congregate: Papa's Pizza in Craig.

They were boyfriend and girlfriend for about five months, chatting online when they couldn't be together before the stress of their long-distance relationship and their age difference caused them to break up. Rachelle again took the initiative, dumping him, he said, in an e-mail while he was in summer school in Fairbanks in 2003.

Her next boyfriend was a Craig High School boy named

Ian Lendrum who had arrived on the island in 2002. They met while walking home from school and started dating in the summer of 2003. Rumor had it that her problems with Ian started around the same time she met Jason. But in recent months, as Rachelle returned to school and her busy schedule, Jason seemed to have drifted out of her life—until Don Pierce saw him in the principal's office that afternoon.

McPherron then discovered that Rachelle may have seen Jason again that day. After Rachelle got the news from Chief See about her mother's van and went next door to the Pierces' with her father, a worried Don Pierce called her friend Stephanie Claus to ask if she could be with Rachelle.

Stephanie came over, and the girls hung out there with their friend Amanda Vosloh and Don's son Phillip Pierce, who is six months older than Stephanie. Despite the tumultuous events of the past twenty-four hours, Rachelle was back to acting "very normal," recalled Stephanie, who was interviewed by police. "She was very calm and just like she'd always been."

The subject of her missing mother hung in the air, but "Rachelle said she didn't want to talk about it," recalled Stephanie. "Phillip and Amanda and I didn't push her. She explained that her mother's van had been found on Monday and that she didn't want to talk about it, that she wanted to leave the house and to do something fun to get her mind off of it."

The trio sampled the few activities available to teens on a Monday night on Prince of Wales Island. They browsed at the Voyageur Bookstore in Craig, went to the boat harbor, then took a drive, with Phillip at the wheel of his sister's car. They left Craig, went past the Viking Lumber Company sawmill, and headed toward Klawock, where the island's only convenience store—the Black Bear Market—is located. "There's not a lot of places to drive within the town," Stephanie said.

Until now, Rachelle's behavior seemed normal enough, her friends accepting that she wanted to get her mind off her troubles. But halfway to Klawock, Rachelle announced, "I need to take a crap," and asked if they would stop at the Klawock school.

She went inside and emerged five or ten minutes later, saying she had seen Jason. She again made a crude remark, this time about how badly the bathroom now smelled and he'd have to clean it up, but it was OK because he was well paid as a janitor.

They turned around and went back to Craig, going into Papa's Pizza, where Ian Lendrum worked, for about forty minutes before returning to the Pierces' house.

The most provocative information came from Rachelle's friend and volleyball teammate Katrina Nelson, who was on the trip to Anchorage. Katrina recalled that Rachelle borrowed her cell phone about four times, usually to call to her mother.

"She said she called 'Red,' " said Katrina.

She didn't know who Red was, but Katrina knew Jason Arrant had red hair, and she suspected it was him. So did Sergeant McPherron and Trooper Claus.

CHAPTER FOUR

Ian Lendrum was asleep when detectives knocked on his door at ten a.m. on Tuesday, November 16. Startled awake, Ian raced downstairs before he realized he wasn't wearing a shirt. He went back upstairs to dress, then returned to the front door to let the investigators in. He started a pot of coffee to clear his head.

Ian was worried. The rumor sweeping the island was that police wanted to arrest Rachelle's former boyfriend. At the time of Lauri's murder, Ian fit that description. From the outset, he insisted to detectives, he had nothing to do with Lauri Waterman's murder. He had always gotten along well with the Watermans, had remained friends with Rachelle even after they broke up, and had even been with her that week to help comfort Rachelle.

He said that on Sunday, the day Rachelle was to return from Anchorage, he called her house a couple of times but got no answer. It was unusual for Rachelle to be unreachable, so he finally went to the house in the evening and found Rachelle with her father.

"Me and her were downstairs and watched a movie," he recalled later, recounting what he told investigators. "I just remember being really worried and stuff." Rachelle, he said, seemed "distressed" and "looked like she was going to cry."

He asked her what was wrong. "She just couldn't speak.

She was worried about things," he said. "She said she had to go upstairs and make dinner for her dad."

Only later did he find out that Rachelle's mother was missing.

Investigators asked Ian about his history with Rachelle. He said it was uncertain exactly how long they were together— "Just seemed like forever," he said—and he couldn't pinpoint the date they broke up.

Ian had been part of Rachelle's circle of friends who played the ultraviolent science fiction video game Halo and Dungeons & Dragons, first at the homes of Rachelle and Ian, then over the summer of 2004 at the computer store in Craig where Rachelle worked. Rachelle was the only girl among the D&D players, who included Ian, his friend John Wilburn, Jason Arrant, and Jason's best friend—and the owner of the store—a six-foot-five-inch, 280-pound bearded giant named Brian Radel. The group took their game-playing seriously, each player assuming a fantasy identity as they immersed themselves in make-believe adventures.

"She was a thief," Ian recalled, "Brian was a warrior, and Jason was a vampire, and I don't remember what John was." (John later said, "I myself prefer spell-casting roles.") They would keep their characters for about two weeks, meeting sometimes daily over the summer, scarfing down pizza from Ian's store, Papa's Pizza.

The interview with Ian complete, detectives compared notes. In recent months Rachelle's life had split into two— the D&D crowd on one side, the choir/sports girls on the other. While not unusual for a teenager to belong to more than one social clique, in Rachelle's case the dichotomy seemed particularly stark. Her girlfriends knew little of Jason Arrant and even less of Jason's friend Brian Radel.

Rachelle's volleyball teammate Katrina Nelson told investigators she thought she had heard the name Brian but didn't know if Rachelle had mentioned him or somebody else. Katrina couldn't place the face. Rachelle's parents knew even less. Detectives would find out that Lauri once visited the computer store over the summer while Brian was working there. Whether Lauri took notice of the big man wasn't known. About a week later Brian bought food from Lauri while she was working at a snack stand at a Fourth of July fair, but again, it wasn't known whether she noticed him.

Bob Claus knew more. He remembered first seeing Brian Radel when Brian was ten years old. Brian's father was a gunsmith who did work on the trooper's shotgun. The Radel shop was in the family compound, a run-down homestead-type spread with children—apparently Brian and at least one sibling—running around dressed in camouflage. Claus seemed to recall the Radel children had been home-schooled and trained in military tactics. His lingering impression: "Think *Deliverance*."

When Jason was older, he had been seen around town with Brian, the two big men hard to miss. Claus related his thoughts to McPherron. He didn't know where Brian lived now, but the compound where he grew up was in Thorne Bay, not far from where the van was found.

"I was really concentrating on the two men," Claus recalled. "What I saw were these two people were associated with Rachelle. She couldn't have done this. But they could."

McPherron agreed. "Because of Trooper Claus's information regarding the problems between Lauri Waterman and Jason Arrant and the problems that it caused in the family, they seemed to be a very logical place to start," he said. With the investigation stretched thin, McPherron called in two more detectives to find Jason Arrant and Brian Radel and try to get initial interviews to determine their whereabouts on the night of Lauri Waterman's murder.

One phone call to Jason Arrant's parents' house brought him to the trooper post in Klawock. He arrived at noon on Wednesday, November 17, while the investigators were still speaking to Ian Lendrum and Rachelle's friends and searching the Waterman house. He met with one of McPherron's reinforcements, Trooper Cornelius "Moose" Sims, who flew in from the investigations bureau in Soldotna, south of Anchorage.

Although he appeared voluntarily, Jason made it clear that he was not happy about what was going on. The same rumors troubling Ian Lendrum had reached Jason, no doubt sparked by Rachelle's friends' questions about him. Jason complained that the latest rumor was that he had already been arrested for the murder of Lauri Waterman, and nothing could be further from the truth.

In a brief conversation with Sims, Jason explained that, like Ian, he had once dated Rachelle, but they called it off to avoid problems with her family.

Sims asked him where he was at the time of the murder.

"Saturday night," Jason said, thinking. "I believe that was the night I was out, hanging out with my buddy Brian. I stayed out in Hollis that night because I had had a few drinks and it was storming. I figured I should probably just crash instead of trying to drive home."

Jason said the pair spent the day tooling around the island, leaving Brian's place in Hollis at about two thirty p.m. Brian's residence of late had been a room in the home of a retired sawmill worker named Lee Edwards. Jason drove his pickup because Brian didn't have a vehicle. The two men arrived in "town"—what everybody called Craig—around four p.m. on Saturday; they bought munchies at the grocery store, stopped in a clothing shop, and hit other spots in Craig before driving to Klawock, then back to Hollis, where they got drunk and spent the night. Jason awoke around seven a.m. and drove to his parents' house in Klawock, arriving around eight a.m.

Sims tape-recorded Jason's statement and had a few more requests, to which which Jason readily agreed. He allowed Sims to take a DNA sample by swabbing the inside of his mouth, provided fingerprints and allowed for photos of his shoes to be taken for comparisons in case any footprints were found at the Waterman house or elsewhere.

Jason left the trooper post, then returned within minutes,

saying he had just thought of something. He told Sims that Rachelle had once dated a boy named Ian Lendrum.

"I was there when she broke up with Ian," Jason said, "and Ian got kind of scary."

Finding Brian was also easy. Using the address provided by Jason, Trooper Dane Gilmore, who also had been sent in from Soldotna, and a trooper who worked with Claus in Klawock, Walter Blajeski, drove to Hollis and knocked on the door of Edwards's house, a three-bedroom, woodstove-heated home that still appeared to be under construction. It was about 1:45 p.m. and Brian was there alone. As with Jason, the troopers asked Brian for his whereabouts the night of the murder and he gave an account similar to his friend's: they had gone to stores in Craig and Klawock, then spent the evening at his place drinking. When Brian woke up the next morning, Jason was gone.

When asked about the murder of Lauri Waterman, Brian said it was the first he had heard of her disappearance. The island rumors hadn't reached him out in Hollis. He said he didn't have a television or read the papers, so if it had been reported, he'd have no way of knowing. (In fact, the case had not yet reached the media.) Brian agreed to having his mouth swabbed for a DNA sample, had his boots photographed, and posed for a picture of himself.

After the interview, Blajeski huddled with Gilmore. Blajeski had also long known Brian and was surprised at how he looked. Back at the trooper post, they showed the picture to Claus.

"Mr. Radel is a very distinctive man," Claus later recalled. "He's huge—large across the chest and shoulders, strong and tall, and goes close to three hundred pounds. He had a distinctive bushy unkempt reddish-brown hair and goatee . . . He was a sight to see walking down the street in Craig."

The man looking up at him in the photo was somebody else. Brian had shaved off his hair and beard.

Under instructions from McPherron, the troopers didn't

press Jason or Brian on their alibis, any animosity with the Watermans, or, in Brian's case, his new appearance. For now, McPherron wanted to establish—and lock in—their alibis while not letting on that they were under suspicion. That both men were big enough to easily overwhelm a woman of Lauri's size didn't escape notice. The plan was to double-check their alibis by interviewing the clerks at the stores they said they had visited and to speak with Lee Edwards. The detectives were also calling the airlines to confirm the travel accounts of Rachelle and Doc Waterman. Soon they'd set up follow-up interviews.

But before they could get back to Jason, Jason got back to them.

At five thirty p.m., Craig police received a call from the Klawock School near the trooper post. The dispatcher relayed the message to Claus.

"There is a man holding everyone inside the building," the dispatcher said.

Sensing this had to be linked somehow to the Waterman case, Claus and McPherron made the short drive to the school, where the situation was considerably less dire than described. In the school office the investigators found the school's janitor, Jason Arrant, trembling and crying.

The investigators turned on a tape recorder and asked what had happened.

"I went around to the side of the building so I could walk up the hill to the Dumpster," he began, "and I hadn't gone more than about ten steps and someone grabbed me from behind and got a handful of my hair and pulled my neck back and I felt a blade at my throat. He told me that if I didn't stay away from Rachelle, there was going to be another accident. And while he was talking to me he was running the blade across my throat."

Jason described the weapon as a serrated knife, and he showed the troopers a red mark on his throat left by the blade.

The two investigators searched the school and spoke to people. An electrician fixing the basketball scoreboard who had wandered into the parking lot to get his tools at the same time as Jason's reported assault said he didn't see anything. The principal, who was standing on the porch and had a good view of the parking lot at the time, also saw no attack. Claus and McPherron walked with Jason through his reenactment, looking for footprints or other signs of a scuffle, but could see no evidence other than the injury to his throat, which appeared superficial.

(At one point a man who lived nearby came out with a shotgun to assist the investigators, but he was sent home.)

Claus and McPherron were soon convinced that Jason had made the whole thing up. They allowed Jason to go home but knew that wouldn't be the end of it. Jason would certainly tell his mother, the police dispatcher, who would be suspicious if the troopers didn't file a report.

Claus called in a fake "Be on the lookout" for a man with the description given by Jason. But the real focuses of their investigation were Jason Arrant and Brian Radel. The one person still alive linking them was Rachelle Waterman. The investigators called her house to set up a follow-up interview. The questions this time would be more pointed.

CHAPTER FIVE

"You want a cup of coffee?"

Doc Waterman was playing host to three police guests on Tuesday night. They were at Doc's house just after seven thirty p.m. on November 17, 2004. Sergeant Randy McPherron's face gave Doc the answer.

"Drinking coffee all day, huh?" asked Waterman.

"Yeah," said McPherron, "that's the last thing I need."

The sergeant had arrived with Troopers Bob Claus and Dane Gilmore to conduct what he had told Doc on the phone earlier in the day would be routine interviews in the murder investigation. New information had come to light in the last two days and the investigators had follow-up questions for Doc and Rachelle to fill in the gaps.

McPherron would later acknowledge he hadn't been truthful, leaving out his belief that Rachelle knew more about her mother's murder than she was saying. The new information came from Rachelle's friends and related to what seemed to be her suspicious behavior the last two days and additional details about problems with her mother.

"Did you wanna talk to me first?" asked Doc.

"What we like to do is maybe divide things up," said McPherron, "have Dane stay here and talk with you and have Rachelle come with me."

The sergeant introduced Gilmore, saying he was sent in

from his post in Soldotna. Doc recognized him from when the trooper spoke to the Pierces next door.

Doc said, "OK."

Then, to Rachelle, McPherron said, "How ya doin'?"

Rachelle said she was doing fine, and McPherron asked Doc if it would be all right to interview Rachelle at the police station this time.

"I've talked with her about it," said Doc. His daughter agreed.

"Super," said McPherron. He gave his cell phone number to Doc and said, "If there's a problem, just give me a call. We just wanna go down there and talk. We'll be out of the way and private. Nobody will bug us."

Doc again said, "OK," accepting McPherron's explanation. It was another piece of deception, McPherron actually wanting Rachelle alone, isolated, and uncomfortable—without her father or a lawyer. By law, McPherron only needed Rachelle's permission to speak to police without her father, but the sergeant again didn't want to tip his hand.

Rachelle put on her shoes and jacket and got into the patrol car, where McPherron reminded her to put on her seat belt for the short ride to the Craig police station.

McPherron radioed the dispatcher "10-6"—code for "I'm busy, don't bother me"—and gave his location as 602 Oceanview. Overhearing, Rachelle corrected him, "You know this is 604, right?"

"Six-oh-four, right," said McPherron.

"Yeah," said Rachelle, "I thought you said 602."

"Oh, did I?"

"Yep."

They drove down the hill and in the next mile passed the major landmarks of Rachelle's fifteen years: the marina where Brian Radel kept his boat, the T-shirt shop where Rachelle once worked, the junior high school, Papa's Pizza, the Thibodeau Mall where Brian had his computer shop, then up another hill toward the little brown police building on Second and Spruce streets.

Along the way McPherron made small talk, telling Rachelle, "My oldest daughter's name is Rachel. So I've been having a hell of a time. Every time I would try to write your name, I write R-A-C-H-E-L."

"Yeah, Rachelle is a French version of Rachel," she said.

"Do you speak French?"

"A little bit, because we had a foreign exchange student here last year with a friend of mine."

"That's the one living with the Clauses, right? Bob's daughter?" asked McPherron. The trooper had told him of the French exchange student.

"Yeah," said Rachelle, and McPherron said, "Wow, that's cool." Rachelle said she was planning to go Germany next summer—the trip her mother had been raising money for with friend Janice Bush at church—and McPherron asked if Rachelle spoke German. She said she didn't but wasn't worried because "everyone in Europe, you know, speaks English."

They talked about foreign languages and colleges; McPherron said his daughter was at the Art Institute of Seattle and that "I'd like to see her come back to Alaska, 'cause I miss her."

They pulled into the back parking lot reserved for police cars, got out, and met Claus. They entered through the rear door and went down a hallway past the glass window to the left that opened to the dispatch center, where Jason's mother worked, and into the squad room. Chief See's office was located on the right, and down the hall was a waiting area where the front window to the dispatch office was located on one side and the DMV office on the other.

They went another few feet into a meeting room on the left.

"Why don't you grab a seat there, make yourself comfortable," McPherron told Rachelle. "You need a glass of water?"

"I'm fine, thanks."

McPherron left her in the room a minute while he discussed with Claus the recording system in the room. The room was small, windowless, claustrophobic, and wired for video, which was how McPherron wanted it. His patrol car banter with Rachelle was all a calculated effort to build trust and rapport, softening Rachelle for an interview that could likely turn nasty quickly.

The investigators returned and took their seats, old family friend Claus next to Rachelle and McPherron across from them. Claus placed his digital recorder on the table, as did McPherron, so they'd have an audio backup to the video recording from a wall-mounted camera.

For the benefit of the camera, McPherron announced the time in military fashion—"1947"—and said he was "10-6 at the Craig Police Department" with Rachelle Waterman and Trooper Claus.

He looked at Rachelle.

"You can call me Randy, you know," he said.

"Randy?"

"Yeah, we don't need to be real formal here. And I believe you know this guy," he said, pointing to Claus.

"Yeah," she said.

"And I do need to record our conversation, OK?" he said. "Not a real good note taker. I wanna make sure I get everything."

The note-taking remark was another fib: he wanted an on-video acknowledgment from Rachelle that she was aware she was being recorded; otherwise he would have needed a warrant for a secret recording. He also wanted to memorialize anything she said to use against her in court, if necessary.

With the small talk over, McPherron began the interview in earnest. He explained that since they had last spoken the night before, he had come up with "a laundry list of questions" about her mother's "behavior" and "her lifestyle."

"The fancy term for it is 'victimology,' " he said. "Kind of give me a general description of her. I mean: What is she kind of like? Is she conservative?"

"Conservative in some areas," said Rachelle. "I would say conservative to more old-fashioned."

As she had the previous night, Rachelle spoke of her

mother in the present tense. She said her mom "has a very good temper," that "she's usually pretty happy" and "she volunteers a lot."

"She used to smoke like a long time ago. She drinks socially," said Rachelle—a wine cooler at most when friends drop by. "She's not a bar hopper or anything like that."

McPherron asked about Rachelle's relationship with her mother. "It's pretty good," said Rachelle. "I mean, we have our normal teenage mother-daughter stuff. She doesn't like my black fingernail polish."

The sergeant had been briefed on Rachelle's new fashion sense from Claus and from the interviews with her friends, the black clothes and studded leather collars she had been wearing for about a year now. He didn't press the issue yet, allowing Rachelle to speak.

"We have a good relationship," she continued. "We talk actually a lot compared to what I know about my friends and their mothers. . . . I do confide in her."

Her mother's relationship with her father was similarly good "as far as I know," though she had "heard rumors" of infidelity by her dad. But it was only a "hunch" and there could have been an innocent explanation, she said.

"I think maybe my dad was just, you know, going out, staying really late at work more than normal, going out for long drives that he just kind of started up the last few months," she said. "He hasn't really done that before. . . . Just off behavior for him."

As for her mother's routines, Rachelle said she always left the house carrying a medium-size purse bought from JCPenney along with a matching checkbook-size wallet. Her purse normally contained keys, checkbook, tissues, and makeup.

"She wears her [jewelry] during the day but she takes it off when she gets home," Rachelle says. "She puts it on, like, when she goes to school or to work."

McPherron did all the talking in the interview; Claus watched and listened. The sergeant spoke in a low, calm voice, sometimes almost a whisper that contrasted with Rachelle's eager-to-please voice punctuated with a nervous giggle. With each question, Rachelle appeared to build confidence. About fifteen minutes into the interview, the questions moved from her mother toward her.

McPherron asked for her e-mail address; Rachelle provided it, explaining that it was inspired by the Narcissa, her favorite flower, and the jersey number she wore for basketball and volleyball.

Still positioning himself as Rachelle's friend, McPherron shared that his wife's e-mail was a mix of words created because her maiden name was Fisher and because as a child she moved nine times all over the state.

"That's clever!" said Rachelle.

She said she was more computer savvy than her mother. Asked if her mother sent instant messages, Rachelle for the first time showed a flash of sarcasm. "She doesn't know how to save a picture off her file: How could she figure out how to chat?"

McPherron used the computer questions to throw the first curve. "You know, obviously we've gotten your computer," he told her. "We need to look through the files on the computer. We're just looking for any information we can find that may help us find out what happened."

He asked for her computer password.

"'Craigsucks,'" said Rachelle. She added nervously, "Really funny."

Asked what she used her computer for, she said she stored "pictures, hand drawings, schoolwork, music, and games." McPherron noted that he had a search warrant to check the computer, so if there was anything embarrassing, she should tell him now. She said that, no, it was only "female conversations in my chat."

"Kind of getting back to relationships," said McPherron, "we've kind of gotten some information from other sources that there's been a little friction between you and your mother."

"Uh, a little," said Rachelle. "Just over this and that."

"Like, what are the bones of contention?" asked McPherron.

"Uh, that Jason fellow," she said. "Like, we were friends

for a while. We had kind of talked about being together, but I don't—it's depending on who you're asking." She went back to sarcasm. "I've also had four abortions, apparently, so it depends on who you talk to."

McPherron just said, "Mmm-hmm," and let her talk.

"And then," Rachelle continued, "we realized that, you know, age difference. It's too big. And then my mom found out later, and she's, like: You're talking to an older guy. And I'm, like: Yeah. You know, it was just kind of—she [was] a little bit shocked, I guess, that I was talking to this older guy about that kind of thing, even though it was very brief."

"So, how did that make you feel?"

"I totally understood her position," said Rachelle. "I mean, I would be the exact same way if I had a daughter. But, I mean, I agreed with her."

"How do you feel about your mom's role in your life?" asked McPherron, adopting Rachelle's present tense about her dead mother. "I mean, we were teens once. I have teenagers. I know there's sometimes resentment."

"Well, I mean, sometimes I don't agree with why I can't go out with my friends," she said. "But, I don't know, she's pretty fair and she's open-minded."

"Any other relationships you had that she's disapproved of?"

"Well, with every boyfriend she probably disapproved in the very first, but, you know, she got to know 'em."

Rachelle said her mother didn't like Kelly Carlson "'cause he had an eyebrow ring and a tattoo," but she came around. Her mother had never been unreasonable and, even when Rachelle did something wrong, her mother "could only really ground me, like, a few times."

Even with Jason, Rachelle said, "She actually agreed with [us] being friends. She said: Yeah, you know what, we'll have a talk and maybe he can come over and watch a movie."

As Claus listened, he felt that Rachelle was again downplaying the level of animosity toward her mother and misrepresenting her relationship with Jason. Rachelle said nothing of Jason meeting her at school the day before or of Rachelle stopping by the Klawock school to see him. McPherron would return to the subject later, but backed off and moved instead to the days surrounding the murder.

Rachelle said that she called her mom from the volleyball tournament in Anchorage when she arrived on Wednesday.

"She was really excited to hear from me," she said. Her mother was going to the chamber of commerce dinner and Rachelle was surprised she'd be attending alone. Rachelle repeated her account of returning on the Saturday flight from Anchorage to Juneau, coincidentally getting on the same connecting flight to Ketchikan with her father, then taking separate floatplane flights to Hollis and driving home together. The airlines confirmed her account and McPherron ratcheted up the pressure by moving to a more delicate subject.

"We need to ask," McPherron said. "Now, I'll throw this out first, OK, just so you understand where we're coming from." The detective stopped himself. "I'm sorry," he said. "I guess I should have gone over this again. You know we had talked before and you understand you have a right to have a parent here if you so desire?"

"OK," said Rachelle.

"You understand you don't have to talk to us if you don't want to? You can leave at any time you want—or here in this room just for privacy's sake. And if you wanna go, we'll gladly give you a ride home?"

"Yeah," she said.

"Or you can leave on foot, whatever you'd like to do," he said, "but there's some hard questions we need to ask. And I think you're mature enough to take 'em."

"All right."

"And so you understand: your mother is dead," he said.

"Yeah," said Rachelle.

"And, based on what we've found, that this is not an accident. Your mother did not die in a car crash."

"Yeah."

"Your mother was killed."

"Yeah."

"By somebody. And that's what we're here to find out."

"Yep," said Rachelle.

He told her that the next few questions would pry into her personal life and deal with issues like sex and drugs.

"You're not going to get in any trouble for anything like that," assured McPherron. "OK, we're not here to judge your lifestyle or anything like that."

"And it's confidential?" asked Rachelle.

"We're just here to find out what happened to your mother," he said, dodging her question. "So I wanna make sure you understand that you don't need to be afraid to talk to us about certain issues. I mean we're all essentially adults. You're this close to being one."

"A couple of years," said Rachelle.

He told her the investigation had now provided a "clearer picture as to what happened and who might be responsible for this"—and that one of those people was Jason.

He asked her again about their relationship.

"Just friends," Rachelle repeated. "We're, I mean, like I said before, we had an interest in each other, but it was brief and we decided, you know [with the] age difference, maybe when we're older and are not, you know, this young—"

McPherron interrupted her. He told her that while he understood some young people may feel uncomfortable talking about sensitive issues, "This is very, very severe. This is the biggest thing there is. And we need to find out what happened. And we need everybody to tell us the absolute truth."

He said that he and Claus had been cops a long time and they by now "get a pretty good idea of when somebody's being straight with us and when somebody's trying to be deceptive with us."

He then asked her about her relationship with Brian Radel.

"We became friends but, I don't really—I mean, I talk to him," Rachelle said.

"You ever party with either Brian or Jason?" asked McPherron.

"I have shared an alcoholic beverage once," said Rachelle.

"Smoke any dope, anything like that?"

"Hmm, with Jason, once."

"Has there been any sexual contact between you and Jason and/or Brian?"

"Nope," said Rachelle.

"None at all?" pressed McPherron.

"Nope," she repeated.

"So, why," he asked, "would Jason and Brian tell us that they're having sex with you?"

Rachelle suggested, "Trying to make their egos inflate?" She said the most she ever gave Jason was a "kiss on the cheek."

McPherron didn't drop the issue. He asked her again why Brian would claim to have had sex with her.

"That's really gross, because I've never had any interest in him whatsoever," she said. She acknowledged Brian had a "crush" on her, but "I don't think he'd ever pursue it. I mean, probably the age thing and just 'cause when I met him I was dating his friend"—Ian Lendrum.

Neither Jason nor Brian had acknowledged dating Rachelle, much less having sex with her. It was an interview technique—legal and widely considered appropriate and ethical among police detectives—that McPherron would use repeatedly in the case: lying to get the truth. The tactic drew on his military experience. As a training officer in the army during the waning years of the Cold War, McPherron was an expert on the enemy, teaching a class about the then Soviet military. During battle simulations, he played on the enemy side.

Trooper Bob Claus took over the questioning and picked up on the deception. He told her that police had scoured her house for fourteen hours and looked at "everything that's on the computer," which also wasn't true.

"I'm not a gossip," he told her, a statement that would resonate with a fellow island resident. "You've never heard a word of gossip out of my mouth."

"No, I have not," Rachelle said.

"I don't tell things to my family," he said, a reference to Rachelle's friend, Stephanie. "This is between you and me and Randy."

McPherron asked, "So, how many times have you had relations, sexual relations, with Jason? Has it been less than five?"

Relenting, Rachelle admitted, "Yes."

"When did these incidents occur?"

"Like, do you want specific place and time?"

"If you recall those, yes, because it could be of importance."

"Once in his truck—I don't remember what time, it was probably evening. Once in the bathroom of the building where I used to work. And once at his house."

"Did you have genital intercourse?"

"Yes."

"Did you have anal intercourse?"

"No."

"Did you have oral sex?"

"Yes."

"You gave him oral sex. Did he give you oral sex?"

"Yes."

"But it's less than five times?"

"Yes."

"And when did these incidents occur?"

"This summer."

She said she also was intimate with Brian. She said she didn't have intercourse because his penis was too big— "Girth," she explained—but they had oral sex at his house the previous spring.

"We fooled around, I guess you'd say, and that's it."

"In any of your conversations with Jason," the detective asked, "did you ever say anything about, you know, you're mad at your mother, that she's running your life, you wished she was out of the picture?"

"I said that I was mad at her, but I've never said I wanted her gone," said Rachelle.

"I'm not accusing you of anything," said McPherron, "and I'm convinced that you are not a willing participant in what's happened. But it's very clear to us that Jason and Brian are responsible for your mother's death, and we're trying to figure out why it keeps coming back to you as an unwitting catalyst."

"I highly doubt Jason would do anything like that," Rachelle said. "He's offered to talk to her because she used to hit me occasionally."

"Would Brian wanna get that involved in your life?"

"He's one of those people where he would do a lot for somebody he really doesn't know."

"How far would he go?"

"To the end," said Rachelle. "He is a very dedicated, loyal person."

"We're talking murder," said McPherron. "He would kill somebody?"

"Probably," said Rachelle.

"If somebody asked him to help him do it?"

"Or even on his own."

But Rachelle insisted that Jason couldn't have been involved because she called him at his house from the pay phone in the lobby of the downtown Marriott in Anchorage "very late," perhaps two a.m. on Sunday, when the murder likely happened.

"I was really bored. I couldn't sleep. I knew he'd be up," she said. They spoke for about forty-five minutes to an hour.

"What was the gist of the conversation?" asked McPherron.

"How's volleyball going? How's Craig? New Halo 2 game?" she said. "That kind of stuff. Just BS-ing."

The detective continued to push the view that Jason was involved, telling Rachelle about the assault Jason had staged earlier in the day. He pressed Rachelle on why, if Jason were innocent, he would make a "100 percent crapola" story.

But Rachelle pushed back. "I don't know," she snapped. "I'm not that smart, I guess."

"Just speculate," said McPherron. "Why do you think somebody would do that?"

"Why don't *you* tell *me*?" she shot back, her tone now more confrontational. "I've never known him to get, you know, angry. Never. He gets irritated when he doesn't get a cigarette, but that's about it."

McPherron offered a way to determine once and for all if Jason was involved in the murder: have Rachelle talk to Jason and Brian while secretly wearing a wire.

Aghast, Rachelle asked, "You'd have me ask them?"

"Yes," said McPherron.

"That seems kind of dodgy."

" 'Dodgy'?"

"Dishonest," she said.

"I know on the surface it appears—"

"Dishonest," she answered.

"Well, I don't know if that word would be right," said McPherron. "It's sneaky."

"Yeah," said Rachelle.

"The law allows us to sometimes lie to people," he told her, "just in order to get to the truth."

"It seems wrong to me," she said.

With Rachelle resisting, Claus appealed to her sense of community pride. He told her that the case had to get resolved because "people are scared to death" that a killer was still on the loose.

"People are sleeping with guns. People are paranoid. People are chasing people out of bars 'cause they're the wrong color, 'cause they think this is some kind of stranger thing," he said. "So if we can go quickly, we can put a stop to this."

And nobody was more at risk than Jason and Brian. "I would be afraid for these guys," he said.

Claus was vastly overstating the reaction. One man had raced to the Klawock school with a shotgun when he heard about Jason's assault report, but otherwise life proceeded as quietly as usual on the island, not counting the hum of the rumor mill. But the approach worked. Rachelle was in tears, the magnitude of what the detectives were suggesting sinking in.

"It's not your fault," McPherron told her. "It's, like, is it the water's fault that it flows into the rocks and freezes in the winter and breaks the rocks? It's the water that's doing its thing, right? Your mom's death is not your fault."

"But if I told them—"

"Don't blame yourself," McPherron said.

"No offense," she said, "you did a really good job of making me feel like it was my fault."

"So, why did these guys want to get rid of your mother?" asked McPherron.

"I don't know," Rachelle sobbed.

"Your mom's never done anything to them other than disapprove of you being around them, right?"

"Right," she said.

"Do you know if she's ever confronted either of 'em and told 'em to 'stay the hell away from my daughter'?"

"No."

"Now, obviously both of them knew you and your dad are out of town, right?"

"I don't know if they knew my dad was out of town. They knew I was," she said. "I might have mentioned it."

McPherron asked her to try to remember what she said to them. The last time she spoke to Jason, she believed, was that previous Tuesday—the day before she went to Anchorage—when she saw him at the rehearsal for the community play, *The Importance of Being Earnest*, in which Jason played Dr. Frederick Chasuble. They spoke about her trip to Anchorage the next day.

"Do you think you told him Dad was going to be gone too?" asked McPherron.

"I might have mentioned it," she said, "like, a while ago, but I really don't recall. But it might have come up."

That's not all she told Jason and Brian. Under relentless questioning, Rachelle acknowledged what Claus had suspected—that she and her mother clashed more frequently and intensely than she had previously said, with their differences over more than clothes and dating. In recent months Rachelle had developed an interest in Wicca, she told the detectives.

"What's that?" asked McPherron.

"Just a religion that we believe," she said. "It's kind of like hippie mixed with what you call magic. We believe the earth has spirits, and perform spells."

"So, how did she deal with that?" asked the detective.

"She'd get angry and fight—well, not really fight, but, you know, she'd say you shouldn't do that. A lecture," said Rachelle. "And she'd hit me."

"Explain," said McPherron. "I mean, slap you across the face, kick you in the shin? What do you mean?"

According to Rachelle, the abuse took various forms: her mother hit her legs with a baseball bat and tried to push her down the stairs—"but I caught myself." Her mother also "came to me with a knife once" while in the kitchen cutting up meat for dinner. She ran and hid in her room.

"Did you ever push her back or slap her back?" asked McPherron.

"No," said Rachelle. "I'm too much of a coward." She never told her father and for all she knew he never found out about it.

"You ever tell Jason and Brian about these incidents?"

"Yes," she said, "I just told 'em that she was abusive."

"Did you give 'em any details about that?"

"Not really, just, you know, that she pushed me occasionally. I didn't really say exactly what happened."

"Did you ever say anything like 'I wish someone would straighten her out, get her out of my life'?"

"No, because I didn't want other people interfering 'cause I was embarrassed."

She also told Jason that she had been "depressed lately" about "things with my ex"—Ian Lendrum—as well as troubles at school and nagging health problems, including a sore back.

"You were in a very bad place?" asked McPherron.

"Like, a bad place in my life," she said.

Rachelle told Jason and he in turn "probably told Brian, 'cause that's who he confides in." With each statement Rachelle implicated Jason and Brian, creating a scenario in which the two older men tried to protect the depressed girl from an abusive mother by resorting to murder. The more the investigators listened, the more they came to believe that Rachelle held the men in her thrall, the ties both emotional and sexual.

"Sex is a big motivator," Claus told Rachelle.

"Particularly for young men," added McPherron.

Rachelle downplayed that aspect of her relationship with them. "Yeah, but there's enough people on this island," she said. "That's really not a hard thing to find."

"Hard to find a nice-looking sixteen-year-old girl to have sex with, you know? I'm not saying this is true—"

"Yeah, right," she said.

"I'm just trying to understand what's the driving force behind this," said McPherron. "What is making this happen?"

"I think they're also worried about me because I had contemplated suicide," she said. She confided this to Jason about two months earlier. "It was: My life was crappy, everything's going wrong, that kind of teenage melodrama bullshit," she said.

Brian could have misinterpreted that if he heard about it from Jason. Rachelle said, "I don't know how far he'd take it."

The detectives thought they already had the answer. They had been talking to Rachelle for nearly an hour. It was time for a break, they told her. Claus and McPherron walked out of the interview room, leaving Rachelle alone. It was another interrogation technique: let the subjects stew in their private thoughts, talk to themselves, make admissions thinking nobody is there to hear—even though all the time the video camera was trained on Rachelle.

But Rachelle said nothing. She waited patiently for the detectives to return after several minutes. After conferring in the hall, they decided to play tough.

Rachelle had earlier provided an alibi for Jason, saying

she spoke to him from Anchorage on Saturday night for more than an hour and that he was at home. That wasn't what Jason and Brian had said, McPherron told Rachelle.

"Their story," he told her, "is that they were together Saturday night, Sunday morning, and that Jason drove out to Brian's house some time between two and four p.m. Saturday and spent the remainder of Saturday at Brian's house. They came back into town and do a little shopping, but they did not go back to Jason's house: they went to Brian's place in Hollis and stayed there the rest of Saturday night watching TV. They crashed there. And then Jason gets up in the morning and comes home, ten-ish. Now, that doesn't seem to match what you were telling us about the phone call, does it?"

Rachelle said, "Nope."

"What's the discrepancy here?" asked McPherron. "Who's being honest with us? Did you call him?"

"No," Rachelle admitted.

"Why did you tell us that before?"

"I was scared," she said.

In fact, she said, she had not spoken to Jason on Saturday night. She had talked to him Tuesday before the trip. They didn't get in touch with each other until the day she returned, Sunday, when they chatted online. By then her mother was dead.

"Why did he show up at your house?" asked McPherron.

"Because I called him from the school because I was upset and wanted to talk to somebody."

"Why did you choose to speak to him?"

"Because I didn't think he was doing anything. I really didn't want to pull my friends out of class."

Rachelle was caught in a major lie. McPherron wanted to leverage that.

"I appreciate you being honest with me," he said. "I need you to be absolutely honest with me with everything. Your credibility is on the line here."

"Yes, I know."

"You need to tell us everything," said McPherron. "We do not believe you are responsible for your mother's death but somehow you are the catalyst for the events and we need to find out what that is. And I think you may know."

"I don't know," she insisted.

"We're not blaming you for anything, and it's not your fault what happened."

"You have a funny way of saying one thing and saying the other."

"No, I'm not trying to confuse you or trick you," McPherron said. He explained that the law has "a lot of degrees" of responsibility, and that while somebody could be the cause of a person's death, it could still be inadvertent or unintentional rather than killing somebody "deliberately with malice and planning and forethought." He didn't tell her, but that's the legal definition of "murder."

The more he lectured Rachelle, the more irritable she became. She repeatedly told him she had no idea why Jason and Brian would want to kill her mother. When McPherron asked, "What is making these guys tick?" she shot back, "I don't know. I'm not telepathic."

All Rachelle knew was that the men were "not typical sex-driven people," that they were only occasional drinkers, that they never dabbled in cocaine or LSD, that they played Dungeons & Dragons and other fantasy games but nothing overly violent.

"Are they into pornography?" asked McPherron.

"I don't know. They're guys. Probably."

McPherron said, "We've been talking quite a while. I'm sure you're getting tired. Your dad's probably worried about you. There's one more thing we do need to talk about."

He asked one more time for Rachelle to secretly record a conversation with Brian and Jason. All she would have to do is call Jason, tell him it's very important, then follow a script of questions.

"Time is of the essence," said McPherron. "The longer we wait, the more hysteria builds, the more of a chance that they will get spooked and won't want to talk·to anybody."

"And frankly," added Claus, "I'm worried about Jason. Jason is acting really strange lately. Jason [did] an attack on himself, cut his throat with his keys or his own fingernails to make it look like he was attacked, told us a story, which all by itself is a crime."

"Yeah," said McPherron, "he's committed a crime already."

"If he's willing to hurt himself," said Claus, "implicate himself or commit a crime just to do this, with the amount of pressure that's on him now, I'm afraid he's gonna hurt himself, do something so reckless that other people will hurt him."

"All we're after is the truth," said McPherron. "Like Bob's saying, I'm just as compassionate as he is."

Rachelle made a face.

"Oh, don't roll your eyes at me!" chided McPherron. "Are you willing to help us?"

"I still want to think about it."

"Well, how long?"

"Can I give you my answer tomorrow afternoon?"

"That's a long time. How about tomorrow morning?" pressed McPherron.

"I don't know," she said. "I'll think about it. You kind of pissed me off, making me feel really bad."

"Well, I'm sorry about that, but unfortunately that's my job."

"I know, but I don't like being told—"

"The truth?" Claus offered.

"No," she shot back. "You're telling me I killed my mother."

"We're not saying you did it," said McPherron. "These two people that we know killed your mother and for some reason something is motivating them to do that."

Claus said, "The only nexus, the only connection, is you. And the only way to smoke them out quickly is you."

"The ball's in your court, kiddo," said McPherron. "You can do something rather than sit on the sidelines now. You can get involved. We need your help. . . . The rumors are running. The last thing we need is an ugly mob pointing the finger, blaming Jason, and deciding to do a little vigilante justice on this guy."

"You've heard the rumors as well as we have. Jason can't

even go to work," said Claus. "Middle school kids are calling him a murderer in the school."

"I would like until tomorrow lunchtime," Rachelle said. "That gives me tonight, tomorrow. I'll still be tired, so I won't be able to give rational thoughts. I know I'm gonna go home and cry and go to bed. I might be able to think rationally after sleep."

"Your father wants to know," McPherron said. "Your mother's family is desperate to know. You brother wants to know. This community wants to know. Life is tough sometimes. You get in dilemmas. How we deal with our dilemmas is what makes us human beings or scumbags. And I think you're a human being."

Rachelle held firm. She wanted to sleep on it and go to school as usual. McPherron tried to talk her out of that.

"You're either gonna focus on school or be distracted by your friends."

"I highly doubt that I'll be distracted. . . . I don't like missing class." She said she also had a math test the next day.

"We can fix it for ya," said McPherron. "We can get it so you can take the test again."

"No," said Rachelle. "I mean I like to go, just go there and get my work."

"That doesn't make sense," said McPherron. "Why?"

"Get my work so I can have it done for the next day of class. All I wanna do is get my homework."

"OK."

"I'm sorry, I'm a student."

"I understand that, but—"

"I don't like falling behind."

They left it that the police would talk to her at noon the next day—Wednesday—and get her decision. Then they would tell her father what they're doing.

"Do we got a deal?" asked McPherron.

"Yeah," said Rachelle.

"Shake on it?" asked the detective.

"OK."

At 9:52 p.m., McPherron drove Rachelle home, nearly two

hours after picking her up. He walked her up to her front door, where they met her father.

"She looks a little agitated," said Doc Waterman.

"Long talk" was all McPherron said.

The detective left Rachelle at home without telling her father anything more.

CHAPTER SIX

Craig, Alaska, is a very old town. The native Tlingits arrived around the time the ice age glaciers were still receding. One Indian artifact was dated 10,300 years old. They were later joined by the Haida Indians, who in the early twentieth century worked in the fish saltery owned by a white man. The saltery prospered and by 1907 lost its original name, Fish Egg, and adopted that of the business owner, Craig Miller. When a salmon cannery and a cold storage plant were built, workers arrived, and with them came houses, a post office, and a school, all erected on the steep hills of town. Timber joined fishing as the island's prominent businesses and, by the late twentieth century, so did tourism, sports fishing, and hunting.

Today, Craig retains what Fodor's travel guide calls a "hard-edged aura fast disappearing in Inside Passage towns," still retaining the feel of the little village where herring eggs were collected. No cruise ships come here, sparing Craig the cheesy jewelry and souvenir shops that line Ketchikan's waterfront. The totem poles in Klawock, Hydaberg, and Kasaan villages recall their ancient Indian history. They face the sea and tell in carved cedar creation myths and historical events. This is the real Alaska. A person could find his peace here amid the salt air and spruce, the cold, quiet nights where the lapping waters on the rocky shores and the purr of an outboard are the only sounds. The sunsets over Bucareli Bay are the stuff of poetry.

But to some, Craig might as well still be called Fish Egg, a stinky nothing town with 1,200 gossips and no movie theater or McDonald's. Its most famous former resident is the Playboy reality star Holly Madison, and she has long since left town and doesn't advertise her Prince of Wales Island roots.

Among those who professed to fall into the category of Craig haters was Rachelle Waterman. She hinted as much during her police interview when she revealed her computer password was "Craigsucks." But that was just the beginning. Rachelle regularly expressed her burning displeasure with all things Craig in an Internet blog. She had referred to it briefly during her police interview, telling the cops she had a LiveJournal account that is "like an online journal type of thing." It was called smchyrocky, she said, a "combination of weird nicknames I got."

What she didn't tell them was the other title—My Crappy Life—and that she referred to her hometown as "Hell, Alaska."

Sergeant Randy McPherron and Trooper Bob Claus could be excused for not following up on what she wrote; they were more interested in her e-mails and instant messages, things they knew about and understood. Late 2004 was the Bronze Age of social networking. Blogging could still be done in the privacy of a teen's bedroom for a select audience of peer-group friends and fellow travelers, far away from the prying eyes of teachers, parents, and the police. There was no evidence that Rachelle's parents—or any other adult on the island—knew about her blog.

But thousands of others did see a note posted at 10:56 p.m. on Wednesday, November 18, 2004, and the impact was dramatic. A bizarrely offhand revelation sent shock waves through the Internet and focused a harsh and often unflattering light on Craig, Alaska. It would also provide a context—and potential clues—to Rachelle's mother's murder.

* * *

Before there was MySpace and Facebook, before Twitter, FourSquare, and iPhones and iPad apps, there was Live-Journal. Launched in 1999, LiveJournal was an outgrowth of online dating and social networking services such as Friendster and school alumni search sites like Classmates. com. It offered the best of social networking: users could create a profile of personal information, make lists of new friends, and reach out to old ones. But LiveJournal had a revolutionary feature: the ability to keep an online diary that people could read and comment on.

At 7:50 p.m. on Monday, September 15, 2003, Rachelle typed her first words on her LiveJournal blog: "I'm a newbie."

"This is my first journal entry," she wrote. "What can I say, I'm a virgin (or am I?;)."

From the start, her blog would have all the hallmarks of a teen online journal, from the winking sarcasm to the slap-dash punctuation, misspellings, and mild expletives. She was a rebel without a dictionary, and her frank entries would have shocked her parents' friends and neighbors while also providing an intimate and poignant view of island life. One of the first people on her friends list was her boyfriend Kelly Carlson, who also kept a blog and who saw nothing unusual in Rachelle likening Craig to hell. He would later say, "Anyone who lives in a lot of these towns in southeast Alaska doesn't think very highly of them."

From the very beginning, Rachelle struck a melancholy tone. One of her first posts dealt with losing a close friend who was about to leave Prince of Wales Island for college in Washington State. Rachelle wrote that she snuck out of the house from 2 p.m. to 8:30 p.m. to spend a final day with her friend, driving around the island to let her say goodbye. They ate and tried to find a cat at the beach to feed but it wasn't there. Then her brother Geoffrey also was in Washington for college. She felt alone and sad. "Sniff sniff," she wrote. She tried to distract herself with homework and choir practice, but it was no use. She likened her mood to "PMSing without the bleeding."

But as would be typical throughout her blog, her teenage

emotions rebounded. "Woohoo!" she wrote after an illness to return to sports training, running ten minutes nonstop. In another post, she looked forward to a weekend without homework, a lunch of pizza and a night with her favorite junk food, Cheetos. She signed off with a pet phrase: "Yeyness in a box."

This was followed by another emotional dip. In October she felt somebody wrongly accused her of something—she didn't give her readers the details—and Rachelle said wanted to curl up in a corner and die. Just as quickly, there was another rebound. A week that had left her feeling depressed and "bitchy" brightened when her teacher brought chinchillas to class. With a smiley-face emoticon, Rachelle wrote of how she loved petting the critters and watching them take a dust bath. The week ended with a Sunday night dance where Rachelle had to laugh at one "pathetic guy" who wanted to slow dance with every girl, including her. A suggestion by somebody that she try out for cheerleading also had her in stitches. She got her braces off and was so happy licking her teeth all day. Halloween night was a blast—she and some others egged a house—and her volleyball team earned a trip to the state championships the next month. "WEEEE!!!!" she wrote.

The only thing bringing her down in the late fall of 2003 was that her commitments to the school volleyball team kept her too busy to perform in the school production of *Winnie the Pooh*. Volleyball meant road trips, which were grueling in Alaska: early morning wake-up calls, harsh weather, stomach-churning flights in small planes. But for Rachelle it was worth it: she could get out of Hell. The best trip was to Anchorage, which she described with wide-eyed wonder, telling her blog readers that the state's largest city had everything tiny Craig lacked, including a movie theater, where the team saw *School of Rock* and a shopping mall, where the team hit the Hot Topic store and Rachelle bought a " 'Johnny the Homicidal Maniac' shirt."

The long downtime in airports and ferry terminals also allowed her catch up on homework, listen to music, and mingle with the state's more colorful characters from remote villages. She wrote of a "moron" from Whale Pass and a guy from Nakauti who was "kinda hot" but had a bad habit of talking to her chest instead of her face. She fantasized at how she could get back at him. She would wear tight jeans and a low-cut fishnet tank top, and lean over the counter and tell him she was a lesbian. She suggested she could wear a T-shirt announcing she was only fifteen years old and if anybody tried anything they'd go "straight to jail."

Looking back, her references to being wrongly accused and the object of sexual fascination by older men seemed ominous. But none of what she wrote about in late 2003 would foretell the crisis in which she was immersed a year later. As the winter of 2003–2004 gripped Alaska, the blog took on a darker tone. She wrote of a rare dusting of snow in Craig that washed away with an "evil rain." She tried to keep her spirits up by staying busy. She sold Christmas trees, worked at a local bazaar and watched DVDs of Jim Carrey movies, *X-Men II*, *Great Expectations*. She traveled to Juneau for an Academic Decathlon competition, finishing in fourteenth place, lamenting that she could have done better. She performed in both the choir and the orchestra in the high school holiday concert.

As it always did, the pendulum swung back. Her brother's return home for the holidays lifted her spirits. They went to the pizza restaurant and watched *Bruce Almighty* again. For Christmas, she wrote, she got "some really cool shit" that spoke to her personality: CDs, two books by Edgar Allan Poe, a copy of *Macbeth*, candy, a new coat, pajama pants, a camera case, lotion, candles, drawing supplies and her best gift, a desktop computer with a color printer. "HOLY CHRIST ON A CRAPPER," she wrote, using another pet phrase. The computer came with preinstalled software for her digital camera.

Two presents, however, spoke to simmering troubles at home. She received a new leather collar and a book of Wiccan charms. Her newfound interest in Wicca concerned her mother and father, whom she called "parental units," taken apparently from the Coneheads sketch on *Saturday Night Live*. Her friends didn't get Wicca, either, which she found "irritating," especially those who called it a fad. She took to lecturing her blog readers on what it really meant to be Wiccan, saying she was not motivated by becoming "popular" or "cool," but had a serious interest in it. She explained that she wasn't worshipping Satan or evil, but quite the opposite.

As for the religion in which her mother raised her, Rachelle criticized Catholicism for what she saw as its intolerance of gays and others, though her most serious complaint focused on having to get up early on Sundays to go to church. She needed the rest. By early 2004, Rachelle was tired and stretched thin. She was on the volleyball team, the basketball team, the honor choir, and the Academic Decathlon team. She was trying out for the community play and kept a demanding school schedule. She was so exhausted that one day she fell asleep at school during World Geography and dreamed that she was driving a carload of kids. When her friend smacked the desk to wake her up, in her dream the car crashed.

Final exams and an Academic Decathlon competition amped up the stress level, and she warned her readers not to expect to see too many updates. She was so tired and cranky that a couple of days later at school, after she finished an essay, she went in the hall to take a nap, feeling a cold was coming on. That's when a boy made an unfortunate decision to ask her if she was Wiccan. When she said yes, he asked if she would then be willing to join him in an orgy ritual. Rachelle chewed him out to the point he cried. Her only regret, she reported to her blog readers, was that she didn't also kick him in the groin.

As the pressures of her schedule mounted, Rachelle clashed more with her mother. Rachelle described her mother as a perfectionist who had to paint Rachelle's room a particular shade of robin's-egg blue in December, paying close attention to the corners. "Whatever," Rachelle said. By February 2004, it was one battle after another, with Rachelle complaining that her mother was finding new reasons to torment her. When Rachelle got a 92 percent on a Spanish test, which she described as "just fantabulous," her mother instead took issue with Rachelle's weight. Rachelle's slender, athletic mother—Lauri had been good in sports and had a trophy collection that rivaled her daughter's—wanted Rachelle to go on a diet, according to the blog, which Rachelle felt was unnecessary.

Lauri Waterman also didn't like Rachelle's penchant for wearing black clothing and leather collars. When Rachelle decided to take her look one step further by getting a tattoo, she said nothing to her mother. One day in February, Rachelle heated up a paperclip and burned a pentagram into an upper buttock, hidden so her mother wouldn't find it. She got assistance from a friend she didn't identify and the pain "sucked massively," but she was proud of the outcome. She said she showed it to an anonymous someone—as a birthday gift.

By late winter and early spring of 2004, Rachelle had entered her worst emotional stretch. She wrote of "little pieces of shit" piling up to the "breaking point" and making her want to cry. She said she didn't know whether to curl up under the covers or kill somebody or herself. After one particularly nasty argument with her mother—Rachelle had gotten in trouble over something at school—she locked herself in her room. Her mother tried to make peace by offering her a CD and asking if she was depressed.

"I kinda did say yes," Rachelle wrote.

After researching depression on the Internet and discussing it further with her "female parental unit," Rachelle wrote that she was prescribed Prozac. She thought the medication would be "happy pills," but the effect was the opposite, making her feel "hairy" and "stoned" but also so "horny" she had to masturbate twenty times. This reference was the first of what would become several increasingly profane and sexually explicit posts. She started using the F-word more frequently and told her audience she would soon post naked pictures of herself from her digital camera.

Despite the antidepressants, her fights with her mother

intensified. They clashed over grades, her wardrobe and sports. Begging out of playing softball, Rachelle didn't like the coach—she said he taught the same thing over and over that she already knew from T-ball. Rachelle won that argument and focused on volleyball, only to fight again over what Rachelle would wear to the spring prom. Rachelle wanted to wear an "awesome" black velvet Japanese dress, but her mother told her she was too ugly and fat to pull off the dress, she wrote. She said her mother could "bite me." Her mother pestered her to go fat camp over the summer. She told her "silly mother" she would be the skinniest one there and get hurt when somebody sat on her.

But as it had in the past, the emotional pendulum swung back. In the spring of 2004 she got a job at a T-shirt shop in Craig called Q-Tees. Hard work agreed with her, and she relished creating a new filing system, coming up with shirt designs for her friends, being trusted enough to open and close the store, and getting her twenty percent manager's cut of the profits. Then her "brother bear" returned home from college for the summer. "Goodness in a can," she said, using another favorite phrase.

As the weather warmed, so too did relations with her mother. Lauri didn't even get angry when Rachelle received a C in math. Her mother made her pancakes—though Rachelle couldn't help noting it was from batter left over from pancakes made for her father and brother. She wondered whether "pod people" had taken over her mother.

It wouldn't last. Just days after that post, on June 15, Rachelle got in trouble over something not specified. Her mother went "psycho bitch" and Rachelle fled to a friend's house to spend the night. But then her mom "freaked out" and wanted her home, in case the neighbors found out her mother had banished her. Rachelle was grounded for three days. When she was allowed out of her room, she hated her mother more than ever. She mocked her mother by taking a huge bite out of her toast at breakfast and telling her how good it was. She vowed to herself—and her blog readers—to get out of the house.

When school was out, Rachelle got a second job, this one at the computer store. She wrote she was hoping to learn computer graphics for ten dollars an hour—"WOO it should be fun," she wrote. She described her mood as content and cryptically referred to an anonymous kind person in her life who did "something so small" that made her feel "all better." Rachelle made it through the summer without getting grounded again. She kept busy at the T-shirt shop and computer store and had a Fourth of July celebration at the beach with family and friends. Rachelle's blog went quiet for weeks on end; July had no entries at all.

As the weather cooled and the new school term approached, Rachelle's mood soured again. By late August, she resumed her blog to announce that she was depressed again and wrote a dark poem that spoke of "contemplating death" and wondering if she would "live to see the stars." She tried out for one of two female leads in the community play, which was being produced in the high school auditorium, but didn't get either. Rachelle complained the roles were written for eighteen-year-olds but went to older women. She called the director "retarded" and settled for working on the sound crew.

Her junior year brought another demanding class schedule: Academic Decathlon, advanced literature, US history, advanced calculus, chemistry and band. The varsity volleyball team met each day for practices and frequent travel to other towns and islands. Her sports itinerary included trips to Juneau, Metlakatla, Petersburg, and Anchorage. She was selected to be in the school's honor choir, which Rachelle announced with an enthusiastic "YEYNESS" on her blog, but singing in the choir also required more practice and travel, with an upcoming trip to Haines, a small town more than 200 miles to the north.

A few days into the new school year, Rachelle had the flu and complained again about feeling alone. She asked her blog audience if anybody else felt like there was nobody to "connect with" or to "comfort you when you find out you might die." She posted a depressing poem called "Ode to Suicide," about pain that ate away at her body like lye and left her yearning for relief. Even her depressing poem depressed her. "Wow I suck amazingly at poetry," she wrote.

In October, she was grounded again, this time for two weeks with more restrictions on her computer, because, she said, she got an 89 percent on a math test and her parents found her Wicca books. When she finally got back limited computer privileges, she announced her liberation as if she were a freed prisoner. She invited friends to the regional high school volleyball tournament being hosted in Craig. She repeated that she was lonely and that the world hated her. But when her volleyball team placed second at the Region 5 regional tournament, earning the players a trip to the state tournament the following weekend in Anchorage, a celebration broke out in the gravel streets of Craig. The team rode around town on a fire truck with ten cars behind them honking. The girls sucked in helium from the balloons decorating the fire truck and yelled in funny voices. A dance followed the regional tournament where not even "kinda sucky" music could keep Rachelle down. An ex-boyfriend tried to put the moves on her, but that didn't bother her either.

Three days later she and the team were off to Anchorage. A sprained ankle in practice put her in a brace and did not bode well for her performance in the state finals. She had piles of calculus homework that nobody could help her with because it was too advanced. She also felt another cold coming on, and packed up on flu medication. But no matter: her sights were set on a visit to the Hot Topic store.

On Sunday, November 14, Rachelle wrote in her blog at 6:10 p.m. that she had returned from the road trip. She said she was still feeling sick, that the team finished in fifth place, and that she had bought some "incredibly awesome boots" that went to her knees.

She wrote nothing of coming home to find her mother missing. Her blog didn't mention her first half-hour talk with Sergeant Randy McPherron or her longer, intense interview that left her in tears. It was only the next morning, on Wednesday, November 18, that Rachelle found a computer and posted her one and only message about the event that would rock the island and turn her life upside down:

"Just to let everyone know, my mother was murdered. I won't have computer acess [sic] until the weekend or so because the police took my computer to go through the hard drive. I thank everyone for their thoughts and e-mails, I hope to talk to you when I get my computer back."

It was the last blog post she'd make.

About five thousand people would comment on the entry. It would make Rachelle a celebrity in cyberspace and leave the town leaders stunned. That Doc and Lauri Waterman's overachieving daughter could write so candidly, so crassly, of such private matters—and so unflatteringly of Craig—defied explanation. That she'd dash off a note about her mother's murder as an explanation for the loss of her computer and hard drive struck many as just plain cruel. Most people had never even heard of a blog. Gossip flourished but rarely left the island's shores. Soon, parents in Craig, like elsewhere in America, would be keeping a closer eye on what their sons and daughters were putting out on their computers.

Examined in a vacuum, Rachelle's My Crappy Life blog was neither incriminating nor exonerating. Never in all of her complaints about her mother did Rachelle say she wanted to kill her or wanted anybody else to do it. The names Jason Arrant and Brian Radel never appear. But if Rachelle was the catalyst, as detectives McPherron and Claus repeatedly suggested to her, then the blog offered insights as to why. Police interviews with her friends and family would fill in the rest of the picture.

From what she told police, the two prime suspects in her mother's murder entered her life in the spring or summer, at the very time that her depression worsened and her fights with her mother were becoming more frequent. If these two men who loved fantasy games wanted a real-life damsel in distress, Rachelle made for an attractive candidate.

The Watermans' neighbor Lorraine Pierce told investigators that in the winter of 2003 Lauri was "very concerned" about her fifteen-year-old daughter.

"She felt that she was depressed," Lorraine recalled. "We had discussed what the signs were. We had discussed even the possibility of the type of help she would need. We discussed what the difference between a psychologist and a psychiatrist was. We discussed what the availability was in Ketchikan for her, whether the doctor would be a female or a male."

As with many other services, psychological help was a three-hour ferry ride away, since there were no mental health professionals on Prince of Wales Island. At the very least, Lauri and Lorraine considered, Rachelle might need a break from the relentless cold and rain.

"It was very dark here," Lorraine recalled. "We had discussed maybe extending her trip to see her grandparents in the summer to get her out of Craig a little bit more, maybe attend another volleyball camp or something like that to help pick up her spirits and be in some sunshine."

Rachelle's father also noticed a change in his daughter. "She painted her nails black, she had a preference for black clothes, she wore a collar sometimes with studs on it," her father later said. He knew that her new look corresponded with a growing interest in Wicca, but "we never had a very long discussion about that." All he knew was that Wicca was "nature-based," that Rachelle burned incense and candles, and that his wife didn't like it.

"In matters of religion, Lauri was a little more conservative than I am," said Doc later. "She was raised [with] a strict Catholic upbringing and she pretty much believed everything that she had been taught growing up."

For all his volunteer work with the school and Girl Scouts, Doc had only a vague idea of what was going on with his daughter. Lauri handled the day-to-day child rearing and what he called the "minor discipline." For "major discipline, she would come to me and ask me to be the enforcer," Doc would recall.

Rachelle was grounded twice, as she had reported in the

blog, though Doc gave different accounts. The first time came over the summer when around midnight Lauri woke up to let the cat out and noticed that Rachelle wasn't in her room. Lauri awakened Doc to investigate. It appeared Rachelle had slipped out through a window in the lower-level family room.

"Lauri had noticed some leaves and grass on the window sill. That was her first suspicion," Doc Waterman later said.

They waited up until Rachelle came back around two thirty a.m. or three a.m. "I believe she confessed," Doc Waterman said. "She was confronted with hard evidence." Rachelle claimed she had been at the ballpark, which made no sense to her parents. "There's nobody at the ballpark at two o'clock in the morning," her father said.

Rachelle was restricted to school and her bedroom for several days. She couldn't leave the house but could stay on her computer, her parents still oblivious to her blogging.

She was punished more severely the second time she was grounded, the incident Rachelle wrote about in October, though again Doc related a different version of events. He told police that Rachelle had snuck out for a second time, returning with a story that she had gone to a friend's house.

"She was—and I don't know if I have it all exactly straight—she was trying to put a good spell on the house because her friend was having some kind of problems," her father said. "This was related to her Wiccan."

Her parents didn't believe her and took away her computer privileges in addition to banishing her to her room.

Rachelle's ex-boyfriend Kelly Carlson got the Rachelle side of things. He told detectives that Rachelle complained her mother—it was always her mother—would ground her for getting bad grades, would be condescending toward her, would put her on a diet limiting her to three meals a day and no snacks.

For all her ranting about her mother in the blog, Rachelle never explicitly accused her of physical abuse, though one entry may have hinted at it. On June 14, when Rachelle wrote her mother "went psycho bitch on me" and grounded her, the post ended with this line: "I even got to fly . . . down the stairs." Rachelle listed her current mood as "sore."

She was more open about it in conversations with her friends.

"I do remember at one point, I don't remember exactly what was said, but Rachelle had said to me her mother had pushed her," Kelly recalled later. "I can't remember if she tried to push her down the stairs. I believe she did."

Rachelle never asked for help and Kelly didn't do anything about it.

"I know they had problems," her friend Amanda Vosloh recalled. "It was more like a mother/daughter arguing a little bit. I never saw Lauri arguing with her daughter. Lauri wanted to protect her, and Rachelle wanted something else. . . . She would talk about how her mom thought she was fat and would not feed her sometimes because she thought she was overweight. I never really believed that."

Rachelle also confided to Amanda that her mother had hit her, but she "never emphasized that." It would be said in passing. "She said that her mom had tried to knock her down the stairs," said Amanda.

Like Kelly Carlson, Rachelle's girlfriends did nothing because they didn't believe her. "She said some things to me about her mom that didn't seem like they were always true," recalled Stephanie Claus. "She told me that she would be grounded and her mom wouldn't feed her, and that to me seemed entirely inaccurate. She got grounded because she got a B-plus on a math test because a B-plus wasn't good enough for her mom, and that didn't seem right to me."

As fond as he was of Rachelle, her former boyfriend Ian Lendrum shared the skepticism. He knew that Rachelle and her mother fought and yelled at each other, and that Rachelle was grounded a couple of times. Then she told him "that her mother hit her and stuff like that," he recalled. "She said her mother pushed her down the stairs or shoved her or something." Rachelle showed him bruises and what she said were marks from her mother grabbing her, but he didn't think much of it: she also had bruises from volleyball.

John Wilburn, a boy who played Dungeons & Dragons with Rachelle over the summer, recalled that Rachelle said her mother beat her and called her fat. Rachelle even said something to the effect of "I wish my mother would die," but Wilburn thought it was just "normal teenage angst."

It appeared that only one person took Rachelle's claims of abuse seriously, according to John. "I recall Jason saying he wanted to protect her."

CHAPTER SEVEN

The big man was sweating.

"I'll be honest with you," Sergeant Randy McPherron told Jason Arrant, "I don't think this assault occurred. I don't think it happened. In fact, I know it didn't happen. It didn't occur."

Jason squirmed. "Yes, it did."

"It didn't happen," McPherron repeated.

"No," said Jason. "I didn't make it up."

"Come on. Look at me," the detective said. "We have witnesses."

"They didn't—"

The detective interrupted him. "They saw nothing! I'm telling you, you made this up."

On Thursday, November 18, Jason was at the Klawock trooper post trying to convince McPherron and Trooper Bob Claus that an unknown assailant really did attack him with a serrated knife at the school the night before.

By now Jason's name was mud on Prince of Wales Island. Teachers were talking to police. Rachelle's friends were talking to police. Rachelle herself had sat for an interview. The chamber of commerce members, the coaches, the church congregation, the merchants and fishermen—everybody had come to the conclusion that Jason Arrant had murdered the sweetest, most wonderful person on the island.

The pressure was getting to him. Jason told the investigators how the island was closing in on him, how he'd never be able to show his face if he didn't come forward with the truth.

McPherron said he didn't believe him—didn't believe that he was attacked at the school and didn't believe that he had nothing to do with Lauri Waterman's murder.

Jason fought it, but his resolve weakened. He appeared to wilt before the detectives' eyes. Finally, he admitted that he made up the attack story, but clung to his alibi the night of the murder. He said he was drinking beer at Brian Radel's place.

No, said McPherron, you weren't. You were involved in the murder. "Was it your idea?" asked the detective.

"I didn't do that," Jason said.

"Jason, I know you did."

"No," he said weakly.

Jason slumped.

"So," McPherron said, "what happened? What's your role in this?"

Jason paused.

"I—" he started. "I know what happened out there."

When Jason was finished giving his account of the night of the murder, a change came over him. Color returned to his face.

"It's actually a huge load off my mind," he told the detectives.

"I can tell, you look a lot better," said McPherron. "You looked pretty burned down."

In his third meeting with police, Jason had given up his best friend.

Several hours later, at five p.m., Sergeant Mark Habib was hooking Jason up with a microphone and transmitter under his clothes. The equipment came from Habib's duties on a regional drug task force in which he worked informants and did undercover operations. Once fitted, Jason drove his truck toward Hollis. Ahead of him, in an unmarked Suburban, were McPherron and Habib. Behind him in another vehicle was Claus.

After the interview at the trooper post, McPherron had obtained a judge's warrant allowing the surreptitious recording of conversations with Brian Radel. Jason had continued to deny killing Lauri, saying instead that Brian committed the murder. By the time Jason found out about it, Lauri was already dead.

Jason's cooperation was vital. The investigators didn't just want Brian to make incriminating statements on tape, they needed him to. They had little else on which to build a case. Rachelle had claimed to know nothing about the murder, and Jason backed her up in the face of stern questioning by McPherron.

"Absolutely not," insisted Jason.

"Why?" asked McPherron.

"She's just not that kind of a person."

"You want this relationship to continue, don't you?"

"I do."

"I think you love her, don't you?"

"Yes, I do."

"Would you do anything for her?" asked the detective. "Would you lie for her? Have you lied for her?"

"I don't think she's involved in this, if that's what you're asking," said Jason.

Brian was another story. Jason professed to be shocked that his friend had killed Rachelle's mother. Jason admitted he withheld the information from police out of fear and confusion, and now agreed to help implicate Brian.

The officers got to the house first, parking the Suburban across the street near the tree line to await Jason.

They were all set to go, when the operation faltered. Brian strolled across the street toward the officers' Suburban carrying a flashlight. Habib got out of the vehicle and shined his own high-powered police flashlight in Brian's eyes to blind him. If Brian saw him, he'd know that Habib had come outfitted in full tactical gear: dark navy blue fatigues, Kevlar vest, night vision goggles, and an assault rifle.

Brian squinted in the light. He asked what was going on.

"I'm looking for the Johnson residence," Habib said.

It was a feeble lie, but Brian didn't ask any more questions, for at that moment Jason's truck pulled up in front of the house. Brian went back across the street, and the two men went into the house.

Jason had been given a list of instructions by Habib in undercover practices, and immediately proceeded to ignore all of them. To begin with, he had been told to avoid any ambient noise while talking to Brian so that the recording would clearly pick up his words. Instead, the TV blared in the background, and for much of the time all the detectives could hear was an episode of *King of the Hill*. From what little they could make out, Brian was jumpy and paranoid, convinced police were onto him and had bugged the house, but he didn't say anything about the murder.

Jason ignored another instruction. When Brian asked for a ride to Thorne Bay to meet with his brother, Jason agreed. Habib had implored Jason to stay in the house, where he would be both protected by the officers across the street and within radio transmitter range. Instead, the detectives listened to Jason telling Brian, "I'll drive you down there."

The detectives saw the men leave the house. Jason smoked a cigarette before the men got in his truck and drove away, with the police following. Due to the truck and traffic noise, little of the conversation during the half-hour ride could be understood, but one exchange was salvageable.

"All right, man," Jason told Brian, following a script of questions, "just, you know, if it comes down to it, and they try to pin this on me and Rachelle, even though we didn't have nothing to do with it, what are you going to do?"

Brian answered, "I'll probably jump up and try to convince them that I did it."

After leaving Brian at a gravel turnout to be picked up

by his brother, Jason drove back to the Klawock trooper station to return the recording equipment and get a ride home. The investigators huddled. Jason's admissions and Brian's comment on the tape left little doubt that both were involved in the murder, with Jason likely downplaying his role.

The detectives had enough evidence to arrest Brian, but the case was weak. They had no hard physical evidence—no fingerprints or blood that could be tied to Jason or Brian—and no eyewitnesses. They couldn't even know for sure where the murder took place.

What they had were words. Rachelle acknowledged she told Jason about the abuse by her mother, Jason acknowledged that he knew that Brian had killed Lauri, and Brian was overheard saying he was willing to admit that he did it.

If investigators were to build a tighter case, they were going to have to get the three to talk some more. They would have to act quickly, before the trio could compare notes, come up with reasons to remain silent, or hire lawyers.

Just after midnight, McPherron and Claus knocked on the door of Jason Arrant's parents' house. Jason's father Doug answered.

"Howdy," said McPherron.

"Hi," said Doug.

"How you doing today? I'm Sergeant McPherron, and you know Bob Claus, don't you?"

"Nice to meet you," said Doug Arrant.

The men went into the house. Jason was there.

"Hi, buddy," McPherron said. "I have a few more questions for you."

"Sure," said Jason.

"Is there some place we can talk privately?"

"Just go to my room or out on the porch there," said Jason.

"Your room sounds good," said McPherron.

Claus would later remember it as looking like a twelve-year-old's bedroom, with action figures assembled with care and shelves of video games. A dog followed them.

"What's your dog's name?" asked McPherron.

"That's Scruffy," said Jason.

"Scruffy, OK," said McPherron. "Why don't you have a seat. Just a few things we need to run by ya."

In fact, the detective had much more in store for Jason. He signaled this by telling him he had the right to remain silent, the right to have an attorney present, and that anything he said could be used against him in court.

"Having these rights in mind," McPherron said, "do you wish to talk to us now?"

"Yes," said Jason.

The questioning then began, with McPherron taking the lead and Claus listening and jumping in at times. It began on friendly enough terms, with McPherron asking Jason about Rachelle. Jason loved her and listened to her, giving her claims of abuse the attention her other friends didn't.

"Did you believe all the stuff that she was saying?" asked McPherron.

"I believed the abuse 'cause I saw the bruises," said Jason.

"What bruises? Where were they on the body?"

"I saw some bruises on her arms and a couple on her legs and a couple on her back."

"Did Rachelle ever say anything like her parents were gonna sell her into slavery or something like that?"

"She did tell me that," said Jason. "They had actually discussed that. I wasn't sure whether to believe that or not."

As they spoke, it was well past midnight, and the strain began to show not only on Jason but on the exhausted McPherron.

"OK, so did you discuss these things with Jason?" the detective asked.

"I'm Jason."

"I'm, sorry—Brian," said McPherron. "I haven't slept much in the last few days."

"Understandable," said Jason.

The interview so far had not told the investigators anything they hadn't already heard from Rachelle, so McPherron shifted the focus to the hours leading up to the murder. Jason said that he and Brian went to stores in Craig and Klawock that Saturday afternoon. He insisted he saw nothing sinister in the fact that Brian was loading up on things like duct tape, gloves, and towels.

"What did he tell you all these supplies were for that he was buying?" asked McPherron.

"He told me that they were gonna be cutting up a deer," said Jason. "[He] said that he used to use the same stuff all the time when he was working at Mel's Meat Market place that has since closed down."

When they returned to Brian's place, however, they didn't drink beer and watch TV as Jason had originally said. Instead, Jason helped cut Brian's hair.

"He told me he was just tired of it being too long and he didn't wanna pay for a haircut," said Jason.

"OK."

"Because he was—he's always been kind of scruffy."

Then, at about midnight, Brian asked for a ride to the marina in Craig, where he had a broken-down boat he had been sleeping in. After they arrived, Brian had one more request: he wanted Jason to pick him up at an old logging road near Thorne Bay later that night. He gave him directions but no explanation.

"What did you think was going on?" asked McPherron.

"I wasn't sure," said Jason. "I kept asking him, but he told me just to trust him, that he needed my help. I mean, I've known him for years."

"What did you suspect was going on?"

"I honestly suspected that something was fishy, but I had no idea that it was—that it was *that*."

Out of loyalty, Jason didn't press the issue and did as he was asked.

"And when he shows up with the body in the car, that's the first time you realize that this was murder?"

"Yes."

Jason said he then watched in horror as Brian set fire to the van with Lauri's body inside.

McPherron said he had a problem with that story. He said that Jason was lying. What really happened was that Jason knew all about the abduction and "you guys were going to get rid of the body."

"No," Jason protested. "I did not have any idea. If I'd known, I would have never done it."

"Well, Jason, I have some problems with that because, you know, initially you told us several lies."

"I understand that. And I know that makes it lot harder for you to trust me," Jason said, "but, I mean, we can go down and do a polygraph right now. I had no idea he was gonna do something like this."

McPherron refused to accept his answers.

"You knew that he was gonna grab her, kill her, and you guys were gonna get rid of the body," he told Jason. "He filled you in on the plan before you departed."

"No," Jason said.

"Jason, you're not gonna help yourself by continuing to lie to us, OK?"

"I'm not lying."

"Well, you did lie. You even fabricated an assault."

"I know that," he said. "I know that destroys my credibility. But I'm not lying now."

"You knew when you left Hollis that Lauri was gonna be dead by the end of the night?"

"No, I didn't."

"Yeah, you did."

"No, I didn't.

"You honestly expect us to believe that after all these lies?" said McPherron. "You sat on this for four days. Four days of knowing exactly what happened, who's involved, and you did nothing about it?"

"That's because by the time I'd already seen the body, I'd already given him the ride, and I was already up to my neck in shit," said Jason. "I was terrified of this whole thing. But I did not kill this woman. I did not."

Claus then took a turn at questioning him.

"I look around your room, your place, the little I know about you from the last couple days of conversation and stuff," the trooper said. "You're a smart guy. You're a logical thinker. You play games and watch movies and things that require you to follow, to use clues to follow a logical sequence of events. What would a reasonable person do, who didn't have the guilty knowledge, when someone presents them with this set of facts: I'm gonna buy duct tape. I'm gonna buy towels. I'm gonna buy gloves. I'm gonna have a little bag with tools in it. And you're gonna drop me off in the middle of the night?

"What is the reasonable person to think?" continued Claus. "Is something good gonna happen? Is this criminal activity? A reasonable person is going to figure out all this stuff. You're too smart for this, Jason. . . . You get to the top of the hill, he opens the door, you see a body. You don't go down the hill? You don't leave Brian there?"

"You saw that road," Jason said. "You know how narrow it is. By the time I would have got half way turned around, he'd be a yardin' me out of that truck and breaking my neck."

"How do you know that?" asked Claus.

"Because he's obviously capable of murder," said Jason.

"Look around you, man. You're too smart for that. You can't expect us to believe that?"

"You've already made up your mind," said Jason, "but I'm telling you the truth."

About forty-five minutes into the interview, McPherron finally said, "If this is the position you wanna take, then so be it. Carry this millstone with you—I'm not gonna try and stop it. We have a warrant for your arrest, OK? We need you to stand up, please."

Claus had the warrant in his pocket. He had secured it from a judge before they went to Jason's house.

"Where are your shoes at, Jason?" asked Claus.

"They're out in the living room," he said meekly.

"Let's wander out there," said Claus. "You can put your shoes on, then what I'm gonna do is put handcuffs on you outside the house. You have any ID or anything that you wanna bring with you? You might wanna leave money or whatever here, but you can bring your wallet. Do you have anything in your pockets at all besides that ID card?"

"Nothing in my pants pocket," said Jason. "I've got my cigarettes and my coat back there."

"You won't be able to smoke when you get to the jail," said Claus.

"Just leave them behind," added McPherron.

"Leave the lighter as well," said Claus. "Any tools, knives, anything like that?"

"Keys with an edge on them?" said McPherron.

"I can give you a copy of the warrant," said Claus. "I can give it to your father if you'd like."

"That's fine," said Jason.

As the detectives were about to lead Jason out of his room to take him to the police station where his mother worked, he said, "Wait."

The troopers stopped.

"Let's have a seat," Jason said. "You're right. I was digging myself deeper."

Claus let go of Jason. They took their seats in the bedroom and the interview resumed.

"So, when did you know what Brian was going to do?" asked McPherron.

"I don't know exactly," said Jason, "but several days."

About a week earlier, Jason said, Rachelle had told him she was traveling to Anchorage for the volleyball tournament. "And then she just mentioned offhand that her dad had to take a business trip too," he said.

"So the opportunity presented itself?" asked McPherron.

"Yes," said Jason.

"When did you relay this information to Brian?"

"Shortly thereafter."

"And that's when you guys resolved: OK, this is when we're gonna do it, when we're gonna kill Lauri?"

Jason said, "Yeah."

"Did Brian agree to do the hands-on, the killing part?" asked McPherron.

"Yes," said Jason. "He didn't want me to have any part in that."

"Why is that?"

"Because he didn't want me to see it," said Jason. "I guess he was trying to protect me from that. I couldn't even hardly put my own dog down when I had to."

According to Jason, the plan called for Brian to break Lauri's neck, but "I don't know if that's actually how it ended up happening." Brian told Jason the killing would occur close to the Forest Service 3012 road, but didn't say exactly where. They would dispose of the body by torching the van with Lauri inside it.

"I was afraid that Rachelle wasn't safe with her mother," he said. "And that one day things were gonna go too far. She was gonna get hurled down the stairs and not get back up."

"So you planted the seed in Brian's head?" asked McPherron.

"Yeah," said Jason. "And then he's the one that ended up working out the details. We'd actually tried to think up different things."

Of the murder plans they had first discussed "nothing really seemed feasible" for a couple of months. And when Rachelle told him she had stopped having problems at home, their plotting "seemed to boil down a little bit."

Then Rachelle told him recently about getting "hurled down the stairs again" and "threatened with a knife" by her mother.

"Brian and I decided that she needed to be safe," said Jason. "And he worked out a plan and relayed it to me. . . . And then we carried it out."

"OK," said McPherron.

Jason said, "I'm gonna be in jail for the rest of my life, aren't I?"

"Well," said McPherron, "I don't know that. But I appreciate you being honest with us finally."

Jason said, "I just wish I had done it that night."

"Done what?"

"Just dropped him off and come down, told you guys what had really happened," he said. "I can't take that back now, but it's been eatin' at me. And now I'm just in worse trouble."

"Well," said McPherron, "the truth is—what the truth is."

For all Jason's newfound candor, questions nagged at McPherron and Claus, all of them relating to Rachelle. For two men to be willing to kill for her, she had to have offered something special.

"Was there ever a threesome?" suggested McPherron.

Jason appeared genuinely taken aback. "No, absolutely not," he said.

"So you loved her that much?" the detective asked.

"I still do," Jason said.

It was over for Jason Arrant. He put on his shoes and coat and reached for a cigarette.

"Is there any possibility that I could have just one of those before we leave?" he askd.

"Yeah, sure," said Claus.

"Just take one butt," added McPherron.

As Jason lit up, McPherron asked one more time, "Just to be sure now, did you ever tell Rachelle what was gonna happen?"

"No," said Jason through cigarette smoke.

"And she was never privy to any of these discussions about how we're gonna do that?"

"Not with me," he said. "She might have been with Brian."

"'Might have been'? Did he ever say she was?"

"No, but I can't say whether he did or not."

Claus clamped the cuffs. "You can continue to smoke while I get this done," the trooper said.

"One more drag and let's go," said McPherron.

Jason's mother, the police dispatcher, watched in horror. "I didn't know you guys were taking him," she said.

Claus gave her a copy of the arrest warrant and led Jason to the patrol car for the twenty-minute ride to the police station in Craig. Shortly after one a.m., Jason was placed in a cell.

CHAPTER EIGHT

The Lauri Waterman case was slow to attract media attention. Prince of Wales Island has one newspaper, the weekly *Island News*. Supported by ads for concrete contractors, a septic tank maintenance company, beauty salons, the floatplane charters and Doc Waterman's business, Island Reality, the paper keeps locals up on changes in fishing regulations, the tide tables, and events at the library and senior center, but didn't have anything on the murder.

There are no television or radio news stations in Craig. People with cable get their TV news from Anchorage stations, which wouldn't carry the story for days. Those with satellite dishes pick up the news from Seattle or Denver.

The first paper with the story was the *Ketchikan Daily News*, which arrives on the island each morning in bundles carried in the small cargo sections of floatplanes. Under the headline "Body Inside Burning Van Is Identified," the article said that troopers were investigating Lauri's death as a "possible homicide." Doc told the paper of returning home from Juneau to find his wife missing. The story made no mention of troopers' suspicions about Rachelle, nor was it able to include by deadline the overnight developments, including the arrest of Jason Arrant after he admitted to helping dispose of Lauri's body.

Another major development in the case also didn't make the morning papers. Jason's undercover operation provided enough evidence to get an arrest warrant for Brian Radel. Trooper Bob Claus tracked down Brian at his mother's house and, after a brief discussion, handcuffed him and drove him to the Craig jail, where he spent the night in a cell near that of his longtime friend.

Brian had told Jason he was willing to take the fall, and by Friday afternoon troopers had collected circumstantial evidence against both men. Irving Langmaid, a clerk at the Black Bear Market, a convenience store in Klawock that sells everything from fishing tackle to frozen dinners, told investigators that both men—whom he knew—came into the store on Saturday and bought two rolls of duct tape. Security video at the nearby Klawock Liquor Store showed Jason and Brian buying a bottle of wine at 4:52 p.m. that same day. A search of Brian's mother's house turned up a black hat, and a search of Lee Edwards's house turned up electric hair clippers, a clump of reddish hair, and ashes in a five-gallon bucket near the woodstove.

At two p.m. on Friday, Brian was let out of the cell and escorted into the same interview room where Rachelle had been two days before. As he sat down with Sergeant Randy McPherron and Trooper Bob Claus, Brian said he was willing to make a full voluntary statement on video explaining in detail how he kidnapped and killed Lauri Waterman.

He spoke in calm, matter-of-fact tones. When McPherron read him his rights and reminded him he had the right to remain silent and to have an attorney, Brian waived them both. "I can understand. I figure it's not a problem because I'm planning to plead guilty when this gets to court anyway," he said. "I have no problem talking to you guys."

McPherron got out a pad of paper and asked Brian to help him diagram exactly how he got into the Watermans' house.

"I realize I'm not the world's greatest drawer here," he said, scratching out a diagram. "Here's the street, here's the garage doors, here's Lauri's minivan parked in the—was it nosed in?"

"Nosed in," said Brian.

"Here's the access door with the cat door. Could you show

me—I'll use a different color marker—exactly where you got in the house?"

"Absolutely," said Brian.

Brian said he broke into the two-car garage around twelve thirty a.m. or one a.m. "through the first window I came to," which he struggled to open. He fumbled in the dark garage, afraid of turning on the light and being exposed to neighbors, before he found a door to the house. He tried to jimmy the lock with a butter knife, two of which he'd brought for that purpose, but "I could see that wasn't gonna work."

Crouching on the floor, he reached his arm through the cat door and tried to get to the doorknob on the other side, but came up short. "So I took the cat door out," he said. With the extra room, he could reach the knob with his fingertips and "pulled the door slowly open."

He found himself in the Watermans' lower-level family room with a TV, a sofa, beanbag chairs, and a card table, though at the time he wasn't sure where he was. He had no map, even though he wanted one, and he "didn't have any idea of the layout of the house," having been there only once, briefly.

In the darkened house, he found the stairs to the second floor—the main level with the living room, dining room, kitchen, laundry room, and bedrooms for Rachelle and her brother, Geoffrey.

"I looked around that floor, checked different rooms there, and I could see that there wasn't anyone in that area," Brian said.

Going to the top level, Brian quietly cracked open a door and saw Lauri in the master bedroom.

"She was asleep at the time," he said. "Then she got up and closed the door."

Brian feared she had heard him. He hid around the corner just in time not to be seen, and stayed there, motionless as best he could in the dark, for the next ninety minutes.

"I really psyched myself up considering what I was going to do," he said. "Was I going to go through with it?"

At about three a.m., he decided to act.

"I came up. I had the flashlight shining at her just in case she turned around, so that you know, blinded, because I didn't have any idea of hideaway guns or whatever," he said. "So I came up. I had a cloth in my hand, put it over her head, pulled it sideways, and just held it around her mouth."

"So that action woke her?" asked McPherron.

"That action woke her."

With his huge body, he pinned her down to the bed. He didn't say anything to her and she didn't say anything to him. She didn't resist.

"Then what happens?" asked the detective.

"I had duct tape in my pocket," he said. He put the tape over the cloth gag, then bound her wrists behind her back the same way.

"When did the rope come into play?" said McPherron, remembering the fibers found on and around the bed.

"The rope didn't come in play until I had her tied up completely," Brian said. "It was during the process of moving her around. Anytime I was away from the bed, she had two hands tied behind her back so that I could look around the room so I still had some sort of control."

"So she's lying there. You've now gagged her, tied her wrists behind her back. Did you tie her feet up then?"

"Yes."

"The cloth first, then the duct tape?"

"Yes."

"Why that particular way?"

"So that I wasn't going to leave bruising or abrasion," Brain said. "Not to leave any residue of the tape."

He then bound her wrists and legs with rope, which he described as old, bristly, greenish, muddy rope that had been lying on the side of the road. She was wearing green panties and a flannel nightdress. He held the other end of the rope like a leash while he went through the dresser drawers to find something for her to change into.

"So you wanted to get her dressed? Why is that?"

"Because, if things had gone the way I would have wanted 'em, I would have made this look like an accident."

"Like a driving accident you mean?"

"Yeah."

"OK, makes sense," said McPherron.

Holding her with the leash, Brian found an item in the drawer and asked Lauri, "Is this your clothes?" She nodded yes. He untied her enough to change into a "shirt or whatever."

McPherron asked, "Did you have sex with her?"

"No, I did not," said Brian.

"Did you touch her?"

"Other than to simply grab her on the shoulder, no," he said.

Wearing rubber gloves, Brian helped Lauri get dressed, taking off her gag so she could answer questions: at one point he wanted to know where her purse was.

With Lauri Waterman now dressed, he tied her hands again behind her back, had her put on shoes, tightened the rope around her wrists, and told her they were going downstairs to show him where her purse was. They went into the kitchen for the next part of his plan.

"I went and searched the refrigerator," he said, "found a thing of wine, got a glass and simply filled it up, told her to drink it until the bottle was empty."

"What'd you do with the glass?" asked McPherron.

"The glass went in the sink."

"What'd you do with the bottle?"

"The bottle went in the car. Should be in the front of the car," he said. In fact, it was a melted blob. "It was in the front seat." He had no use for the bottle of wine he purchased earlier in the day; it was disposed of later.

Around this time Brian looked at his gloves and realized he had made the first of several blunders that night.

"The left hand one got ripped," he said; that accounted for the tip of rubber police found.

"And when did that happen?" asked McPherron.

"That's when I was putting the duct tape on."

"You just left it there?"

"It wasn't until I got downstairs that I saw that it had been ripped," he said, "so pretty much figured at that point I was probably screwed."

Carrying the wine bottle, Brian led the bound and gagged Lauri into the garage, where he told her to get into the minivan. He ordered her to lie sideways across the back passenger seat. Now, apparently drunk from the wine, she lay on her right side, her gagged face pressed against the seat back. Brian tied her bound hands to an armrest.

He ran back upstairs for a once-over, still remembering that missing glove tip, but he couldn't find it.

"I was in a hurry to try to get out of town before it got too light," he said. He packed his gear into a trash bag he had brought and tossed it on the seat behind the one where Lauri was tied. The last thing he did at the house was to reattach the cat door, then got into the van.

He removed Lauri's gag to ask her where the electric garage door opener was. She told him it was on the sun visor. He drove out of the garage, closed the door behind him, and headed out of town, past Klawock, until he go to the T in the road, turned left, and drove about a half hour until the pavement turned to gravel. He went another twenty minutes on gravel toward Naukati. Much of the road was winding and unpaved. Lauri, her stomach full of wine she was forced to drink, bounced around in the backseat but never said anything.

Brian pulled over into a turnout on the left side of the road, unsure exactly where he was.

"There's a creek or a river or something," he said. "There was trees all around." He recalled a small bridge just beyond where he pulled over.

It was occurring now to Bob Claus that although Brian had grown up on Prince of Wales Island, he had never been to this area before. Less than an hour's drive from his home, Naukati is one of only a handful of communities on the entire island, but for Brian, the trooper said later, "this was the end of his known universe."

Brian said it was now about four or four thirty a.m. He

opened the sliding side door of the minivan, pulled Lauri out, and set her down on the gravel on her knees.

The plan was to fill her with wine and make it look like she died in a drunk-driving crash.

It didn't go as Brian had hoped.

He tried to break her neck with his bare hands, but although he heard a crack, she was still moving and breathing.

He then pummeled her neck with a red flashlight, and still she didn't die.

Finally, he covered her mouth with a cloth and pinched her nose and held on to her.

Through it all, Lauri never resisted, never screamed. But at one point she said to Brian, "Can I ask you a question?" She seemed dazed or drunk or both.

Brian recalled, "She just kept repeating that. She didn't say anything else."

"And did you reply?" asked McPherron.

"I stopped and said, 'What?' And she just kept repeating that: 'Can I ask you a question? Can I ask you a question?' "

"OK," said the detective, "she's on the ground, you're pinching her nose and covering her mouth: Did she finally stop moving then?"

"She stopped to a certain point, but she wasn't dead yet," said Brian. "But I figured I was running out of time. I figured if I had to, I'd take her to another location and finish her off. I figured likely she was dying. Because of the throat, she was going to die anyway. So I put her back in the vehicle."

"Did you see any blood? Did you see any swelling?"

"There was blood. I saw some marks on her throat. There was some marks on the cloth."

Her feet and hands were still bound when he loaded her back into the van's backseat. She was in the fetal position. He got into the van and drove to the 3012 turnoff, where he had told Jason to wait for him. By now it was about five a.m. and just starting to turn light. It was raining softly but there was no wind or fog.

He saw Jason's truck. From the intersection, Jason followed Brian up the logging road. Brian pulled over and cut the bonds from Lauri.

"Did you ever check to see if she was dead yet?"

"Yes, I did."

"Why'd you do that?"

"Because I wasn't exactly interested in burning someone alive. I decided I was gonna kill her, but I figured I'd finish her then." He said he would have suffocated her again. He checked for a pulse and didn't feel one.

"And just to confirm," asked McPherron, "did Jason ever lay hands on her?"

"No, he did not," said Brian.

"So then you soaked the body pretty thoroughly in gas?"

"Yeah."

"Then put some in the car?"

"I soaked the front seat, all the seats, anywhere I'd been sitting, where my feet might have been."

He left the wine bottle and her purse in the car, but took out his break-in gear—the butter knife, duct tape, etc.—which was in a trash bag. Just then the car rolled down the side of the hill a few feet. He went down the bank, poured more gas in the van, ran a trail of gas up the hill, and went to get a lighter from Jason's truck, about fifty yards away.

When he returned, he couldn't find his gas trail because the ground was wet from rain. He went back to Jason's truck and found a roll of paper towels, which he lit and threw into the van.

"Did Jason stay in there or was he up by you helping?"

"He was by the car."

"So he never goes up to where the vehicle is?"

Brian said Jason never left his truck.

The fire took about thirty seconds to catch and then the van "basically blew up," Brian said. "And at that time, I ran down the hill. Jason was freaking out, and we left."

It was, to be sure, a full and complete confession, enough to convict Brian Radel of first-degree murder and put him away for the rest of his life. His story was corroborated by the physical evidence: the rope fibers, the glove tip, the melted wine bottle, plus the witness accounts from the clerks at the convenience and liquor stores.

To the troopers, Brian came off as a stone-cold killer with no conscience. He affected the attitude of a man who didn't care what happened to himself, chillingly honest and straightforward about the deed he had committed, willing to answer any question, ready for the consequences.

And yet, McPherron and Claus felt he was still holding something back. Despite his denials, Jason seemed deeper into the murder plot than Brian was suggesting. Why else would Jason just happen to have had a gas can and paper towels that night? And what of Rachelle? Her name barely came up, and yet this murder was all supposedly done to protect her. McPherron had more questions.

"Obviously you know we've arrested Jason," McPherron told him. "Was it his idea initially to kill Lauri?"

"He planted the seed," Brian acknowledged, "but past that, he had nothing to do with any sort of planning. I mean, there wasn't a bit of this that was his planning."

"He was kind of the idea man and you were the follow-through?"

"Yeah."

"I understand also this occurred over a period of several weeks to a month that you guys are plotting this? You guys discussed different scenarios of how you would do this?"

"Yes."

"How to get in the house, how to kill her?" asked McPherron.

"Again, it wasn't really discussed," Brian said. "I came up with different plans of what I was going to do, and again there wasn't a plan that Jason actually came up with."

"OK, so it was more like bouncing ideas off of you?"

"Yeah."

"So, then, was the original plan to make this look like a car wreck?"

"The original plan—it went through a lot of metamorphosis. I mean, we went through stages where [it was] my personal desire of trying to find blackmail or something, just something to possibly blackmail her with."

"And this is a means to get her to stop abusing Rachelle?"

"Yes," said Brian.

The detectives were now an hour into the interview when there was a knock on the door of the interview room. A voice from the hall summoned McPherron. The sergeant left for a few moments while Claus continued the interview.

"Sorry," said Claus, "these things happen. You know, this is kind of intriguing me. What kind of ideas did you have?"

"Pretty much anything," said Brian, "from the outlandish, unaffordable. Explosives."

"Lots of explosives around here," said Claus.

"Due to the lockdown on the kind of explosives that I'd want, it would be highly limited," said Brian. "I wouldn't be looking for the stuff that you get at a blasting pit."

"You'd get tagged by the ATF or by Homeland Security or something because of recent events?"

"Yeah."

McPherron came back into the interview room.

Jason, he said, was being interviewed at the same time elsewhere in the station.

"He's finally told us the truth about everything," the detective said, "and this involves Rachelle. He gave her up."

CHAPTER NINE

It was noisy in the jail. The cell that Jason was in had a door, but the other cells have only bars, and the inmate population was making a racket.

"Hey, guys, hold it down," shouted Sergeant Mark Habib to the other inmates as he went inside cell number five, where Jason sat on a cot.

Among those investigating the murder, Habib knew the most about Jason. He knew his parents: Doug worked for the utility company, and Linda had worked for the police department for ten years. Over the years, Jason would stop by the station and talk to Habib about police work or their shared interest in electronics. Habib had overseen the installation of computers in the police station, and Jason was a whiz at computer games. Jason had recently purchased a high-end gaming computer, now in police custody after a search of his bedroom. For a time Jason had expressed an interest in becoming an officer and gone on ride-alongs with Habib. They didn't socialize, but were friendly enough that Jason once stopped by Habib's house to pick up a DVD movie for his mother.

"Look, this is very serious," Habib told Jason. "This is not a juvenile drinking party that we're investigating. This is not a burglary. This is a very serious thing. Who do you think they're looking at? Whose mental state is the evilest of all here?"

Jason mumbled that it was probably him.

"Why do you think that?"

"Because . . ." and his voice trailed off.

"It probably has something to do with the fact that you basically deceived them yesterday and gave them a little bit," Habib said. "These guys are not dumb. You cannot beat them. This is what they get paid to do. That's why they sent the investigators of the crime lab in now from Anchorage. These are the *CSI Miami* guys, OK? They're not dumb. There's more to this shit. This ain't over. This is not over. There is still one more person out there running around free. You two have been scammed. You two have been scammed, bottom line."

"What are you talking about?" asked Jason.

"What about Rachel?" asked Habib, mispronouncing her name.

"Rachelle?" Jason asked.

"Rachelle, rather," said Habib. "She's running around fat and happy right now. She's not showing any remorse. She's laughing at school. And this has concerned me from day one. It's concerned them: Why is she running around happy? Why is she not crying and bawling that her mother is dead? Her mother never beat her. Her mother never mistreated her. Do you know how many juveniles, how many adults like you, I interviewed in the last five days?"

"Probably quite a few."

"That have been in the same position that you are." Habib said. "She's going and telling them that she was abused, her mom beats her, her mom mistreats her. I've got kids her age and over telling me that her statements to them are: Mom says she's fat and won't feed her dinner. I mean, come on. Not hardly. Not hardly."

Habib told Jason that he and Brian were "covering for her ass" and that nobody believed that Jason and Brian came up with the murder plot on their own.

"Not happening," Habib said. "I don't buy it. I *won't* buy it. And I won't stop until we find out the truth. This did not happen. She put you guys up to it. Jason, she's running around, fat and happy right now in that goddamn school."

Habib said he'd been to Rachelle's school every day that week, and each time, Rachelle was seen at the main office, craning her neck through the window to find out who he was interviewing.

"She's all over this, man," said Habib. "Now, you may be bullshitting these guys, but you don't know them and they don't know you. You're not bullshitting me, because I know you. And you know me. And that girl had something to do with that. That girl put the seed in you guys' brain. That girl played you guys."

As the other investigators had done earlier, Habib was exaggerating to get Jason to talk. The sergeant hadn't been to the school every day and witnesses had described Rachelle's behavior as changing wildly during the week, from crying fits to moments of odd giddiness that a friend attributed to denial. None of her friends had described her as coldly as Habib did, though it was true that when Habib was interviewing one of Rachelle's friends in the principal's office, he had spotted Rachelle outside, craning her neck in an apparent attempt to see who was in there with him.

"Now, you tell me I'm wrong. I mean, hey, either way, why should I care, Jason?" asked Habib. "The state of Alaska has you and Brian on murder in the first degree. Murder one. That's as high as it goes. I should walk right out of here and say, 'Hey, case status: fucking closed, man. These morons got played and she's walking fucking free.' But I have more respect for your mother than that."

It was an insult, Habib told Jason, to expect anybody to believe that Jason and Brian killed Lauri on their own without telling Rachelle about it.

"You making me a common fool?" asked Habib.

As Jason listened in the cell, Habib gave a heavily edited version of the witness statements collected that week.

"She says to her girlfriends: She probably got drunk and drove off a cliff," said Habib, though actually Rachelle had said her mother probably died in a drunk-driving accident on the basis of the wine bottle left behind. "Where was

Lauri at? Where was Lauri's body found?" said Habib. "Inside of the van. Where was the van?"

On a cliff, Jason said.

"What did Lauri have in her bloodstream?"

"Alcohol," guessed Jason. Habib didn't tell him the autopsy found no such thing. Because the remains were so badly burned, the results of an alcohol-level test were inconclusive.

"Now, I've been doing this for sixteen years," Habib lectured Jason. "I know people. I know their behavior. Human nature. Human nature is what I do. That's why these yahoos sent me to school for all this stuff. For some sick fucking reason I've got a knack for it. I can read people inside and out. I can read when people don't make sense."

Jason cast his eyes down.

"Look at me," Habib said. "Her comment to her friends at school Monday morning? Come on. There's more like that out there that we've got. That's why this isn't done yet. Just because you're in jail and Brian's in jail does not mean these guys are going home. This case is not over. Now, right now, they're interviewing Brian again. That's why I'm talking to you back here. They've asked me to meet with you. Why do you think they're going after him?"

The mention of Brian got his attention. Jason had no idea what Brian had been saying to police.

"Well, they're just trying to find out if Rachelle communicated with him," Jason said.

"Well, do you suppose?" asked Habib.

"Like you are," said Jason.

"I'm not trying to find out, Jason. I know," said Habib. "They know she had something to do with this. They've seized everybody's means of communications. They've seized everybody's phone records. They've seized everybody's computers. And you know as well as I do, you can delete everything you want off of a hard drive, is it gone?"

"Not unless you zero it out. Not unless you zeroed the drive," Jason said. "That doesn't even work all the way."

"These—these computers," Habib said, fumbling through another set of lies, "they're bypassing the Anchorage Crime Lab. They're going right to the Federal Bureau of Investigation's crime lab. Homeland Security and FBI. I've got half your e-mails already printed out. This is before we even seized your computers. You know who's the stupid shit and left that crap on her computer?"

"Rachelle," said Jason.

"Yeah," said Habib. "And you know who's the stupid shit and used computers at school?"

"Rachelle."

"All this is making you look right now, Jason, is that you two assholes, you two evil older men, took her mother," said Habib.

The computers would be sent to Alaska's crime lab for examination, not to any federal agencies. The only e-mails and letters they had were some that Doc Waterman had found printed out in Rachelle's bedroom. Still, the tactic was working, Habib's claims about their mountain of evidence starting to sink in with Jason.

"Whether she's convicted of this or not, you guys still get charged with murder in the first degree. Bottom line," said Habib. "The question is whether this chick, who plays people, this up-and-coming black widow, goes free."

His voice dripping with sarcasm, Habib painted a picture for Jason of Rachelle's life after she let Jason and Brian go to prison.

"She's thinking about college, graduating from high school, going to prom, moving on in her life, being able to come and go as she pleases now because Mom's out of the picture, because Mom was the only responsible one in the family," said Habib. Rachelle, he said, was thinking: "Dad's too busy out there running around having affairs. Dad's not going to care what time I get home from school. If he thinks I'm going to clean house and do all the laundry, he's crazy. I'm not taking on my mom's old duties."

Habib said, "This is from a girl whose frickin' mother

just died. She's showing no remorse whatsoever. You are showing a thousand times more remorse over Lauri's death than her own daughter. Now, do you want to tell me about it? Because without someone telling us, we're going to have to try and pull all this crap in, but in the meantime, she is still running free."

Jason made another attempt to defend Rachelle, but it was halfhearted. He was beginning to crack.

Finally, he admitted he had more of a hand in the murder plot than planting a seed. In fact, he said, the planning started shortly after Rachelle told him of the beatings. With a newfound resignation in his voice, he added, "Whether or not they happened, I don't know anymore."

"They didn't," said Habib, "but go ahead."

"First we tried to get her to take legal routes, like emancipation or just go into child protective services," said Jason. "She claimed that she had already tried that and no one believed her. Things kind of simmered down after a while. They weren't really having any more problems at home. Then things started up again. And I asked her what she wanted done, what she wanted me to do to help her. She said it would be better if her mother was out of the picture. And I'm apparently a goddamn idiot."

"Well, you're a goddamned idiot if you let her get away with it," said Habib. "Partner, you're a damned idiot if you let her get away with it. And I'd have more respect for you if you say, 'Hey, I fucked up.' "

"I'm aware of that," Jason said. "I did."

"But you're letting her get away with it. You're letting her get away and her playing you."

"Yeah, I know."

"She told you that it would be better if she was out of the picture. Well, she said more than that. Keep going."

"I'm trying to recall exactly what was said," Jason said. "I know she wanted her dead."

"How do you know she wanted her dead?" asked Habib.

"She told me she wanted her dead."

"How long ago was that?"

"Few months."

"She told you when her and her dad were going to be out of town?" asked Habib.

"She did," said Jason.

"What did she say to you then?"

"She told me that it would probably be a good opportunity to take care of things."

"Like what?"

"To kill Lauri."

"What did she say exactly to you?" asked Habib.

"I'm having trouble recalling the exact words of the conversation," said Jason. "But she did know it was going to happen. She was planning on it happening. And she did confirm that we were going to do it."

Rachelle called him just before she left for Anchorage and asked if he and Brian were all set. Jason told her yes, that Brian had worked everything out.

"Did you tell her how you were going to do it?" asked Habib. "She's got the comment of her mom was probably drunk and drove off a cliff."

"I told her that alcohol was probably going to be involved."

"Like how?" asked Habib.

"Well, Brian mentioned that he should probably get Lauri drunk to make her more pliable," Jason said. He quickly added: "He didn't rape her or anything, if that's what you're thinking."

"No, no, no, no," said Habib. "Make her more pliable?"

"More cooperative, yeah."

"And he said that to us already," said Habib. "When Rachelle and her dad get back, when was the first time you talked to her or communicated with her?"

"She phoned me the day she got back," said Jason.

"And what did she say to you?"

"She said that she noticed her mother wasn't home, and I told her it was done."

"You said it was done? And what did she say?"

"She didn't say much," said Jason. "Sigh of relief."

Habib had heard enough. He told Jason, "Let's take a break. I've got to check some notes." That's when the sergeant went down the hall and knocked on the door of the room where McPherron and Claus were interviewing Brian Radel.

When McPherron came out, Habib gave him a recap of the jail cell interview. McPherron returned to the interview room telling Brian that Jason had given up Rachelle. At first it seemed to have no effect on Brian, who continued to insist that Rachelle was in the dark about the murder plan—as far as he knew. He repeated that he never spoke directly to Rachelle and that anything she said came to him through Jason.

"So he was the go-between?" asked McPherron.

"Yeah," said Brian.

"So she did say: 'Kill my mother for me'?"

"Again, I can't say that she did," said Brian.

"Did she ever relay to him: 'We're going to be gone this weekend'?" asked the detective. "'Now would be a good weekend to do it'?"

"Jason told me that he had been informed that they were not going to be there over Friday and Saturday," said Brian.

"And that she had given orders that this was the time to do it?" asked McPherron.

"No, she never actually gave orders that this was time to do it," said Brian. "At least, I didn't hear any. Once it got to that stage, the plan of execution was my call."

"You were basically given the task of doing the dirty work? You willingly agreed to do this?"

"I did not want murder on Jason's conscience."

"And then the same thing for Rachelle?"

"I'd never assumed she would ever be involved."

"You understand what a conspiracy is?" asked McPherron.

"Yes," said Brian.

"Everybody has a role in it. Obviously, you're the guy who did the deed, but these other people assisted you?"

"No, no," Brian said.

"Well, she's in on it?"

"Yeah, but—"

"She's the catalyst. She's the driving force?"

"What I'm saying is, when it came to planning, she was definitely not involved in the planning," said Brian. "I did not want her to know anything. Because just like I knew I was taking a risk simply having Jason involved, every single mouth that knows anything is one more mouth that can talk."

"Right, OK. I understand. So you basically kept her out of the loop because you don't want her to talk?"

"Yeah. I figured, the more people that knew something, the more likelihood they would respond, for example, if you're questioning them. If they knew something, their eyes might light up. If a person doesn't know any specifics about it, they can't give anything away about it."

"But that still makes them a conspirator nonetheless?"

"Right, I understand."

McPherron reminded Brian about a statement he made before they sat for the formal interview: "I keep my promises, no matter how long it takes."

The detective asked, "Who did you promise that?"

"I had given a promise to Jason and previously to Rachelle that if I'd [been] asked to do anything—at that time I hadn't actually meant murder—I would do it."

"You told that to Rachelle?"

"At one point, I told Rachelle," said Brian. "Apparently, she spoke to Jason . . . and Jason came to me and asked me and I said OK."

"Because Jason didn't have the stones to do it?"

"I can't say exactly why he came to me, other than the fact that we were very close friends. I was his blood brother and had made promises in the past, that if you ever need something, I would do it."

"So she's for sure, she's in on the starting phases of this?"

"From what Jason tells me, yes," said Brian.

"Then you get this idea, you run with the ball."

"It's the simple fact that I had studied sort of different military and police enforcement over the years, so I knew more what we might need done," said Brian. "I actually didn't like any of the plans, it was just a matter of time and just doing it. Personally, I didn't think it was well enough funded or anything. I just didn't think it was going to work."

"Funding? What's that?"

"It takes money to get items that you want to use to do something like this. I didn't have lock-picking tools. I didn't have anything that was professional."

"Did Rachelle ever provide any money?"

"No, she did not," Brian said. "I provided money. Jason—he got the fuel."

"I see. He basically paid for gas. For his truck or the gas for the fire?"

"He did not pay for the fuel for the fire."

"That's the stuff he borrowed from Lee? Took from Lee?"

"Yes," said Brian. The gas came from Lee Edwards's house, but Jason didn't know what it was for until he got out to the logging road.

"After the fact, was Jason in communication with Rachelle?" asked McPherron.

"I asked him some questions about that," said Brian, "but I never actually got an answer on it. So I don't know. From what I could tell, it seemed like he had not. . . . I have no clue if he did or not. I didn't have much contact with him other than a couple of phone calls asking how he was doing."

No matter what Jason said, Brian wasn't going to give them up. McPherron looked to Claus and asked, "Have any other questions?"

"Not right now," the trooper said.

They slapped handcuffs on Brian, who grimaced. "I was wondering if you might know," he asked, "is there a nerve or anything down there that can get pinched by handcuffs."

"It's possible, I suppose, why?" asked McPherron.

"It's nothing major," said Brian. "I'm just like numb on the side. I was wondering if I'd twisted it or something."

"Let's see how it goes in a couple of days," said McPherron.

Brian said, "Oh, I'm sure it's not gonna kill me."

CHAPTER TEN

On Friday evening, five days after Lauri's burned remains were found, Brian Radel stood before Craig town magistrate Kay Clark for his initial court appearance on murder charges. The courtroom in the red building that also housed Brian's old computer store was packed. Among those watching were Don Pierce and Doc Waterman. The newly bald Radel was escorted to his seat, where he quietly listened to Clark read the criminal complaint written by Sergeant Randy McPherron accusing Brian of murder in the first degree. The charges were based almost entirely on statements made in the last twelve hours by Brian and Jason.

Aside from the judge, there were no lawyers physically in the courtroom. Because of the vast distances between cities and villages in most of Alaska, it's customary for attorneys, and sometimes judges, to make appearances via telephone, even for such serious matters as sentencing. Over the courtroom speakers, Ketchikan district attorney Dan Schally could be heard requesting a cash only bail of $250,000. It may as well have been $250 million. Brian told the magistrate he was self-employed and made $15,000 in the past year. He listed his assets as fishing gear and an old boat. He had no attorney and hadn't tried to find one. The magistrate appointed a public defender from Ketchikan to represent him.

Brian had always valued loyalty, and while the rest of his life would likely be spent in a prison cell, he felt a certain pride. He had promised to Jason, Rachelle, and himself that he would liberate Rachelle from her horrific mother, and he had succeeded. Moreover, he had done everything he could to spare Rachelle and Jason any burden. Brian took the fall, but he could also take the credit.

It was only much later that he came to realize that Jason, his blood brother, was rapidly abandoning the code of honor that Brian had thought they shared. During the interrogation, the police had told him that Jason sold out Rachelle, but Brian didn't believe them. He knew Jason was weak—that's why Brian carried out the kidnapping and murder alone— but he hadn't appreciated how weak.

While Brian was standing before the magistrate, Jason was sitting in an Alaska State Troopers patrol car with Bob Claus talking almost nonstop. Jason, too, faced a life sentence, but he never felt more free, unburdening himself not only of the details of the murder but of a lifetime of pain and frustration as a socially awkward fat kid on a remote island.

After giving yet another statement to investigators at the police station, again without requesting a lawyer, Jason agreed to take a drive to show where everything had gone down that weekend. Claus loaded a video camera and a tape recorder and led Jason to his truck. They pulled out of the police station to a restaurant, where Claus bought Jason a cheeseburger. Jason also was allowed to smoke and stop for bathroom breaks. If Jason got any ideas about escaping, there was an armed trooper in the backseat and a chase car behind them with officers.

They left Craig and drove to the high school, the ball field on a bluff to their right. Through puffs of cigarettes, Jason shed all pretenses: he and Rachelle were knee-deep in the murder plot from beginning to end. This was not the first time they had tried to kill Lauri Waterman; just the first time they succeeded. They had talked about putting Lauri's feet in cement and tossing her off a boat. They had come close to storming her house and shooting her. Each plan was abandoned for one reason or another.

But one murder attempt nearly came off. As they approached the turnoff to the school, Jason revealed that about four weeks earlier, on an afternoon in late September, Brian was at this location, crouching in a stand of trees with a high-power rifle. The plan had been to gun down Lauri after she dropped off Rachelle for volleyball practice. But Brian had trouble with the gun and the mission was aborted. Jason said he informed Rachelle in an e-mail, using the code phrase "hunting trip," and promised to try again.

The sun was now setting as they continued on the road past the sawmill, where mountains of spruce, stripped of their bark and branches, stood near the road; across the street were monitors testing the air for dangerous fumes. Arriving in Klawock, Jason confirmed that he knew exactly what Brian had in mind that previous Saturday as they purchased wine, towels, duct tape, and a pair of small, cheap flashlights.

After the thwarted assassination attempt, they settled on a plan to stage a drunken-driving accident by kidnapping Lauri and forcing her to drink wine, then driving her off a cliff or a ridge on a remote road. When Rachelle told him that she and her father would be gone over the weekend, they knew they had their window of opportunity and, in Brian, the perfect man for the job.

As Jason talked about the murder, Claus realized that his prime suspect was a man-child, at twenty-five no more mature than any of the teenagers he hung out with. Jason told Claus about his sad and unsettled childhood. He was ten years old when his family moved from Oregon to Prince of Wales Island, where they lived first in Craig for a year or two before moving to Klawock for another two to three years. The family moved back to Oregon, where Jason finished middle school, then returned to the island for his high school years in Hollis. When he dropped out of basic training in the Marine Corps, he came back to Craig, washing dishes at Ruth Anne's for about a year before moving to Yakima, Washington, with a couple of friends, where he worked in a plastics plant. That went nowhere, and in a year he was back in Klawock sweeping floors, cleaning toilets, and taking out the trash as a school janitor.

Claus picked up on what a psychologist would later describe in court: that Jason was a lonely and troubled child who struggled to make friends and establish lasting relationships with peers. Moody, socially isolated, he retreated into comic books, video games, and pornography, battling depression. He felt so numb that as a teenager he would cut himself just so he could feel something. By the time he was an adult, he was consumed with paranoia fueled by pot smoking.

Jason's one enduring friendship was with Brian Radel, whom he met when they were both about thirteen or fourteen at the Echo Ranch Bible Camp in Ketchikan. A few years later they reconnected by chance at the meat market in Craig where Brian worked, bonding over computer games and D&D. When Brian opened Dark Wolf Computer Design, Jason helped him on calls to people's homes to set up their systems.

When Jason met Rachelle in February of 2004, he was, in all likelihood, a virgin. His father had warned him to stay away from her, telling him, "She's jailbait." But Jason fell hard. The first time he saw her, she was with her boyfriend Ian Lendrum. Rachelle told Jason she was in the process of breaking up with Ian. Jason saw his opportunity, and the two began quietly seeing each other over the summer, even as Ian thought he was still with Rachelle.

Jason had a strong physical attraction to Rachelle, and one day he asked her to send him nude photos of herself. She complied, striking poses suggested by Jason. Soon their relationship, as Rachelle had said, became sexual. It was when he saw bruises on her body that he found out about the abuse Rachelle suffered at home.

Dating a teenager proved challenging, as Jason opened himself up to a statutory rape charge and Rachelle feared being ostracized by her friends and punished by her family. They met when they could, where they could: in the computer shop, at the T-shirt shop where Rachelle worked, and on Brian's boat. By August they had their first separation when Rachelle went on vacation to her grandparents' house in Washington State. It was then that she revealed, while they chatted online, that she also once had a relationship with Brian. Until then Jason thought they had just been friends.

The beginning of the school year brought more complications. Brian's store went out of business and it became almost impossible to see Rachelle. They communicated by instant messaging, e-mail, and through letters. One of their Dungeons & Dragons friends, a high school boy named John Wilburn, served as messenger, delivering Jason's typewritten letters to Rachelle's locker and bringing Rachelle's handwritten notes back to Jason. In exchange, Jason got Wilburn pornographic movies. Jason was so desperate to be near Rachelle that he joined the community play, where she was on the lighting crew. The prospect of being on stage terrified him, but at least he could see Rachelle.

From Klawock, Jason led Claus to the next stop, a gravel pit several miles outside of town. This was to be the rendezvous spot. Jason said he waited there for hours on Saturday night and into Sunday morning, chain-smoking cigarettes while waiting for Brian to kidnap Lauri and drive up with her in the van. In the gravel, Claus collected cigarette butts matching the brand that Jason smoked and photographed the area.

Jason said that he had finally grown tired of waiting, drove back toward Craig, turned around, and returned to the gravel pit. He repeated this trip several times before seeing oncoming headlights from the van. Jason directed Claus to their next stop, taking them from the paved road onto the winding gravel road that lead to Naukati. Eventually they stopped at a pullout on the left just before Yatuk Creek.

It was here, Jason said, that Brian killed Lauri. Jason said he had lied earlier when he claimed that he met Brian at the logging road after Lauri was dead. Instead, Rachelle's mother was still alive, bound in the back of the van. Claus directed Jason through a thirty-five-minute video reenactment of the murder, the production values poor because darkness had set in, but the horror of the attack came through.

Jason described the tied-up Lauri kneeling on a garbage bag on the gravel: they thought the staged drunken driving would be more convincing if she had no dirt on her. In the illumination of Jason's truck headlights, Brian first tried to snap Lauri's neck, then pummeled her with one of the little flashlights, then suffocated her. Jason confirmed everything Brian had said, with the exception that Jason witnessed it. Claus searched the area with a flashlight, but in the days since the murder, the gravel road had been regraded, obliterating any sign of violence.

The last stop on Jason's tour was on the other side of the island, a pullout near Thorne Bay where he said they burned some of the gear they had used in the murder. While Jason stayed under guard in the truck with Claus, two troopers found a fire pit about two hundred yards off the road. Amid the ashes and blackened kindling were unburned pieces of pink rope, white cloth, gray duct tape, partially melted, gloves and burnt socks.

Back at the Craig police station, the investigators, including McPherron and Habib, were discussing how to proceed. DA Schally sent the investigators an e-mail saying he was satisfied with the state of the case.

"We currently plan on presenting the Radel and Arrant charges to the grand jury on Friday, Nov. 26, 2004, because Thursday, Nov. 25, is Thanksgiving," the DA wrote in an e-mail at 4:35 p.m. Friday to the investigators. "If we can develop charges against Rachelle Waterman, that case should be presented to the Grand Jury at the same time for multiple reasons."

That was a big if. So far, the case against Rachelle was shaky. Even while implicating themselves, Jason and Brian still minimized her role. None of the other people they interviewed, neither her school clique nor her Dungeons & Dragons friends, knew anything about her being involved a murder plot aside from her complaints about her mother and strange behavior after returning from Anchorage. The closest to an incriminating statement came when Rachelle admitted she lied when she gave Jason an alibi.

The investigators decided their best course of action was to interview Rachelle again, this time more aggressively. Trooper Bob Claus bowed out. He felt his anger rising during Rachelle's last interview because he was certain she was lying to his face. He didn't think he could hold in his emotions in a second round. So Sergeant Mark Habib would play second chair to McPherron if Rachelle agreed to talk to them.

The pair went looking for her. They stopped into Brian's arraignment but didn't see Rachelle. Next they drove to the Pierces' house, arriving a little before five p.m., and knocked on the door. Lorraine Pierce answered.

"Is Rachelle here?" asked McPherron.

"She is," said Lorraine. "Do you want to come in?"

As they entered, McPherron saw Rachelle.

"Hi, Rachelle," he said.

"Hi," she said.

"How you doing?"

"I'm OK."

"Good, well, as you know, Brian got arrested."

"Yes," she said.

"And he's just been arraigned. We talked just a little bit last night and there's a few things we need to run by you. Would that be OK?"

Rachelle said, "Yeah."

"Would you mind coming down with us to the police station where we talked before?" asked McPherron.

"Sure," she said.

"Be a little more private down there."

Rachelle said, "Let me get a coat."

While Rachelle did this, Habib made small talk with Lorraine Pierce.

"How you doing?" he asked. "I've been meaning to stop by and see how you're doing."

Lorraine said she was glad about the arrests of Jason and Brian.

"We're glad too," he said. "It doesn't resolve anything, but we're really glad, too."

Rachelle came out. Lorraine asked, "You're going to go?"

"Yes," she said. "I'm going to go with them."

Lorraine said, "OK."

"We're just tying up the loose ends," McPherron told Lorraine. "We've got some things to run by and confirm."

Habib added, "The rule of thumb is you just can't have too much evidence, you know."

"I know," said Lorraine. "We want you to."

"Where's Doc?" asked McPherron. "Did he go to the arraignment?"

"He went to the arraignment," said Lorraine, "and I just assumed that so many of his friends were there that they're just visiting and whatnot. He'll be back in a little bit."

"All right," said McPherron. "We'll just—we'll be down there, if he wants to know."

Rachelle said to Lorraine, "See ya," and left the house.

Rachelle got into the back of a patrol car smelling of fast food—Sergeant Habib had made a hamburger run—and the two detectives munched on dinner while driving to the police station.

"We've been kind of eating on the fly," McPherron told Rachelle over his shoulder. "It's been a busy day, busy couple of days. So, how are you holding up?"

"I'm doing OK," she said. "I watched about five disks of *Family Guy*."

"I guess the memorial service for your mom is Sunday?" said McPherron. Rachelle said it was. "Will I be able to go out tonight?" she asked.

"Well, of course, that'll be up to your dad," said the detective. "And depends how long it takes. It may take us a little while to run through this. We've got kind of a laundry list of questions to ask you."

Rachelle groaned.

"Little cooped up, huh?" asked McPherron.

"Yeah," she said.

"We'll try not to keep you confined too long."

The morning after she disappeared, Lauri Waterman's burned van was discovered by a hunter on an abandoned logging road. *(Courtesy: State of Alaska)*

An active community volunteer, Lauri Waterman was 48 years old when she was killed. *(Courtesy: Brian Wallace/ZUMA Press)*

Former Alaska Trooper Bob Claus returns to the gravel turnout where Lauri Waterman was brutally beaten to death. *(Courtesy: Michael Fleeman)*

Craig, Alaska, is a close-knit community of 1,500 people on Prince of Wales Island. *(Courtesy: Michael Fleeman)*

Rachelle Waterman was 18 years old when she went on trial in 2006. *(Courtesy: Brian Wallace/ZUMA Press)*

Lauri Waterman was asleep alone in her home, her daughter and husband both out of town, when she was awakened by her assailant. *(Courtesy: Michael Fleeman)*

My Dearest Daughter,

Im sorry things between us are tense right now. Please don't feel like I think your a bad person, because your not. I know I worry way too much about you but thats what Moms do when they love their daughters as much as I love you.

You know those commercials on T.V. where they tell parents to always know what your kids are doing? I take that to heart. I really think parents need to stay in their kids lives and know whats going on.

I feel you pulling away from us and friends and everything. I want us to be close and you be able to tell me things or just talk about nothing or anything.

I wish you understood how much your loved. How proud

In a handwritten note found on Rachelle Waterman's nightstand, her mother expresses her love—and concerns. (*Courtesy: State of Alaska*)

A standout student, Rachelle played volleyball and basketball and took part in the music program at Craig High School. *(Courtesy: Michael Fleeman)*

The Trooper Station, in Klawock, Alaska, where Bob Claus worked. *(Courtesy: Michael Fleeman)*

Brian Radel confessed to horrible actions—but how much did Rachelle Waterman know? *(Courtesy: Brian Wallace/ZUMA Press)*

Madly in love, Jason Arrant believed Rachelle Waterman's stories of being abused by her mother. *(Courtesy: Brian Wallace/ZUMA Press)*

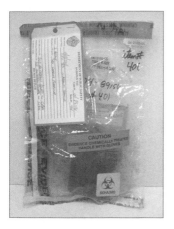

This cheap red flashlight was used to kill Lauri Waterman. *(Courtesy: State of Alaska)*

Rachelle Waterman was accompanied by her father, Carl "Doc" Waterman, outside the Lemon Creek Correctional Center in Juneau, Alaska, after her release. *(Courtesy: Brian Wallace/ ZUMA Press)*

After her murder, the Craig High School ball field was named in honor of Lauri Waterman. *(Courtesy: Michael Fleeman)*

As they neared the police station, they talked about movies and television shows, making the same kind of small talk before Rachelle's previous interview, which had ended with her angry and in tears. Habib shared he liked the Discovery Channel and the History Channel, even though it "drives my wife nuts." Rachelle said she liked the *Princess Bride* and the *Godfather* movies and asked the detectives if they had seen the latest *Lord of the Rings* film.

"Sad to say, I fell asleep in number three," said Habib as the cruiser pulled into the back parking lot of the police station.

"It was just too long," added McPherron. "They needed an intermission or something."

They got out into the November cold and walked through the back door of the station and down the hall to the same interrogation room. The video camera was turned on. Rachelle was asked if she needed to use the restroom. She said she was fine.

"Good," said McPherron. "I'm hoping this won't take long."

Rachelle yawned. "Pardon me," she said, explaining the stress of the week had left her tired and not feeling well.

McPherron began.

"Like I said before, there's a few things that we've uncovered, and we need to get some clarification from you," said McPherron. "You are the one person that could probably help us, given your relationship in all this."

Rachelle yawned again, then apologized.

"All right," said McPherron, who also was exhausted. The interview with Jason had gone into the early morning, then he handled the paperwork for Brian to be charged. He was eating the take-out cheeseburger while speaking with Rachelle.

"First of all," he said. "I'm going to go ahead and read you something here. OK?"

Her read her her Miranda rights. "Do you understand each of these rights as I've explained them to you?" he asked, just as they do in cop shows.

No yawn this time. Rachelle answered, "Yeah."

"Having these rights in mind, do you wish to talk to us now?"

She didn't answer at first. "Well," said Rachelle, "I'm curious: Why are you reading this and you never did before?"

"Some things have come up," said McPherron, "and I just want to make sure you understand what your rights are before we go any further. Do you also understand you have a right to have a parent, your father, present?"

"Yes," she said.

"Do you want to talk to us? Do you want your dad here?"

"No, I'll talk to you," she said. "I'm just curious: Why are you doing that?"

"I'm just trying to be cautious," said McPherron. "I just want to make sure you understand fully. I mean, you're not quite an adult, but you're almost there. You're here speaking with us voluntarily?"

"Yes."

"Excuse me," said McPherron, "I should never try to eat a cheeseburger while I'm talking. I mean, we brought you here, but you're free to go."

"Yeah."

"We're just in here for privacy's sake only."

"I know," said Rachelle.

It was another ruse. McPherron read Rachelle her rights because he wanted to use anything she said against her in court. The privacy was for his benefit; he didn't want Rachelle's father interfering with what was now not going to be an interview but an interrogation.

"You understand," said McPherron, "Brian was arrested late last night."

"Yes."

"He just got done being arraigned. Prior to the arrest, he did talk to us at some length and told us many things about what happened with your mom."

McPherron asked Rachelle again about her relationship with her mother, their arguments over her interest in Wicca and having sex with her boyfriend Ian, her "venting" to Jason and other friends about abuse by her mother, and why she never reported it.

Rachelle told the detective that her mother had a side the rest of the island never saw.

"It's, like, you know, people out in the public probably think my mom would never lose her temper, probably think she never cusses or anything," she said. "But, you know, behind closed doors, other things happen."

McPherron circled back to Jason and Brian.

"I think Jason still loves you, to be honest. He's told us so," the detective said. "And I think he has strong feelings for you. Brian certainly does too. They both care about you and I think they'd do just about anything for you, do about anything you'd ask them to do, including asking them to have your mom killed. Jason's been arrested. Both Jason and Brian have told us everything about the plot, about your participation in the in the plot."

It was, of course, untrue. Brian had said it didn't appear Rachelle knew anything about the murder plot and Jason had portrayed her involvement as minimal. Rachelle started to speak up.

"Just hear me out, OK?" said McPherron. "They told us everything. They told how you came to them about the abuse, how you wanted their help, how you went to Jason first, told him you wanted to get rid of your mom."

Rachelle tried to say something again.

"Just hear me out," McPherron repeated. "Let me tell you what they told us. And then you can talk. Jason figured he needed Brian's help, and that Brian would be the one who would actually do the deed, and Jason would be the helper. But they told us about how this was all planned for months, and about your participation in it. And apparently there's been a couple other failed attempts or plans that didn't come to fruition."

He showed her a piece of paper.

"This is an e-mail we got off of Jason's computer," he said.

In fact, it was an e-mail off of Rachelle's computer that

her father had printed out and given to Bob Claus. The e-mail
had been sent on Wednesday, September 29, 2004, at 12:34
p.m., to Rachelle's Narcissa address. It was from Jason.

Subject: Hey Shell ☺

Hi, how goes it, not much going on here today. I went
down and found Brian so I could chat at him for a bit.
Oh, yeah, and we canceled that hunting trip we were
planning for today. But he said he would like to go
sometime soon. No later than a week from now if he
can swing it, so that should be fun ;).

McPherron asked, "What's the hunting trip?"

"He goes hunting," said Rachelle defiantly. "I remember
this e-mail, but I didn't—I thought he was just going hunting."

"He says 'hunting trip' was a code word for one of the
failed attempts," said McPherron, "where you were going to
have your mom take you to volleyball practice and after she
drops you off, Brian was going to be waiting in the woods
and shoot her. That was one of the attempts."

McPherron told her that there were other plans to kill her
mother and that she knew about all of them. The burning
van was the final successful effort. He told Rachelle that on
Sunday when she got home she called Jason and he gave her
a report on how the murder went down.

"They told all," said McPherron.

Speaking in his calm, soft voice, McPherron stared down
Rachelle.

"Now, I just want you to understand something," he said.
"There's a big difference between being the person who actually commits the crime and the people participating in the
planning of it. Now, I know you participated in the plan."

He showed her the e-mail again.

"We have more of these," he said. "We've got your computer, we got Brian's computer, we've got Jason's computer.
And even though you may delete things, the computer still

saves it, and we're able to find things on computers that people think are deleted. We have experts at retrieval.

"We know exactly what happened up there," he continued. "We know that Jason and Brian killed your mother, that Brian was the one who did the killing. Jason assisted him. But you participated in the planning of the incident. You gave them the information. You approved plans. You let them know basically that you were going to be out of town, that your dad was going to be out of town. You showed them how to get in the house. Brian went in that garage, just as instructed, and he abducted your mother, put her in the van, and took her out, and then Brian ended up killing her. And they drove her up to the end of the road and set her and the vehicle on fire. They've told us everything. They've given you up, Rachelle."

The speech brought Rachelle to tears.

"No," she sobbed, "they offered and I said no. I said I loved her."

"But you did ask [them] at one time to kill her for you?" asked McPherron.

"I had mentioned it," she said. "I wasn't serious. I told them no. I don't want it done because I loved her."

For the next hour Rachelle and the detectives went at it. She cried, she lashed out, she revealed some details, denied others. The door was unlocked the whole time and she could have left whenever she wanted, but she never tried to go. She never asked for a lawyer, she never asked for her father. In fact, she worried that her father would find out about what she was saying. When it was over, Rachelle was exhausted and feeling ill, no longer the confident, snide-talking blogger of My Crappy Life but a scared girl.

CHAPTER ELEVEN

One hour into the interrogation, Rachelle began to lose it. Peppered with questions and accusations, she insisted through tears that she never wanted her mother murdered, even though Jason and Brian had offered to do it.

Sergeant Randy McPherron asked, "Why did you tell them that you were going to be gone that weekend?"

"It just came up," said Rachelle, crying. "It just must have came up in conversation is all."

"Now, listen, Rachelle," lectured McPherron, "you need to be straight with me, OK? You've tried to lie to me in the past, and it's failed right? You've tried to lie to me in the past and it hasn't worked, right?"

She didn't answer.

"Right?" he asked.

"Yes," she said.

"Don't lie to me now."

"Yes," she repeated.

"It's not going to help you to lie to me."

"I told them no. I told them no," she said.

"You've got to tell me everything."

"I told them I didn't want it to happen."

"When did you tell them that?"

"I told them a while ago."

"What's 'a while'?"

"It was weeks ago. Months ago."

"At one time, you told them—Jason—you wanted him to kill your mother, didn't you?" asked McPherron.

"I didn't tell him directly," Rachelle said.

"He remembers the conversation. And he asked you directly, 'What do you want me to do, kill her?' And you said, 'Yes.'" McPherron wasn't bluffing this time. Jason had stated this in his jail cell interview to Sergeant Mark Habib.

"I wasn't serious," said Rachelle.

"Well, he believed it was serious," McPherron said. "What about the assassination? The shooting from the woods?"

Crying so hard she couldn't speak, Rachelle started to say, "I didn't—"

"According to them," interrupted McPherron, "you knew full well what was going to happen. You were riding in the car with your mother, and she was going to drop you off at the school and drive down the driveway, and Brian was going to shoot her."

"I didn't know they were going to do that."

"You approved the plan. You said, 'Yes, go for it.'"

"I did not approve the plan. I did not approve the plan."

"Yes you did."

"No I didn't."

"Listen: I've told you before. No more of this."

"They called me," she said, choking out the words.

"They called you when?" pressed McPherron.

"The day they were supposed to do it," she said. "I didn't know they were going to do it until the last second. And Jason happened to be talking to me, and I said, 'No, don't do it.' That's why it didn't happen, because I didn't want it to happen."

It was a turning point in the case, the first time Rachelle admitted to being aware of the plot to kill her mother and having a role to the extent that she could call off a murder.

McPherron asked, "Why does this plot keep continuing?"

"I don't know," said Rachelle. "I told them, 'I don't want it to happen.'"

"You've been in constant contact with Jason for months now," McPherron said.

"We hadn't talked about it," she insisted.

"Yes you had. You've been talking for months."

"I told them I didn't want it to happen!" she cried. "I love her! I love her!"

"They carried it out, and they carried it out with your blessing and your assistance," McPherron said. "You told them this weekend was a good time to do it: 'I'm going to be gone. My dad's gone. Go through the window in the garage, like I always do, and you can do the deed. And I'll be rid of my mom and I can live my life.'"

"I told them I didn't want it to happen."

"You talked to Jason on Sunday after you got back, and he gave you a status report."

"No—"

"You told your friends Monday, before the body had been identified, that your mom probably died in a drunk-driving accident."

"Because that's what I assumed."

"Because that was what the plan was. That's what they told you the plan was."

"I saw that there was a bottle of wine in the garbage and I thought she drank it because I know my dad wasn't there. He couldn't have drank it. And I saw the car was gone and I assumed the worst because I'm a pessimist."

At this point Sergeant Habib spoke up. "Rachelle," he said, "you knew about it before you knew about your mom's car. You made these statements before the police notified your dad."

"Because I'm a pessimist," she said again.

McPherron jumped back in. "Jason gave you a status report Sunday after you got home," he said. "He called you and told you, 'We have accomplished the mission that you put us on.'"

"I did not do that," Rachelle insisted.

"Yes you did," said McPherron.

"I told them," Rachelle repeated, "I didn't want it to happen."

"I've had enough," McPherron said. "I've had enough of this drama queen stuff. I've had enough of your lies."

Habib said, "Rachelle, you must understand that we are not Brian and Jason."

McPherron said, "We are not idiots. We're not puppets you can dance around."

"So fine," Rachelle said indignantly. "Then throw me in jail. If you think I'm so guilty, throw me in fucking jail."

"I want to know exactly what your role in this is," McPherron said. "And I'm trying to offer you a solution to your dilemma. As I explained before, there's a big difference between the person who puts their hands around a victim's throat and kills her [and] between the person who says, 'It's a good weekend. Go for it.' "

"So instead of ten years I'll get five," said Rachelle.

"Well, it's your life," said McPherron. "You tell me how you want to live the rest of it."

"I just want to have a normal life," Rachelle said. "I want my mom back."

"Well, that ain't gonna happen," said McPherron.

"No shit, Sherlock," said Rachelle.

"You set in motion the events that we are grappling with now. And you need to start thinking about yourself. These two guys have given you up. They gave you up so quick, I couldn't believe it. For two people who claim to love you, they handed you over to us on a silver platter, without thinking twice. They gave you up as soon as we put the screws to them. Now it's your turn."

Rachelle said, "I did call them that weekend when I was in Anchorage, and I told them not to do it."

She told the investigators she called Jason from her friend Katrina Nelson's cell phone: he was the guy named "Red" about whom Katrina spoke to police. Rachelle said that in the call she and Jason quarreled. He told her, "You're just being irrational. You're just being emotional. Don't worry about it." But she told him, ordered him, "No, no, don't do it. I'm serious." She told him that she and her mother were now getting along. Jason wasn't listening to her, thinking she was just overacting. They ended their conversation with Rachelle hanging up on him.

"So you knew it was going to happen this weekend?"

"I had an idea," Rachelle admitted, "but I wasn't sure."

When she got home, she called Jason to make sure he followed her instructions not to go ahead with the murder. "So we're OK?" she asked him. He replied, "Yeah, we're fine."

She took that to mean that her mother was safe and she sighed with relief, thinking her mother was gone because she had an unexpected errand. But then Jason told her, "It happened."

"What?" she asked Jason in a panic. "What are you talking about?"

Jason said, "We did it."

Rachelle told the investigators, "Do you know how horrified I was?"

Habib said, "We can understand that."

"I told them not to," said Rachelle. "I told them beforehand that I didn't want them to do it. They didn't listen to me."

McPherron was less understanding. "You sat there and lied to me, didn't you?"

Rachelle started crying again. "I was scared."

"You knew who killed your mother, didn't you?" said McPherron.

"Yes," she said.

"On Sunday," McPherron said. "You knew it had been done and you knew they did it."

"Why have you got to rub it in my face?"

McPherron told her that she was still withholding information.

"We're about 98 percent there," he said. "But that other 2 percent belongs to you. And I want to know what that other 2 percent is. If you truly do love your mother, you owe it to her to tell us that. You owe it to her to let the world know what really happened."

"I just told you what happened."

"If you have any concern, care for her, you're going to tell us."

"I just told you what happened."

"Rachelle," he said, "do you know what Brian did?"

McPherron was merciless, painting a vivid picture for Rachelle. He told her that Brian abducted her mother from bed, forced her to drink a bottle of wine, tied her up, and drove her out to the middle of nowhere on a wet, rainy night. There, on the gravel, he made her get down on her knees in the gravel and tried to break her neck "because," the detective said, "it looks good on TV.

"But you know what," McPherron said calmly, "it doesn't really work. So he laid her down on the ground and he took a flashlight and he slammed it against her throat about ten times."

Rachelle burst into tears. "Why are you telling me this?"

"Because I want you to understand what happened here," said McPherron. He told her that Brian then got on top of her mother and pinched her nose and put his hand over her mouth until she died. Jason and Brian took her mother to the end of the logging road, poured five gallons of gasoline on her, and set her on fire.

"Now, that's what happened," said McPherron. "And you knew it was going to happen, and you didn't do anything to stop it."

"I told them not to do it!" Rachelle said.

"And after you knew what had happened, you didn't do anything."

"I was scared!"

"You could have brought your mother's killers to justice. You could have handed them to us on a silver platter."

"I was scared."

"And instead you sat there and lied to us about it. And now you expect us to believe you?"

"Why are you asking me questions if you don't even believe me?"

"Because I want you to come to understand what's going

on, and I want you to tell me the truth about your involvement in all this. When did you first tell Jason, 'I want you to get rid of my mother'?"

She sniffled and breathed in deeply. "I don't know," she said. "August sometime."

"Were you still dating him? Were you still having sex with him? What was going on?"

In a small voice she said, "We were kind of, I don't know what you call it, coming to the end of the relationship. We were just thinking: You know what, this isn't going to work."

"So even though your relationship's on the skids, you still ask this guy to kill your mom for you? Is that how it worked?"

"Yes," she said.

The plot came up when she called to ask him a question about the community play. He told her he was planning to kill her mother in the house, and Rachelle told him, "I don't know, you guys. I told you not to kill her before."

The plan resurfaced a few weeks later when Rachelle told Jason that her mother had tried to push her down the stairs. McPherron asked her about Jason's statement that Rachelle's parents wanted to sell her into slavery.

"No, it was a long time ago," Rachelle corrected. "My mom was really mad at me, and they were low on money, and she was talking about selling me for prostitution as punishment."

"You told him this?"

"Yes."

"Well, you got to understand, these guys accepted this as gospel. They accepted this as 'She's not joking around. This is for real.'"

"I wasn't joking around."

"They believed that you were truly in jeopardy, and that the only way to save you from your mother was to kill her," said McPherron. "I mean, these guys were true believers. You had them so wrapped around your finger, they were so in love with you, that they would do anything for you. And he *did* do anything for you."

"I didn't know that Brian was in love with me."

"Well, you'd had sex with him."

"A while ago. I cared for him. And then we ended it. I didn't know he still loved me. I thought we ended that."

"Well, some people react differently, you know."

"That's true."

"When you have sex with somebody, it's quite an experience for some, and not for others. Obviously, both of these guys are real connected to you. They really care about you," said McPherron. "They don't care much now, but they did then. They feel kind of used now, and they feel manipulated, and they feel stupid that a sixteen-year-old girl talked them into killing her mother for her."

"I didn't use them," she said. "I didn't have them wrapped around my finger."

"Now, this has been going on for months, right?"

"Yes."

"And you've at times heard their plans and you knew what was going to happen, knew what was going on."

"And I told them no."

"And you didn't do anything about it, like warn your mother?"

"I didn't think it was necessary because I thought they would listen to me. As you said before, they listened to me."

"They listened to you so good that they were ignoring all other instructions," said McPherron, "which I'm a little skeptical about. If these guys are your servants—"

"They're not my servants."

"Just listen to me," said McPherron. "They'll live and die by what you tell them. If you would have told them no, they wouldn't have done it."

She acknowledged she "had a hunch" they were planning to kill her mother the weekend of the volleyball tournament: that's why she called Jason from Anchorage. But she kept insisting, "I didn't know for sure." But the investigators shot back that they didn't believe her, that she was downplaying her role—and that they had evidence to prove it.

"You can start being honest with us," said Habib. "If you want to make us use all this evidence against you, that's fine," he said. "We'll let a jury see that, and that you weren't cooperative, you show no remorse in this whole thing."

"No," said Rachelle.

"Up to the end, you're going to hold your own," Habib continued. "You're not going to budge. You want to go that route, that's fine. The DA will hear it, the judge will hear it, everybody can hear that."

McPherron added, "You're sixteen, but this is a serious offense, and you will automatically be waived into adult court. Juvenile bets are off now. You're in the big leagues now. This is the real McCoy, no do-over, no restarts."

McPherron urged her to think ahead. "A bunch of strangers are going to look at you and judge you based upon your behavior, based on how you deal with this and how you answer the following questions. What face are you going to show them? The grown-up woman who is looking out for herself and realizes that the jig is up and it's time to come clean? Or Rachelle, who wants to play the little girl that thinks she can lie her way out of anything? . . . We're giving you an opportunity to tell your side of the story, but we need it lie-free, embellishment-free, omission-free. We don't need part of the story. We don't need the part you think we want to hear. We need the whole shebang, starting from day one, when you told Jason that you wanted him to get rid of your mother for you."

"I think it was August," she said.

"It was before school started?"

"Yes," she said. "He said he might use Brian. I wasn't sure for sure."

"But you did approach him and say, 'I want you to kill my mother'?"

"Not exactly," she said. "I just said, 'Sometimes I just wish my mother wasn't here. She causes me so much pain.'"

"But the gist of it was, yes, you did want her dead, and you wanted him to take care of it for you."

"Yes," she said.

Rachelle said she didn't discuss murder plans with Jason,

but didn't object as "different ideas were discussed," some of which she knew about, some she didn't. She never specifically ordered them to kill her mother: Jason instead heard her complaints about her mother, then acted on his own. The plan to shoot her mother outside the school, for instance, probably grew out of a conversation she had with Jason.

"The day before, my mom had gotten angry at me and beaten me, and I told him about it," she said. "And I guess that's when they threw [the plan] together, because they were afraid she was going to do something. And I was honest: I was worried for myself, and I told him then. I said, 'I'm worried. I don't know what my mom's going to do. I'm scared to go home.' And they, I guess, threw it into gear."

She called Jason about three p.m. and was told that her mother would be shot around five p.m. She implored them to call off the plan, but Jason wasn't sure if he could reach Brian. "I said, 'Please try. Please, please, please try.'"

Similarly, Jason decided to go after her mother in October after she related more accounts of abuse. "She was beating me, and I told them," said Rachelle. "And they said, 'Well, what do you want us to do?' I said, 'I don't know. I just really wish she wouldn't hit me, and I wish I could make her happy.' And they said, 'What about the plan?' and I said, 'Oh, I don't know.' I was kind of on the fence about it. And then they kind of started plotting it."

She then happened to mention to Jason that her dad was going to be of town the same weekend she was. That's when she began to worry that the plan was in effect. She called Jason from Anchorage that Friday to call it off, but he said she was being emotional and she'd thank him later. Rachelle responded with "some not very nice things that probably pissed him off," she said. Her harsh words "might've encouraged him not to listen."

She tried to reach him again but couldn't, which she took as a good sign. She assumed he was at a friend's house comforting the friend after an uncle's suicide.

"So I almost felt relieved, you know?" said Rachelle. "I was thinking: You know what, I think it's OK. So I breathed a bit easier. And I got home and she wasn't there."

McPherron asked, "I still don't understand why you weren't raising the alarm flags. I mean, did you tell anybody else about this?"

"No," said Rachelle.

"I mean, weren't you the least bit concerned about it?" he asked.

"I thought it was going to be OK," said Rachelle. That's why she didn't warn her mother when they spoke on Saturday about the chamber of commerce meeting.

"You didn't tell your mom nothing?" asked McPherron.

"I thought it was over," Rachelle said.

"I mean, heaven forbid we interfere with the volleyball tournament, right?"

Rachelle snapped back, "I was done playing by that time, thank you very much."

It was only when she got home and called Jason that she found out what happened. He told her, "Yeah, it's done. We did it. She's gone."

"And I freaked out," she said. She didn't tell police the truth initially because she was scared. "It was wrong and I didn't want it."

When she was told she had seemed to be joking at school after her mother's murder, she snapped, "Forgive me for trying to have a smile in the time of gloom."

The investigators continued to push her for more information, telling her repeatedly that she played a more active role in the plot.

"You're still downplaying. You're still diminishing. You're still trying to squirm out of this."

"I'm telling you what happened."

"Not everything. You're holding back."

"Please, please tell me, then: What am I holding back?"

"I don't need to tell you nothing. *You* need to tell *me*."

"Well, apparently you know more than I do, because apparently I'm holding back."

"I do," said McPherron, "because I've talked to your two partners and they've told me everything. I found all kinds of things out at the crime scene."

She said Jason and Brian were trying to "drag my butt in with them" because "they're angry."

"Oh, they're definitely angry," said McPherron.

"I'm sure Brian's mad because I didn't know he loved me, and I didn't love him back," said Rachelle.

"Jason's the one that's angry," said McPherron. "It's Brian who still loves you. He's throwing himself on a sword for you, you know."

Habib said, "Brian makes no sense to me."

"Brian's a psycho," said McPherron.

"I agree," said Rachelle. "Why do think I broke up with him?"

"Brian is a crazy guy," McPherron agreed.

"You know," said Rachelle, "I broke up with him because he was freaking me out about marriage and stuff."

"Well, he's a man of commitment," said McPherron.

"Yes," Rachelle said. "I realized."

"He promised you he was going to take care of your mom and he did it," said McPherron.

"He didn't listen," said Rachelle. "Jason didn't listen."

"You didn't do a very good job of stopping them, did you?" said McPherron.

Rachelle answered with more sarcasm: "Well, maybe I should not ever be on a debate team."

"You don't need to be a smart aleck with me," said McPherron.

"You don't need to question everything I say, then," said Rachelle.

They bickered some more before Rachelle asked, "So, can I just know: Am I going to go to jail?"

"Eventually," said McPherron. "But I need to understand just exactly what your role in this all is. You are going down with Jason. It just depends on how hard you go down with him. Quit telling me what you think I need to hear. Tell me what happened."

"If I was going to tell you what I think you need to hear," said Rachelle, "I'd be saying everything a whole lot different."

"How would you be saying it?"

"Probably what you want to hear is that I did it myself," she said. "Because right now I'm thinking all you want to hear is I had the most involvement."

Finally, McPherron said, "We can go around and around about this, and we've been talking about it for a quite a while. How about this: How about we take a wee break." He said he'd come back in ten minutes and urged Rachelle to "think about a few things."

"Have you told my dad yet?" asked Rachelle.

"No," said McPherron. "We're going to have to."

"I know," she said. "How long am I going to go to jail? How long?"

"I don't know those things. All I'm after is the truth. That's my job. The diviner of the truth."

After McPherron and Habib walked out, Rachelle sat in the little interview room alone, crying, breathing heavily, blowing her nose.

Eight minutes later Sergeant Habib returned. Habib closed the door, took a seat, and said, "Rachelle, why don't you sit up for me for a second. I want you to wipe your eyes for me. Compose yourself. You're sixteen years old. You're almost an adult. You need to start thinking like an adult, so I'm going to talk to you like one, all right?"

"OK," said Rachelle.

Habib began using the same approach as he had with Jason: talking to Rachelle islander to islander.

"I want you to be very, very clear on this. Very clear," he said. "And I want you to listen to me. We have been working on this for five days now, twelve-hour days. We have crime lab technicians down here, just like you see on TV. It's *CSI*. We have homicide investigators down here, three of them. This department, the troopers here, everybody has been working on this. We have done numerous interviews. We have interviewed your friends. The things your friends have told us is amazing."

"These two [Jason and Brian] have basically 'fessed," he said, and on this score he was truthful. Habib implored Rachelle to come clean with McPherron.

"That man is one of the top homicide investigators and top interviewers in the state of Alaska," Habib told Rachelle as she sniffled. "That's why he flies all over the state from Anchorage to do these cases. He is a pro. He's got the patience of Job. He'll stay on this case 'til hell freezes over. He's not done 'til he says he's done. He's got ya. He's got you. He's got your involvement in the case.

"You have a choice. And this is the only choice you have," Habib said. "This is the only decision you have to make right now. This is not a game. This is not high school: Do you want us to stand up with the district attorney and tell them that you cooperated, you screwed up, you weren't thinking? Or do you want us to stand up and say for five days you've lied to us? Down to the end, when we present all this evidence in front of a jury, you continued to lie to us and bullshit us? Trying to show us you're smarter?"

Rachelle mumbled, "I know."

"Listen to me: Do you want us to do that?" asked Habib. "Do you want a jury to hear that? Do you want a judge to hear that? Or do you want us to stand up and say: 'This kid screwed up.' Or 'She at least stepped up to the plate and was honest with us?' Which one? Those are your two choices."

"The first one," she said in a tiny voice.

"Then you need to start doing it!" said Habib. "We're not dumb. That man is not dumb. You're giving him a little piece here, trying to appease us. I'm sitting over there shaking my head, watching you lie. And it's not helping you any. It's not helping you at all. He's pissed. He's ready to just go for it: Let's do it. You're a kid. It's time to act like an adult.

"Do you want to talk to him again and be straight with him? If you're straight with that man, I will stand up, he will

stand up, and the DA will stand up and say, 'She cooperated.'
It's your choice. That's where we're at, yes?"

"Yes," she said.

"Just show the man a little respect."

On cue, McPherron walked back in the room.

"Hello again," he said.

It was a different Rachelle Waterman, the talk from Habib
having had the same effect on her as it had on Jason. Gone
was the argumentative teen with the smart mouth.

"First of all," she told McPherron, "I'd like to apologize
for being a smart-ass."

"OK," said McPherron.

"A lot of times I speak before I think."

"OK."

"I know you deserve a lot more respect than I've been
showing you. Sorry."

"I can understand that," said McPherron, "appreciate that.
Thank you. The ball's in your court. Why don't you start at
the beginning?"

"The beginning," Rachelle said, "was where I came forth
with my situation. Murder wasn't the first thing we came to.
I was talking about being emancipated and different things
like that."

"OK," said McPherron.

"Then they discussed murder," she said. "And I didn't do
a lot of talking. I did a lot of listening because I didn't know
what to do. So, like I said, it was discussed and I said, 'Well,
let's do it.'"

McPherron asked, "'Let's do it.' For which?"

"For the murder," said Rachelle.

She described a plot that ebbed and flowed. Rachelle
didn't come up with the ideas, but she wasn't out of the loop,
either.

"I wanted to know what was going on," she said.

"Before it happened?"

"Yes," she said. "And so time sort of passed, and things
started getting a little better, and I thought they had kind of
forgotten about it and it started to fade. Then another inci-

dent happened and they start talking about it again, about just 'it' in general. I mean, I didn't know of a certain plot or anything."

When her mother abused her again, she told Jason but didn't want him to hurt her mother. When he asked, "What about our plan?" she told him, "You know what? I don't know. I'll talk to you later."

Rachelle told the detectives, "So I guess he talked to Brian."

"When was this?"

"This was before the shooting one," she said. "And I was talking to him and he said, 'Do you want us?' He told me about the plan, pretty much."

"The shooting plan?"

"Yes," she said. "And, like I said, and I will stand by this to the grave, I told them no. I don't know if that's why they called it off. I don't know if he got to Brian in time because he said, 'I don't know if I can.' I said, 'Please call it off.'"

After she was abused again around October, she told Jason. He started talking about the murder plot.

"This time, I wasn't so sure," she said. "I kind of—I don't know—I was, like, it was appealing in the only sense that I wouldn't be abused, but then I was, like, 'This is my mother. I love her.' So we talked about it, and they knew about the window because I had snuck out before. I just told them, 'Yeah, it's easy to sneak out of my house.'"

"Or sneak in, conversely," said McPherron.

"I guess," said Rachelle. "It's right on the ground floor, missing a screen, it's hardly ever locked. And, well, they probably knew about that before."

"OK, continue, please."

"And before state [tournament], she had gotten angry at me, and another incident occurred, and I told them about it, and they were coming up with this plot."

"What did she get mad at you about?"

"A lot of my black [clothing]. I had also gotten a C in math. And just normal stuff, you know."

"OK."

" 'We don't like black,' " she said, quoting her mother. "And so it had just come up in conversation, you know: 'Yeah, my dad's going to be gone this weekend.' "

She quoted "them" as then saying, "So if we were going to do something, this would be an opportune time."

"And I'm kind of, like, 'Well, yeah, suppose,' " she said. "And then, well, that's when I didn't know if we were going to go to state or not because, of course, I only found out about regionals. After I found out I was going to state, I told them, 'Yeah, I'm going to state! Our team made it. Wee-hee, hoo-hoo.' And I really didn't say anything about a plan. I guess I was euphoric about winning regionals. And then before I left, they said, 'We might do the plan this weekend.' "

"I'm sorry, who said it would be a good time?" asked McPherron.

"Brian—or Jason," she said. "And I was, like, 'Well, yeah, I suppose.' And I didn't know if he was—they were—if it was, like, for sure or not. I was just kind of, like, I don't know. It was just bouncing around in my head. Over the weekend I got worried, and I thought of how, since the last incident, how things have actually gone so much above what they've been in the last year. We were both happy about regionals and honor choir, and we had gotten to spend time on my honor choir trip to Haines."

"Together with your mom?"

"Yes, because she was a chaperone for that trip. And we had got to spend time together there. And so on this call I talked to him about it, and—"

Habib interrupted, "Rachelle?"

"Yes."

"I'm going to stop you there. Remember our discussion?"

"Yeah, I know."

"Evidence, and your total honesty," said Habib.

"I know, I know," she said. "So I called him Friday and, honestly, we didn't even talk about it. I wasn't even—well, at least not that I remember. I told him about my trip. I told him how things were going with the team. And I really don't remember much of that conversation. I wish I did."

"There was nothing about the murder plot?"

"Not that I remember," she said. "I mean, you'll have to forgive my memory."

"Come on, it's a week ago."

Habib chided her, mispronouncing her name. "Rachel, Rachel."

"Rachelle," she corrected.

"Rachelle, rather," Habib said. "I'm sorry, I've interviewed so many people this week."

"I know, I'm seriously trying to remember."

"On that phone call," said Habib, "you did not tell him to stop?"

"No," she said, "I didn't tell him to stop. I didn't even know it was going to happen."

She said she "suspected" it might happen but didn't tell anybody about it. "I didn't know how to. I mean, I didn't know to go to my coach and say, 'Coach, I need to talk to the police.'"

When she got home, she talked to Jason and was stunned to find out they had killed her mother.

"You knew this was going to happen while you were away at tournament, yes?" asked Habib.

"Well," said Rachelle, "I suspected."

"You knew this was going to happen when you were away at tournament? Yes or no?" Habib demanded.

"Know for a fact?" said Rachelle.

"You were pretty darn confident that it was going to happen," said Habib.

"Yes, I was pretty—" Rachelle stumbled.

"Don't split hairs," McPherron jumped in.

"Pretty sure," acknowledged Rachelle.

Habib said, "You didn't tell him: 'Don't do it. I've changed my mind'?"

"I didn't," admitted Rachelle.

"Well, thank you for that," said McPherron. "I'm sorry that took two and a half hours of talking to get to."

There was little left for her to say. The detectives pressed her one last time on her claims her mother abused her. She said she never reported it to police because she didn't think they would believe her.

She was right. McPherron and Habib weren't buying it.

"I've talked to you enough to know that you have a tendency to embellish things and dramatize things a little bit," McPherron said. "I don't doubt for a minute that there was discord between your mother and you. And I don't doubt for a minute that things may have even gotten physical. But I have a real problem with baseball bats and knives and stuff like that. I think that was more talk than it was fact."

When she again said her mom had hit her with a baseball bat, Habib said, "The baseball bat never happened."

"Yes, it did," said Rachelle.

"No," said Habib. "I can't believe it."

"You see how things get exaggerated and blown out of proportion if you're not careful," said McPherron. "A little overacting here can have dire consequences."

Asked if she ever thought she was going to die at her mother's hands, Rachelle said, "Not at the moment."

And that ended the interview. McPherron asked if there was anything else Rachelle wanted to tell them, and she mumbled no. He told that he had to "contact some people to find out what they want done" with Rachelle.

"Am I going to go to jail?" she asked.

"We're going to take you home," said McPherron. "Once we get there, I'm going to have to fill your father in on what happened."

"I'm scared he's going to be so angry," she said.

"I don't doubt that he will be," said McPherron. "I'm going to take your father aside. I'm not going to have you stand there while I explain to him, OK? That sound reasonable?"

"He's going to hate me," said Rachelle.

"I can't control what his feelings are. But if we can salvage anything, we can tell him, 'At least your daughter had enough courage, in the end, to stand up and take the responsibility for her actions.'"

"I don't think I can stand the thought of my dad hating me."

"I know that's a difficult concept to accept."

"I already had one parent that hated me. I don't want another."

"I don't think your mother hated you," said McPherron. "I think your mother hated a lot of the things you did."

"She told me she hated me," said Rachelle. "I think she did."

Habib said, "I think that may have been out of frustration dealing with a teenager. I've dealt with two teenagers. Thank God they're grown up now."

Rachelle asked if they would "tell this to the press."

McPherron said she'd be identified in court papers by her initials, RW, but in a small town like Craig everybody was going to know who it is.

"Can you just say 'somebody'?" she asked. "I really want to live."

"We'll do what we can for you," McPherron. "And by all means, we'll tell everybody who wants to hear that Rachelle finally did tell us the truth."

"That's not going to matter."

"It might in the long run," offered McPherron.

Habib added, "You'd be surprised."

"I doubt it," said Rachelle. "I don't think my dad's going to want to see me."

The investigators told her she would have to remain at the police station until they could handle procedural matters.

"My family's going to hate me," she said. "My whole family's going to hate me. I'm going to be, like, tossed out on my butt."

It was now seven p.m. The remainder of the night would be torturous for Rachelle as she was left alone in the interview room several times while the detectives left to meet to discuss her case. Rachelle had never so much as gone to the principal's office before; the worst trouble she had ever faced was being grounded twice by her parents.

For the next seven minutes, Rachelle sat in the room alone, crying, while the video camera continued to run.

When McPherron returned, she asked, "Do I have to go home?"

"We're looking into that," he said.

"Can I just go straight to a friend's house?"

"We'll see," the detective said as Rachelle continued to weep. Then he left again.

She was left in the room alone for another fifteen minutes.

When McPherron returned, he told her he still didn't know what they were going to do with her. She asked if she was going to jail, and he said he still didn't know, then left her alone again, this time for a half hour.

The pressure mounted. When he returned, Rachelle told him she was having an asthma attack and asked for water.

"I'm having trouble breathing," she said.

She again asked what was going to happen, and again McPherron said he didn't know.

"I don't suppose," Rachelle asked, "you could stay and keep me company?"

The question caught the detective off guard. "I'm sorry, what?" he asked.

"I don't suppose you could keep me company?" she repeated.

"I'm trying to help them get this—" he said, stumbling through an answer. "The more I help the, the less I can—the sooner we can get done, OK?"

"Does it look like I'm going to be in jail?" asked Rachelle yet again.

"We don't know yet, OK?" said McPherron.

Again she was left in the room, this time for seven minutes.

When McPherron and Habib returned, they said they still couldn't say what was going to happen. They left her there again, now for another eighteen minutes.

She poked her head out the door and saw a policeman stationed there.

"Are you, like, my guard?" she asked.

"Yes, ma'am," the officer said.

"OK, just wondering," she said, and closed the door and sat back down in the room, where she sat alone.

After another eight minutes the policeman entered. He said, "You need to come with me, young lady."

Rachelle Waterman was not going home to a friend, not going home to face her father.

Rachelle was escorted to the back of the police station, where she was booked into the Craig city jail. She posed for a mug shot and was fingerprinted and processed. She handed over to her female jailer the few personal possessions she had brought with her that night.

"Do I get to keep my sweatshirt?" Rachelle asked.

"No," said the jailer. "I'll give you jail issues."

"Do I have to get into some jail clothes?"

"Yeah," the jailer said.

Rachelle handed over her jewelry, three silver earrings, which were put in an envelope, and underwent the formal processing into the Alaska state criminal justice system, the dehumanizing transformation from free citizen to inmate.

She answered a series of questions about her health, saying her only problem was sports-induced asthma, for which she used an inhaler, and a sprained ankle from an injury the week before. Otherwise, she said she was free of diabetes, hypertension, epilepsy, drug addiction, alcoholism, mental illness, venereal disease, tuberculosis, hepatitis, and allergies. She said she didn't use IV drugs and was on no other medication than Albuterol for the asthma and, she admitted reluctantly, birth control pills.

"I never told anyone," she said.

The jailer said that somebody would bring her an inhaler, underwear, and the contraceptive pills.

"If there's a jail emergency, who would we call?" asked the jailer.

"My father," said Rachelle.

Rachelle then answered more questions, confirming that she'd never been divorced, lost a job, suffered a financial loss, or attempted suicide, though did say she had once considered killing herself.

"When?" asked the jailer.

"A month and a half ago," she said.

"Is there anything that will make you depressed while you are in jail," the jailer asked, adding "aside from being in jail?"

"No," said Rachelle.

The jailer asked if Rachelle became "seriously depressed," would she be willing to talk to somebody?

"One of you people?" asked Rachelle. "Or a friend?"

"Probably would be a mental health counselor type of person."

"No," said Rachelle. "They creep me out."

Rachelle signed an inventory of her seized belongings and was walked down past a row of cells, some containing male inmates, to her private cell.

She got one last courtesy. The jailers made all the inmates stand and face the wall while she walked by.

At age sixteen, Rachelle Waterman was formally under arrest in the murder of her mother.

CHAPTER TWELVE

On Saturday, November 20, Craig, Alaska, ached as only a small, proud town could. One of their best had been murdered, two of their own had been arrested, and a third—one of the island's brightest stars, with college and career and unlimited possibilities in her future—stood before a magistrate to face charges of conspiring to kill her own mother. Rachelle Waterman's father sat a dozen feet away from his daughter. It was an unthinkable crisis: his wife was brutally murdered in a months-long plot instigated and orchestrated by their own daughter.

Just the week before, Rachelle was giddily shopping with her girlfriends in Anchorage, buying "incredibly awesome boots," as she wrote on her blog. Now she wept as she listened to Magistrate Kay Clark read the charges contained in a criminal complaint: conspiracy and murder.

The Ketchikan Public Defenders Office was appointed to represent her. Bail was set at $150,000—$100,000 less than that of Brian and Jason because she was a minor, didn't participate in the actual murder, and was not considered by the DA's office to pose the same threat to the community as the nearly decade older Jason and Brian. Otherwise, her age gave her no advantages. Alaska's tough murder laws call for anyone as young as sixteen to be tried as an adult. At the time of the murder, Rachelle had been sixteen for about two and a half months. If convicted, she stood to spend ninety-nine years in an adult women's prison.

Sitting in the audience section at the court appearance was *Ketchikan Daily News* reporter Tom Miller, who in his article would describe the sixty-year-old Doc Waterman as "shaken throughout his daughter's arraignment hearing." Miller noticed that when it was over, Doc stood in the aisle, reached out, and touched Rachelle's elbow as troopers ushered her out on her way to the women's prison in Juneau. It was a bittersweet detail picked up by the Associated Press and repeated in stories that would soon sweep the nation.

At 1:30 in the afternoon, the Alaska State Troopers released a statement on their Web site providing the most detailed account of the events leading up to the arrests of Jason Arrant, Brian Radel, and Rachelle Waterman.

"Rachelle Waterman approached Arrant and solicited him to kill her mother, Lauri Waterman," the statement said. "Arrant agreed to kill Lauri Waterman and enlisted the aid of Brian Radel, age 24, of Thorne Bay. Between the solicitation and the actual murder, Arrant, Radel and Waterman plotted several murder scenarios and aborted one attempt to carry out a plan in September 2004."

The statement said that on November 10, 2004, Rachelle told Jason that both she and her father would be out of town for the upcoming weekend and "agreed that it would be a good time to attempt to carry out their plan because Lauri Waterman would be home alone." After Jason and Brian "made preparations" for their plot, Jason dropped off Brian near the Watermans' house, where Brian "abducted Lauri Waterman out of her bed and forced her into her minivan that was parked in the garage."

Brian drove her to central Prince of Wales Island and met Arrant with a plan "to murder Waterman and to stage what appeared to be a fatal drunk driving motor vehicle accident," the statement said, "but after Radel had murdered Waterman they changed their plan." Lauri's body was loaded into the van, driven to the end of Forest Service Road 3012, soaked in gasoline, and set on fire to destroy the evidence. When Rachelle got home Sunday, she was briefed by Jason.

"This account," the statement said, "was developed during interviews with the three defendants over the past four days. During the interviews all three made admissions as to their involvement in the murder. Physical evidence recovered at the various crime scenes corroborated many of the defendants' statements."

The statement was signed by Trooper—and longtime Craig resident—Robert Claus.

He left out some details: that Lauri was forced to drink wine, then was bludgeoned with a flashlight. Claus's statement said "blunt object." And there was no mention of the apparent actual cause of death, Brian choking Lauri with his bare hands. Also missing was any mention that the murder was spurred by Rachelle's claims her mother physically abused her. When the *Anchorage Daily News* ran a lengthy story a couple of days later, it said, "Troopers said they are trying to uncover a motive."

The people of Craig were stunned, the no-nonsense, cop-report prose laying bare these horrific acts. "Everybody is pretty much in disbelief," Trooper Captain Kurt Ludwig—Claus's boss in Ketchikan—told the *Anchorage Daily News*. "The family is pretty prominent." Craig School District superintendent Ronald Erickson added, "This is a big surprise to everybody. We all need to hold judgment until we know why it happened."

It didn't take long before the social networking community linked the arrest of Rachelle Waterman with smchyrocky's My Crappy Life blog. Rachelle's final post saying, "Just so you know" her mother was murdered attracted thousands of comments, some pained. The DrudgeReport picked up the story, as did Web sites with names like SurfWax, Daily Rotten, and Crime 2000. LiveJournal would take down Rachelle's blog, but not before thousands had read it and cached it, leaving it on sites for all to download. Here was a landmark: the first blogger accused of murder. "This isn't a legend, it's a sad tragedy, because this is a no win situation for all involved," wrote a Craig resident using the name usanightmare. But many more were of a less thoughtful vein. "An LJ [LiveJournal] killer! Cool as fuck," wrote a mr. twisty. Rachelle also was memorialized in a song "Van on Fire" by the Washington State rap group Futuristic Sex Robotz.

Rachelle's candid and often unflattering posts on the limited opportunities in "Hell, Alaska" shined a light the locals of this tourist-reliant island—including the chamber of commerce that Lauri Waterman helped the night of her death—would rather not see. This young girl was openly writing of Wicca, masturbation, the creepy guy on the ferry, the cruel treatment of classmates, the snide remarks about friends, and troubles with a "female parental unit" who found her daughter too fat.

As the era of social networking was dawning, this would become the voice of the online generation: sarcastic, dark, angst-driven, complaining, snide, dismissive, ironic, unable and unwilling to bother to spell correctly or use proper grammar. This was the generation for which privacy meant something else, that life could be played out—and commented upon—on the computer stage, the virtual public. This was the generation that didn't just love the emerging waves of reality stars—the bachelors and bachelorettes and Hills girls—but identified with their life-lived-in-public more than their more discreet, off-line parents.

In reporting that people were now "flocking" to My Crappy Life, the *Anchorage Daily News* marveled at how her blog, without filters or editors, was a "fascinating peephole into a world where lock-and-key diaries have been replaced by journals written for the whole planet to read and respond to, a world where voyeurism has been compounded by participation." The story spread around the world, with the *London Sunday Telegraph* commenting on the "pale and pretty" Rachelle, "clever at school and a keen singer," who seemed on the surface to be a "normal, angst-ridden teenager" who, if convicted, would become "the blogging world's first killer."

Police pored over the blog and read thousands of comments from the public. Comparing blog entries with evidence from the investigation, including the statements to police by Rachelle, Jason, and Brian, placed Rachelle's teenage tribulations in a more serious light, but Sergeant Randy McPherron found nothing of evidentiary value in them.

"I don't know if it's just me being a cynical old cop or what, but come on, it's a sixteen-year-old girl doing a journal," McPherron told the *Anchorage Press*, a weekly newspaper that printed many of her blog entries. "You might want to take with a grain of salt what's being said there."

In an interview with the *Anchorage Daily News*, he said that he still didn't have a clear idea why Rachelle wanted to kill her mother. "We couldn't cross that bridge of motive with her," he told the newspaper. "Obviously there was some discord in the family, some problems between mother and daughter," he added. "But there's no evidence that Lauri Waterman was behaving in any way but as a normal parent. She was trying to keep her [daughter] out of trouble. Obviously, Rachelle chafed at that."

By Monday, November 22, the teenager at the center of all this was in Juneau, behind the walls of the Lemon Creek Correctional Center, Alaska's only prison for women, housing both those convicted of crimes and those awaiting court dates. Rachelle was housed with seven women serving sentences and thirteen others awaiting their fate at trial—all adults. She was the only minor in the facility. The grand jury delivered exactly what the prosecution wanted, a smorgasbord of charges, including conspiracy to commit first-degree murder, second-degree murder, kidnapping, first-degree burglary, and first-degree vehicle theft. The only difference between the charges Rachelle faced and those of Jason and Brian, who were incarcerated to the south in Ketchikan, was that the men also had evidence-tampering counts.

Her father remained in Craig, reeling under the weight of a painful paradox. Don Pierce, who was with his old friend

Doc Waterman when they got the news of Rachelle's arrest, said Doc's emotions swirled. "As painful as the loss of Lauri was," Don later told *Dateline*. "I think that the arrest of his daughter was even harder."

Police were not done yet—there were more search warrants to be served and more evidence would come to light—leaving Doc in a bind. He wanted to help solve his wife's murder but he also wanted to protect his daughter. In the weeks and months after Lauri's murder, he coped as only Doc knew how, exhibiting a calm, detached demeanor that perplexed all but his closest friends. Tears came only once in the days after the murder; otherwise, he kept strong and busy for the sake of Lauri's family, who had arrived in Craig for her funeral.

"Doc's a very brave man," Don Pierce said later. "He has faced many things in life that I wouldn't want to face, the Vietnam War being one of them. And in our travels over the island that next week we had talked about it, and [he] told me that it wasn't that he was going to be cold, it wasn't that he didn't want to care, but the only way that he could see getting past this was if he put it in survival mode like he had in the Vietnam experience."

Doc didn't talk about the war, but those who knew him well knew it had been traumatic. "That part of that experience he still had not dealt with and it was going to take a long time for him to get to the point where he would be able to deal with Lauri's death," added Don. "We helped him in those roles as much as we could, but it was a very hard experience for him."

Even as islanders openly expressed anger over Rachelle, Doc did not hide. He went to his real estate office every day, conducting business as usual. Rachelle's brother, Geoffrey, returned from college, faced with the same predicament as his father. Both decided they would stand by Rachelle while also cooperating with police on building a case against her.

In the days after Rachelle's arrest, officers returned to the Waterman house to search for more evidence of how Lauri Waterman was kidnapped. Sergeant Mark Habib checked the garage windows, finding cobwebs pushed up against the glass. This was an indication the window had recently been opened. On the sill he saw what appeared to be a boot print and, outside under the window, a yellow box of spark plugs that had apparently toppled from the workbench when Brian went through the window.

More evidence came from the computers used by Rachelle, Jason, and Brian. Although Sergeant Randy McPherron and Trooper Bob Claus told the three during the interviews that police had a wealth of computer evidence, in fact the analysis was only just beginning weeks after the arrests at the crime lab in Anchorage. Trooper Christopher Thompson, who worked in the computer and financial crimes unit, used forensic software designed for law enforcement that is able to recover documents and photos, even if the files have been deleted. Exploring the dark recesses of the hard drive, Thompson typed in search terms such as "parental unit," "Lauri," "Rachelle," and Rachelle's various nicknames.

The software failed to turn up any of the many instant message notes sent between Rachelle and Jason, and only a few e-mails relevant to the case. But Jason's computer contained something detectives found helpful: a file with Rachelle's name containing nine photographs and four video clips, time-stamped July 12, 2004—shortly before Rachelle left for a summer vacation to her grandparents' house. The photos appeared to have been taken with a digital camera, probably the one Rachelle reported on her blog that she had received the previous Christmas.

They showed Rachelle on her bed taking off her clothes and posing provocatively for the camera with explicit close-ups. The videos featured similar poses, the last one showing a naked Rachelle tapping at the keyboard. A text file contained Jason's instructions for the poses he wanted.

Taken together, the evidence from the garage and the photos and videos corroborated the statements by Jason and Brian. The photos and videos in particular, investigators believed, helped explain why Jason was so driven to help

Rachelle by murdering her mother, supporting the theory by Sergeant Randy McPherron and Trooper Bob Claus that this lonely island misfit was motivated at least in part by sex.

The psychological forces at work became more apparent when Rachelle's school principal turned over a stack of letters from her locker. These were the notes shuttled between Rachelle and Jason by their friend John Wilburn in exchange for Jason securing porn (itself a crime because John was a minor). Intimate and sad, the letters lay bare a grown man's obsession for a teenage love he grew to sense he'd never fully and openly possess.

"If you're reading this around anybody, stop," wrote Jason, adding a winking emoticon. He apologized for an earlier email that may have seemed "a little impersonal" but said he worried that somebody might have access to her messages. He also explained the strange words at the end—he wrote "I love you" in Russian because he didn't think her mom would know what it said.

This letter was undated, but appeared to have been written early in the summer, before Jason and Brian considered violence and were instead cooking up other ways to deal with Rachelle's complaints about her mother. Jason wrote that Brian considered Rachelle's mother "rather materialistic" and referenced something that Rachelle apparently told them—that her mother threatened to sell her into slavery. Jason told her he fantasized about driving up to Rachelle's house in a $100,000 Ferrari so that her mother would "be wanting us together so she might get something out of the deal." He also told her that he and Brian came up with ideas "to nab some large cash," a reference, he later said, to Brian's plans to make $100,000 by growing a rare strain of marijuana. The plan fizzled.

In this letter Jason was growing obsessed with having Rachelle for himself. He fantasized about Rachelle telling him on Instant Message one night to "come and get me." But it wasn't until another letter, also undated, that he specifically spoke of the murder plot. The letter was probably writ-

ten in the fall as Jason and Brian considered either shooting
Lauri or killing her in a staged drunk driving accident. He
told her he'd be "so glad" when the "whole thing with your
mother" was over. He said he realized he wouldn't be able to
see her immediately, but would take comfort in knowing
she'd finally be "safe."

The plot, however, was "stressing the hell out of me," he
said, and added he needed somebody to lean on. Jason's
longing for Rachelle grew more acute as they spent increasingly less time together because school was back in session
and their computer store hangout closed. By late September,
he wrote in another letter, he worried that he would lose her.
He wrote that he feared she'd "take matters into your own
hand" and "just get tired and move on to someone else." He
didn't think she'd do it, but reminded her that he'd be lost
without her.

This letter is dated September 29—the day of the failed
attempt to assassinate Lauri in front of the school.

Although Rachelle's letters to Jason were not as long, she
filled hers with the same aching emotions. "I wish I could live
with you. It consumes most of my thoughts," she wrote in
one undated letter. She said she dreamt of the day her father
"goes off his rocker" and that she could be emancipated. It
was a dream, she wrote, that "helps me get through the day."

Of most interest to investigators were lines they believed
could be referring to the murder plot. Rachelle wrote as volleyball season was winding down, "It"—living with Jason—
"will happen one day, hopefully not long after V-Ball."
Later in the letter, she was more specific. "I'm tempted to
take a hunting trip myself," she wrote, then complained that
her mother was pressuring her to go out with Ian again because he was a good influence on her by not allowing her to
drink or smoke and would tell her mother where Rachelle
was at all times.

Jason replied with gushing letters that went on for pages.
Rachelle's notes began to change in tone and length. "It's
not fair," she wrote. "You send me this huge romantic letter

and all you get is a crappy one. I'm sorry. Lol." Another letter was similarly short: "Not a lot going on. It took me until lunch to finish your letter."

If Rachelle was sending signs she wanted to distance herself from Jason, he didn't pick up on them. "You pretty much consume my every thought, babe," he wrote on October 6, a week after the failed assassination of Lauri Waterman. Even while playing video games, he was wondering what she was doing, how she was feeling and whether she was also thinking of him. "I'm not sure if that's entirely healthy," he acknowledged, "but I just don't care." He reminded her that the only reason he had joined the play was in order to be near her.

Five days later, he wrote that he finally got to talk to her for an extended time. "I wish it never had to end," he wrote. The letter was dated October 11, during the time Rachelle said on her blog she was grounded with "computer restrictions." How they were able to speak isn't explained, but their conversation left Jason yearning for more—and drove him to do "crazy stupid things."

Jason revealed to Rachelle that later that night he parked his truck behind the mall, walked down a trail to her house and found her bedroom window. He described looking through the glass at the blinking lights that he thought came from her computer. His hand was two inches from the window when he stopped himself. He says it would have been "pretty selfish of me" to wake her up at 2:30 a.m. on a school night "just so I can say hi."

He left her house, feeling disgusted with himself, even though all he wanted were a few precious seconds together. "It's not like I was trying to sneak a peek at you," he notes, "since I know you sleep not wearing much."

This nocturnal visit to her house was as close as he'd get to her. The next day, he wrote that he was "pleasantly surprised" to see Rachelle on Instant Message, so he dropped her a message. But she didn't answer. By the end of October, he couldn't stand the separation. In a note he later said he composed at 10:30 p.m. while stoned on marijuana, he told her he was "baked like lasagna" with only one thought:

"Missing you, baby." Filled with self-pity, he fantasized about a nighttime rendezvous or confronting her parents with a speech in which he announced his love for her. But in reality, he admitted he'd probably just end up "like a dumbass" without her. "Reality," he wrote, "you mock me with your cruel destruction of my fantasies."

From his letters, it was clear to investigators: Jason couldn't get over his summer fling with Rachelle—the sex, the naughty pictures, his first real taste of passion. He felt free to write her things like: "I'm practically quaking with excess sexual energy, more of a shudder I guess." He reminded her that she still owed him her "groovy or erotic fiction or fantasy." It would never arrive. No stranger to depression throughout his life, Jason told Rachelle that he almost started cutting himself again, just like he did when he was younger when he needed to feel something besides the hurt. The only reason he stopped from cutting himself was because of a "promise I made to you," a promise, investigators believed, he delivered by killing Rachelle's mother.

CHAPTER THIRTEEN

The weeks after the arrests of Rachelle, Jason, and Brian brought a whirlwind of activity. The trial was set to begin in February 2005. While investigators scrambled to complete the last of the searches and interview and reinterview more witnesses, lawyers toiled to prepare for the trial scheduled less than three months after the murder. After Rachelle, Jason, and Brian appeared at their arraignments in November, all pleading innocent, a trial judge was appointed.

Patricia Collins had been a superior court judge in Alaska for seven years and possessed a background that would be unusual in any other state. An avid sailor, Collins also had worked as a commercial fisherwoman in southeast Alaska. She attended college in the East and received a law degree from Gonzaga University. Most judges come from the ranks of prosecutors, but Collins was unique in coming not only from private practice and academia but by having a background in criminal defense as well as labor law. She worked in private practice in Alaska, running her own law firm in the late 1980s through the mid-1990s, and taught law at the University of Alaska. She also served as assistant public defender for Alaska from 1984 to 1985.

Her court was located in Juneau, but like all Alaskan judges, she was always ready to travel and could also preside over the telephone. The case spilled over multiple jurisdictions. Jason and Brian appeared in court in Ketchikan because that's where they were incarcerated; Rachelle appeared in Juneau because that was the location of the women's prison. The DA's office that handled crimes on Prince of Wales Island was based in Ketchikan, and the court-appointed defense lawyers were located all over Alaska.

The vast distances meant that many hearings were conducted by telephone, and it made for an unusual sight to the uninitiated. If Doc Waterman couldn't attend a proceeding in Juneau, a long and expensive journey from Craig by ferry and plane, Rachelle might be the only party to the case physically in the courtroom. Such was the scene on Tuesday, December 21, when bailiffs escorted Rachelle to the defense table. She was handcuffed and wearing a jail uniform for a morning hearing. The judge's bench was empty—Judge Collins had to be out of town on another case—and Rachelle sat alone listening to lawyers argue over loudspeakers, with the DA in Ketchikan and her own lawyer in Anchorage. The attorneys hashed out pretrial matters, including the question of whether to delay the February 3 trial date.

The hearing covered routine matters and was significant for the fact that it marked the debut of Rachelle's court-appointed lawyer, Steven M. Wells. Burly and bearded, Wells had a passion for fishing and hunting. He looked like he was born and raised in the Alaskan woods, but in fact was a product of California. He got his degree at California Western School of Law and practiced in the state for several years before moving to Nashville, where he shared office space with noted criminal defense attorney Lionel Barrett.

Wells's biography on his Web site tells the rest of the story. "After a while, though, the call of the wild places became too strong to ignore and he moved to Dillingham, Alaska, to be the public defender," it says. "The sole public defender for an area roughly the size of Ohio, he handled every type of case from commercial fishing cases to first-degree murder."

A fishing village of 2,400 on an inlet of Bristol Bay southwest of Anchorage, Dillingham is as far from Southern California as possible, and it served as the stepping-stone to his next position with the Office of Public Advocacy, a state agency providing legal representation for children, the elderly, and adults in custody cases. It also handles criminal cases that the public defender can't take because of a conflict of interest or other reason.

He was a traveling lawyer, representing clients accused of serious felonies, including sexual assault, kidnapping, and murder. The job brought a grueling schedule, bumpy flights on small planes in bad weather, overnights in little inns and bed-and-breakfasts. Like Rachelle, Wells kept an online journal—he called it Alaska Blawg—in which he described the plight of an itinerant defense lawyer for Alaska's indigent.

"On Monday, I might have a sentencing hearing in Bethel and then on Thursday I would have to fly to Sitka to see a client," he wrote. "So while I do not have a great deal of cases, the ones I have require a great deal of work. The work on each case, the distance between cases, and pressure to get them to trial is extremely wearying (is that even a word? I don't know, but it works)."

His tales of travel and work weariness echoed those of Rachelle in her My Crappy Life blog, and from early on Wells showed a strong connection to his young client. Loud and brash in court, Wells immediately went on the offensive, fighting for a new trial date that would give him time to wade through thousands of pages of interview transcripts and hundreds of hours of tape recordings. He complained that there was still much the prosecution had not yet turned over, including materials found on the computers, and that what little evidence he had seen so far amounted to nothing.

"The state of Alaska," he wrote in one motion, "is seeking to convict Ms. Waterman on the theory that she conspired to have her mother killed in a particularly brutal way because she and her mother did not get along."

Wells enjoyed a rare luxury for a defense attorney: a prosecution case with virtually no physical evidence and a client who was hundreds of miles away at the time of the crime. The prosecution was building a circumstantial case based on a conspiracy theory and the credibility of two Alaskan miscreants—a defense attorney's dream. Of all the written material in the prosecution's hands, there was not a single e-mail or handwritten letter from Rachelle, Jason, or Brian, and not one entry in thousands of pages of Rachelle's blog entries that directly referenced the murder plot or the actual killing. The closest the state had was an ambiguous reference to the "hunting trip." The prosecution was still hoping to bolster the case by winning the cooperation of Jason or Brian or both. Private negotiations had begun to strike plea deals that would bring them into a courtroom and provide testimony against each other and against Rachelle.

But those were issues for another day. Right now, Wells simply wanted Rachelle out of jail. By a hearing on December 28 in Juneau, she had been locked up for more than a month because her father couldn't afford her $150,000 bail, half of which was required to be paid in the cash, the rest in stocks or bonds. Judge Collins, presiding in person this time, listened as Wells, speaking by phone from Anchorage, requested that bail be reduced to $50,000, with $10,000 posted in cash. Doc Waterman's voice next was heard over the courtroom speaker, calling from Craig, to say that he could scrape up that much cash from savings and borrow the rest. He added that he and two family friends would supervise Rachelle if she were released. As for whether she was a risk to flee, Wells noted that Rachelle would still be a prisoner of sorts, released to an isolated Alaskan island accessible only by ferry and floatplanes, where everybody knew her. She further posed no threat to the people of Prince of Wales Island, Wells argued. Even the prosecution was conceding she didn't actually commit the murder.

The assistant DA, Dan Schally, calling from Ketchikan, opposed a bail reduction. He said that while Rachelle didn't physically kill her mother, the teenager was the "lead domino" in the murder, planning it for months with Jason and Brian, both of whom she was involved with sexually and who fell prey to her manipulations.

Judge Collins ruled that she wouldn't put Rachelle's father or family friends in the difficult position of monitoring Rachelle, who, if she returned to Craig, could get hurt or even harm herself. "I have to be conscious of the danger to the community," the judge said, and kept bail at $150,000. Rachelle was in tears as she was led out of the courtroom in handcuffs and transported back to her cell.

As the year 2005 began, the pace of litigation slowed. Lawyers next sparred over evidence sharing, and the February trial date came and went. One of the biggest early legal hurdles concerned the nude photos of Rachelle found on Jason's computer. The DA refused to provide hard drives containing the pictures to the defense because the images could be construed as child pornography and the transfer of them could be interpreted as a crime. To protect himself, the DA wanted a court order first. The judge issued one, but the defense complained the prosecution continued to drag its feet in providing the evidence. More legal issues arose, more motions were filed, and a new trial date was set for August 2005.

While the lawyers argued, the three people at the center of the case remained locked in jail. Rachelle's father would never come up with the $75,000 in cash required to get her out, and Rachelle would have to come to terms with remaining incarcerated until the trial—longer if things went badly in court. Jason and Brian never had any hope of making their $250,000 bail and both early on resigned themselves to never seeing freedom.

For Brian, the early weeks behind bars gave him time to pause and reflect. For the first time in years he had been separated from Jason, and as Brian sat in his Ketchikan cell day after day he began to see his old friend in a new light. He explained his thoughts in a letter written to his parents about a month after his arrest.

"I loved and still love Rachelle," Brian wrote. "I've always figured my life would be a small price to pay to protect the ones I love. Unfortunately, I had Jason involved, and he had about as much backbone as a jellyfish."

Investigators and the prosecution fueled Brian's emerging

doubts by telling him that Jason had sold out both him and Rachelle. This violated Brian's sense of loyalty and honor. From the very beginning he portrayed himself as a reluctant but willing participant in the plot to kill Lauri Waterman. The only reason he choked her to death was at the insistence of Jason and to protect a girl he thought both of them loved enough to die for.

After months of off-and-on plea negotiations, Brian made a decision. On Wednesday, June 8, 2005, he appeared in a Ketchikan courtroom to affirm that he had reached an agreement with prosecutors. He would plead guilty to first-degree murder. The conviction carried a maximum penalty of ninety-nine years in prison, but with time off for good behavior he could be out in thirty-three years—when he would be fifty-eight years old and still had some life left. In exchange, he would testify in court.

While Brian wrestled with his conscience, Jason also took stock of his plight. His statements to police had been the primary reason he, Brian, and Rachelle were arrested. As liberating as it was to open up to old acquaintances like Trooper Bob Claus and Sergeant Mark Habib, it brought the very real prospect that he would never leave his jail cell. While Jason was instrumental in the murder scheme, it didn't escape notice that he was not the one who actually killed her. And when investigators got a bead on the three of them and everything was falling apart, it was Jason who was the most cooperative. He even wore a wire and showed Bob Claus where the crime took place.

As with Brian, prosecutors played into Jason's concerns and second-guessing, and about two weeks after Brian's hearing, Jason, too, was in court to announce that he had also reached a deal. Like Brian, Jason would plead guilty to first-degree murder, but the penalty would be less severe, reflecting his cooperation and reduced role in the crime. Prosecutors would dismiss all the other counts against him and he'd face a prison term capped at fifty years. If he behaved himself, he could make parole in sixteen years, when he would be forty-two years old. In exchange, he also would testify.

With the two men reaching plea agreements that left Rachelle. There would be no deal. She conceded nothing and was prepared to gamble that a jury would find that she was guilty of nothing more than bad taste in friends. The strategy relied on the defense being able to find an unbiased jury. Rachelle would soon discover how difficult that would be.

CHAPTER FOURTEEN

In the spring of 2005, the people of Prince of Wales Island were starting to get phone calls from strangers asking personal questions.

"Hello, I am from Hellenthal and Associates," the caller said. "We are conducting a Southeast Alaska public opinion research survey. Your telephone number was randomly selected. The questions I need to ask will take three to five minutes. All of your responses will be completely confidential."

The callers, reading from a script, were instructed to "pause and proceed" with asking if they had the correct telephone number. If not, they were told to end the call by saying, "I'm sorry, I dialed the wrong number."

If they had the right number, they said, "Am I talking to you at a place where you live?" A no answer would be met with the scripted remark, "I'm sorry, I need to talk to someone at a residence," and the call ended.

If they said yes, the caller would lead them through a series of questions: Are you eighteen years or older?

If no, then: Is there anyone home who is eighteen years old or older? If yes, then: May I speak with them? If no, then: When would be a good time to call back and find someone who is eighteen or older?

Finally, the caller got to the point.

"Now, I am going to read to you a list of names of various people. Please tell me whether your feelings toward each of them is very positive, somewhat positive, somewhat negative, or very negative. Or if you don't know who they are.

The list included the names Carl "Doc" Waterman, Rachelle Waterman, Brian James Radel, and James Arrant.

If people hadn't figured it out by now, they would know later: the research firm was polling residents on behalf of Rachelle in preparation for her trial. By law, she was supposed to be tried in the jurisdiction where the murder occurred—in this case Craig, Alaska.

The telephone survey of 377 people found that publicity about the case had saturated southeast Alaska, with 79 percent of the respondents having heard about or learned of what the callers called "a recent case regarding the daughter of a mother in Craig." Of those, nearly 90 percent got their information from the newspapers—the *Ketchikan Daily News* had covered it extensively from the week of the murder—while another 55 percent said they also heard about it through word of mouth. Only a fraction heard about it on television or in a *People* magazine story in early February under the headline "Did This Teen Have Her Mother Murdered?"

No matter how they got their information, it was the talk of the region. More than 80 percent of those who found out about the case had discussed it with family, friends, or co-workers. About 7 percent, or twenty-six of the respondents, knew Rachelle and her father personally, while another nine people knew Jason, Brian or both.

Still, many people didn't know the most explosive aspects of the case. Only 15 percent were aware that Rachelle had "made a statement about the case." Those who did know about it overwhelmingly thought she was guilty. More people—nearly 80 percent of those surveyed—knew that Rachelle kept a blog, but their knowledge of it proved to be sketchy. More than 40 percent believed Rachelle had admitted in her blog to having participated in her mother's death, even though she had not.

The findings with the most impact for Rachelle concerned the conclusion that people had come to. Of those who had heard about the murder of Lauri Waterman, two-thirds said they believed Rachelle was guilty.

Just under 7 percent thought she was innocent, and 27 percent were undecided. The same number of people who thought Rachelle was guilty also thought Jason and Brian—the two men who had already reached deals and wouldn't be going to trial—were guilty.

Rachelle's attorney, Steven Wells, wanted the trial moved. Even the prosecution conceded it would be impossible to justify trying Rachelle in the tiny village where everybody had an opinion and everybody knew everybody else. The next logical venue would be across the water in Ketchikan, but Wells objected to that location too. With the same local paper and many friends and relatives in common, the attitudes of the people of Ketchikan likely differed little from those displayed in the survey of Prince of Wales Island residents, Wells argued. The prosecution asked for Ketchikan, noting in addition to it being the next-closest venue, this site would be more convenient. The DA's office was based there, and both Jason and Brian were incarcerated there, making it easier to get them to court for their testimony.

At a hearing in July in Juneau, Judge Collins said she didn't like the idea of moving the case even to Ketchikan, saying she wanted to litigate a crime in the community where it happened "if at all possible," but she didn't make a final decision. This legal challenge, along with the defense's continued hunt for access to the computer hard drives, delayed the trial date, and now Judge Collins reluctantly reset it for January 2006.

"I don't like continuing the trial," she said at a hearing, complaining that people's memories fade and evidence "tends to become stale." But she saw no choice. The lawyers needed time to prepare. Rachelle was brought into the courtroom in chains and asked if she waived her right to a speedy trial.

"Yes, Your Honor," she answered, and she was sent back to the women's prison.

On August 22, four days before Rachelle's seventeenth birthday, she was back in court in the usual orange jail jumpsuit, her wrists again shackled in front with a chain around her waist, for the most important hearing of the case. Family members had traveled to Juneau to support her. Despite the high stakes, Rachelle appeared relaxed, laughing with her attorney Steven Wells and making faces at her brother and father, according to an account by the Associated Press. When Rachelle complained during the hearing that the chain hurt her back, Judge Collins allowed the restraint to be removed.

At issue was whether Rachelle's police interviews to police would be admissible at her trial. Until now, authorities had said nothing about what Rachelle had revealed in her three sessions with investigators—the short conversation with Sergeant Randy McPherron at her house and the two longer interviews at the police station. The supposition in Craig was that she had confessed to being a part of the murder plot; she had, after all, been arrested. But her exact role—and the reason she gave police—remained unknown.

The prosecution intended to play all three of Rachelle's interviews in court, each one more incriminating than the one before it. The first short interview had Rachelle acknowledging her mother's objections to her friendship with Jason. In the second, longer interview, Rachelle revealed she had sexual relationships with both Jason and Brian, claimed that her mother had physically abused her, and ultimately admitted that she had lied about calling Jason at home the night of the murder. That session ended with Claus and McPherron telling Rachelle she was the catalyst that set the plot in motion, perhaps unwittingly.

It was the third interview that the prosecution considered the most valuable—and the defense most wanted to suppress. This is the one that had McPherron confronting Rachelle with the "hunting trip" e-mail and ended with her in tears, under arrest, and saying that her father would never like her again. While people in Craig already knew most of what she had said in the first two interviews—most assumed she'd had sexual relations with Jason and Brian, and her friends had long heard her tales of motherly abuse—the revelations in the third interview were new. A transcript of the interview, attached to court papers as part of the defense challenge, drew the attention of the local newspapers and the Associated Press. Many in Craig saw her actions—and inactions—as a betrayal that could not be forgiven. No matter how the criminal case turned out, Rachelle could never come home again.

From a legal perspective, her statements formed the heart of the prosecution's case, and Rachelle's attorney mounted an aggressive campaign to have them suppressed. In court papers, Wells argued that Rachelle fell victim to a level of police coercion that fell far outside legal bounds during an interrogation. He also claimed that while the investigators had properly read Rachelle her Miranda rights and gave her the opportunity to have her father present, the teenager was too young, immature, and psychologically fragile to make an informed decision when she waived those rights.

To bolster the defense case, Wells arranged for Rachelle to meet with a child psychologist for eleven hours over two days. Dr. Marty Beyer was a Yale-educated clinician with vast experience with young people in the criminal justice system: her résumé listed work in Alabama, Oregon, New York, Virginia, California, Florida, New Mexico, and now Alaska. Her psychological evaluation explored Rachelle's childhood through her final moments with investigators.

"Rachelle," according to Beyer's report, "is a bright, depressed 16-year-old who shows a complicated combination of independence and immaturity."

Beyer concluded that traumatic events throughout Rachelle's life left her not only scarred but easy prey to an aggressive interrogation. These factors dated back to when Rachelle was in grade school. She developed physically at an early age—menstruation at age ten, acne at eleven, conspicuously large breasts in junior high school—leaving Rachelle plagued with low self-esteem. All this was exacerbated by frequent criticism about her weight from her mother, whom the psychologist noted "was slim."

Her mother also criticized her for getting any grade below an A, favored her brother, pushed her into sports and disapproved of Rachelle's interest in Wicca. Eventually, Lauri Waterman lashed out with more than words, according to the report, hitting Rachelle "with increasing frequency over the summer before 11th grade."

That was the summer that Rachelle met Jason Arrant and Brian Radel.

Rachelle told her therapist, "I was her anger outlet," a victim of her mother's menopausal outbursts. As Rachelle had told police, she never reported the alleged abuse. "No one would have believed me," she told the therapist, and Rachelle was correct. Her friends didn't believe her and, when she finally told police, neither did they.

Rachelle told the therapist she thought of talking to her father about the abuse but didn't think he would understand. The two had a "buddy-buddy" relationship that prevented them from deep conversations, and, besides, "I knew he wouldn't believe me," she told the therapist. When Rachelle complained about her mother, her father "made light of her mother's bad moods," the report says, "so she decided not to complain about her mother's abuse."

But low self-esteem and alleged parental abuse weren't the only traumas haunting Rachelle. Dr. Beyer's report included a shocking claim that placed Rachelle's behavior in a new light, but was one that Craig residents weren't sure they believed.

According to the report, Rachelle says that when she was in eighth grade, while walking home from school one night, she was pulled into the backseat of a car and raped at knifepoint by "someone who did not live in their community."

"The rape was traumatic not just because of the violence, the pain of first time intercourse, and the terror encountering the perpetrator again," the report says, "but also because her mother did not believe her."

Rachelle claims her mother refused to take her to a doctor and wouldn't tell her father. Her mother felt Rachelle had invented the story to avoid punishment for coming home late. After this, according to Rachelle, she didn't trust her mother and worried about acting or dressing in a way that would draw attention to herself.

"I quieted down. I was not as happy. I read a lot. I was a little weird," she told the therapist. "My worst fear was being raped again. I worried about seeing him. I didn't want it to control my life or make me afraid of men. I didn't want it to change who I am."

The rape account could not be confirmed and became one more reason to question Rachelle's credibility. Many in Craig refused to believe that a mother as devoted as Lauri Waterman would have reacted the way Rachelle said she had. The defense psychologist took it at face value as something that Rachelle believed and, therefore, contributed to problems in her emotional development and her depression. Rachelle, Beyer concluded, appeared independent for her age but was in fact as needy as a young teenager, reaching out to boyfriends and friends for the nurturing she didn't get at home.

These psychological forces came into play with tragic consequences in the summer of 2004, the report says. Rachelle showed an immature thinking process in which she "did not imagine negative consequences of friendships with Jason and Brian," the report says. When Jason asked her if she wanted him and Brain to "get rid of" her mother, Rachelle claims, "I played along. I didn't think it was serious."

When they told her they had plotted to shoot her mother, Rachelle dismissed it as their "weird sense of humor. I thought they were joking." When Jason suggested that the weekend she and her father were out of town would be a good time to kill her mother, "I did not think he was serious. I thought it was talk, not a real plan." Rachelle, according to the therapist, merely saw the men as "different" and, despite their fixation on D&D and Jason's drug use, "it had not occurred to her that they would act on these fantasies."

By the fall of 2004, when Rachelle's mother was killed and detectives were asking her questions, Rachelle didn't grasp the Miranda warning read to her, thinking that "right to an attorney" meant she could only have a lawyer if she already knew one. When Rachelle asked in the second interview why the detectives were reading her rights, McPherron brushed it off as "standard" and "just for this interview." Rachelle claimed to have been intimidated by the detectives, that Sergeant McPherron was big like a football player, and that she would have wanted to have her father there but didn't know how to deal in an adversarial situation with authority figures.

Rachelle told Beyer that "I was so confused. I told them the truth but they wouldn't listen. They kept telling me it was my fault."

In the end, the psychologist concluded, Rachelle fell victim to classic "coercive interrogation techniques," leaving this confused girl in shock over her mother's death with no choice but to tell the detectives what she thought they wanted to hear— not necessarily the truth. In her court testimony, Beyer said, "She parroted back the words she had heard."

The prosecution countered that the interrogations of Rachelle were done by the book. The state's argument was presented by a new face in court, Stephen West, who became Ketchikan district attorney when the governor appointed Dan Schally as a judge in Valdez, Alaska. West had taken over the plea negotiations from Schally and now was trying to keep the state's case from being gutted.

Like so many in Alaska, West came from somewhere else, in his case Texas, and the prosecutor still spoke slowly with a tinge of a drawl peppered with "y'all's." Although he lived most of his life in Houston, West had spent three years in Alaska as a child from ages nine to thirteen when his family temporarily relocated, and after he returned to Texas he always wanted to go back north. After getting a law degree from the University of Houston, he took a job with the Alaska Legal Services Corp., which provides free and low-cost legal representation. West worked in civil litigation there, then switched to criminal law, working in the district attorney's offices in Juneau and then Ketchikan. He, too, traveled extensively throughout southeast Alaska and appeared at least once a month in Craig, staying in a bed-and-breakfast near the water. The work exposed him to every aspect of criminal law, from screening incoming cases and drafting appeals to participating in full-fledged murder trials.

At the admissibility hearing he elicited testimony from the three investigators involved in Rachelle's interviews— Sergeants McPherron and Habib and Trooper Claus. They said they went so hard on her because she lied at the beginning, and only reluctantly told the truth over time under repeated questioning. Their techniques, including exaggerating the strength of the evidence, all fell well within the legal and ethical parameters of police interrogations.

In his argument before the judge, Prosecutor West responded to the psychological issue raised by the defense. He said the investigators faced a much different Rachelle Waterman from the naïve, immature, vulnerable girl described by the psychologist. The Rachelle going toe to toe with the detectives was smart—and smart-mouthed—and seemed to fully grasp her decisions. He said the detectives, in refusing to accept Rachelle's lies, were doing their jobs.

"A defendant has a Fifth Amendment right to be silent," West argued, "but doesn't have a right to lie."

Judge Collins took two weeks to make her decision. In early September, she released a thirty-page decision that showed she carefully considered the psychologist's report— and rejected most of it. The judge took issue with Dr. Beyer's methodology, noting she didn't conduct standardized tests on Rachelle that could provide a more objective opinion. Instead, the judge found, the therapist's conclusions came from Rachelle's own statements, many of which had proven to be false. Rachelle, for instance, had denied to the therapist that she had sex with Jason or Brian but acknowledged it, in detail, to detectives. Rachelle also didn't tell the psychologist about the nude photos sent to Jason, which Beyer—in formulating her opinion that Rachelle had body image problems—conceded would have been an area to explore.

"The audio- and videotaped interview process clearly reflects that Rachelle Waterman is intelligent and articulate," the judge said, adding that the detectives followed the proper legal steps, reading Rachelle her rights, making sure that she wasn't harmed or subjected to physical deprivation. Rachelle was free to leave during her second interview, but never did so—in fact, never even asked to go.

The judge raised one concern about how children could be influenced by adults generally, but "it does not, however, render all juvenile confessions involuntary."

In the end, "given the totality of circumstances in [this] case," Collins concluded, "the statements made by Ms. Waterman to Investigator McPherron and Sgt. Habib were knowingly and voluntarily made and she was sufficient of age, maturity and intelligence to make reasoned decisions to provide information to police. No obviously deceptive tactics were used and there was no physical threat or deprivation of any kind."

The murder case against Rachelle was now on the fast track for trial, with her defense having to recover from a major blow.

While public opinion in Craig was squarely against Rachelle, residents cut slack for her father. When Matt Volz of the Associated Press caught up with Doc Waterman in the summer of 2005, the Realtor was trying to live life as close to normally as he could. He was still working with the school board and the Girl Scout council, still busy in his real estate business, spending his free time fishing or sitting alone with his thoughts. He still smoked in the garage instead of the house, still living by Lauri's rules.

Interviewed in his office, Doc told the AP reporter he was trying to "dwell on and focus on the good parts" of his life. He said he had "lost something," but "I had 25 or 30 years that were fantastic." Stoic as always, "I tell myself I'm doing well and sometimes I'm just, you know . . . ," his voice trailing off.

Although the DA was building a case against his daughter, Doc steadfastly supported Rachelle. He would travel to Juneau for her pretrial hearings, sometimes with her brother, Geoffrey, making eye contact from the audience section while she sat shackled in her orange jail jumpsuit. It was Brian Radel who put her up to it, he said, describing the man as "the poster child for reinstating capital punishment." In Doc's eyes, Rachelle was merely a "16-year-old kid [who] doesn't really recognize the impact of everything that is happening" and whose statements to police were bullied out of her.

Rachelle, too, was trying to have some semblance of a life. While in jail, she passed her high school equivalency exam and was applying for colleges. But Doc acknowledged his daughter could never return to Craig. And despite his best efforts to remain positive, his friends conceded that life would never be the same in Craig.

"They aren't going to bounce back," Lorraine Pierce told the AP. "I don't think anybody's going to bounce back. They're going to cope."

In Juneau, Judge Collins considered whether these wounds suffered by Craig, Alaska, from the case were felt too deeply to hold a trial there. She agreed with Rachelle's defense, ruling on January 17, 2006, that the case wouldn't be held in Craig or in Ketchikan. Jury selection would begin in one week in Courtroom D on the second floor of the Dimond Courthouse in Juneau.

CHAPTER FIFTEEN

More than one hundred potential jurors squeezed into Judge Collins's courtroom—another fifty had to stay outside—on Monday, January 23, 2006, to begin the process of finding a panel to consider Rachelle's fate. They were a cross-section of the thirty thousand people in the state's capital: homemakers, teachers, miners, fishermen, and workers in the tourism business.

Government employees made up the largest proportion of the jury pool, since state offices and the legislature are based in Juneau. The governor at the time was Frank Murkowski, but by summer he'd be trounced in the GOP primary by an up-and-comer named Sarah Palin, who would win the general election. The pool was overwhelmingly white, with Native Americans making up the biggest minority group at about 10 percent of the population.

They skewed younger and male: Alaska is the only state where men outnumber women, though the discrepancy is smaller in Juneau. It's a city accustomed to safety and friendly relations with the police. At the time of jury selection, there hadn't been a murder in Juneau in years. Taken together, they came from the same demographic as Craig.

As jurors filed in, Rachelle sat at the defense table with Wells and her father. Gone were the orange jail jumpsuit and handcuffs she had on for pretrial hearings. She now wore a gray blazer with a white turtleneck. At the prosecution table sat Ketchikan DA Stephen West. Throughout the trial, Sergeant Randy McPherron and Trooper Bob Claus would be on hand to assist.

Judge Collins had agreed to allow a television pool camera in her courtroom. This, plus the national attention from the case, brought Court TV, which would stream the trial on its Internet site for $5.95 a month. NBC's *Dateline* had sent producers and a crew for a big prime-time story. CBS, ABC, CNN, and *Extra* also planned to cover portions of the trial. Television stations from Juneau and Anchorage also were on hand, as were reporters from the Juneau bureau of the Associated Press and the city's paper, the *Juneau Enterprise*, which described the courthouse scene as a "spectacle." So many reporters wanted to cover the trial that the court set up an overflow press viewing room with a closed-circuit television monitor.

The media presence raised the question of whether the jury should be sequestered in a hotel during the trial. When Judge Collins asked the crowd of jury prospects to raise their hands if they had heard about the case, most did. Prosecutor West argued against it. He said juror media bias could be weeded out by questioning prospects and dismissing tainted prospects for legal cause. The judge agreed and said she would allow jurors to go home at night with a stern admonition to avoid news reports.

Jury selection lasted two days. Prospects were brought into the judge's chambers to be questioned by lawyers while Rachelle and her father observed. The questions were designed as much to influence jurors as to ferret out bias. Defense attorney Steven Wells not only asked whether any of the Juneau jurors had ever been to Prince of Wales Island but whether they'd be willing to accept the concept that somebody can implicate themselves in a crime by saying things that later turned out to be untrue. Several jurors said they couldn't imagine talking themselves into jail but that a teenager could do so under pressure.

By Tuesday afternoon, both sides had settled on a panel of fifteen, a dozen jurors and three alternates, for what looked to be a two-week trial. Judge Collins swore in the panel and scheduled opening statements for the next day, though testimony would be determined by the weather. A winter storm gripped the state of Alaska, and prosecutor West warned that his first witnesses may be delayed by snow. When the day's session ended, participants exited the courthouse into the early darkness of January in Alaska, where the nights are seventeen hours long even as far south as Juneau.

Indeed, it was still dark on Wednesday, when attorneys, jurors, reporters, and Rachelle Waterman returned to the courthouse the next morning. By law, the prosecution gets the first and last word, and so the case began with Ketchikan DA West standing before the judge and jury to deliver his opening statement on January 25, 2006, just over two years after the murder.

"This case is about Lauri Waterman," he told the jury, showing the panel a photo of her taken on the night of Saturday, November 13, 2004, at the chamber of commerce dinner in Craig. The snapshot captured Lauri in her element: attending a volunteer function, surrounded by friends and neighbors. It had been a gray, rainy night, but she dressed for spring in her tropical skirt.

"Eighteen hours later," West said, "this is Lauri Waterman."

The next photo on the screen showed a blackened skull and charred torso in the backseat of a burned-out minivan.

"She's dead and found in the burned van," said West. "This case is about Lauri Waterman and about three people who planned and then murdered her."

For the next two hours West explained how the relationships between Rachelle, Brian Radel, and Jason Arrant became what the prosecution considered a toxic conspiracy that resulted in the grisly scene before jurors. West played some of Rachelle's interrogation, read letters between her and Jason, and reviewed the legal language of charges against Rachelle.

By eleven a.m. he told jurors, "After hearing all the evidence, the state will be request you to return verdicts finding Rachelle Waterman guilty."

When attorney Steven Wells previewed the defense case, it was not Lauri but her daughter, Rachelle Waterman, who was introduced to the jury.

"A teenage girl," he said. "She grew up in a small town in Alaska, a town of 1,300 or 1,400 people. Essentially, she is just a quintessential small-town teenager."

The villain in this tragedy, he told jurors, was not Rachelle but the two men who already have admitted to being responsible for Lauri's death: "Poor, pudgy" Jason and "the hitman," Brian Radel. These men, he said, can only be believed when admitting to evil, not when blaming a teenage girl for whom they had unhealthy affections.

West concluded his statement by presenting the jury with questions he would answer during the course of the trial: "What did Rachelle intend—not know—but *intend*? What did she actively want and when did she want it? You're going to realize [that] for all her griping, she wants what every teenage girl wants. She wants a good relationship with her mother, who is alive and who is well. When you realize that, you're going to have the courage to come back and say: Rachelle Waterman, you are not guilty."

Rachelle's father wept during the opening statements, wiping his eyes with a handkerchief. The tears, he later told reporters, were for his daughter. "She may be the greatest living victim of all of us."

The prosecution called its first witness, chamber of commerce volunteer Janice Bush, who made it to Juneau despite the snowy weather and recounted Lauri's last night at the awards dinner. She was followed by Scott MacDonald, the young Forestry Service worker who found the burning van, and then Doc Waterman.

Testimony of a relative of a victim or the accused is often a high point in a trial, and the fact that Doc was both the husband of Lauri and father of Rachelle set the stage for an early burst of emotion. But the quiet, low-key Realtor maintained a calm demeanor as he recounted the most horrific week of his life. He also described the tensions between Lauri and Rachelle, and how his daughter's behavior had become increasingly troublesome in the months before the murder, with mother and daughter arguing over Rachelle's growing interest in Wicca, which Doc barely understood.

"We never had a very long discussion about that. It's nature based, uh, not— I'm kind of lost," he said. "The explanation is a couple of years old."

"Was there some friction between Rachelle and Lauri about this?"

"I know that Lauri talked to Rachelle about it. I don't know how much friction. I didn't have the impression there was a great degree of friction over it. It was more of a counseling."

But on one point Doc Waterman was certain.

"Did you ever see her physically hit or strike Rachelle?" asked West.

"No," he said.

"Did Rachelle ever say anything to you?"

"No."

"Did anybody else tell you?"

"No."

"Did you see any injuries on Rachelle that might have come from hitting?"

"She was a very active girl, not only in volleyball—and she'd play football with the boys down at the ballpark on the weekends," he said. "She had bruises nearly constantly."

"She ever say they had come from Lauri?"

"No," he said.

After he left the stand, it was up to Rachelle's neighbor and godmother, Lorrain Pierce, to inject emotion into the trial. Visibly nervous throughout the softball questions from the prosecution, she began to cry during cross-examination.

"Is this hard for you?" asked defense attorney Wells.

"Very."

"Is it hard for you to see Rachelle sitting there?"

"Yes."

With Lorraine and other witnesses, Wells sought to show that Rachelle's behavior was well in line with any teenager flirting with normal rebellion against her parents.

"Was there anything that you ever saw, when you dealt with Rachelle, when you talked with her or anything like that, that made you think she hates her mom?" asked Wells.

"I would not say hates her mom, maybe defy her rules," said Lorraine.

"Frustrated at what she had to live under?"

"Yes, maybe under the rules that Lauri wanted her to follow."

"Would you agree that that's fairly typical for teenagers?"

"Typically," said Lorraine, "it is."

The first day of testimony ended, and on Thursday morning Don Pierce followed his wife to the witness stand. During cross-examination he recalled watching Doc Waterman being told by Craig police chief Jim See that his wife's van had been identified.

Just once that week Don Pierce saw his longtime friend and neighbor break down. It happened after Lauri's identity had been confirmed and Doc dealt with both his daughter's arrest and wife's funeral at the same time.

"He had to put on a strong front for the family from Tacoma that was coming up, he had to play host," said Don. "We helped him in those roles as much as we could, but it was a very hard experience for him."

"He bore it well?" asked Wells.

"He bore it the best he could."

"Kept a stiff upper lip?"

"Yes."

"Is that sort of how Doc is?"

"Yes."

As Wells had sought to do with Don's wife, the attorney tried to make Don into a defense witness. Don Pierce had been a teacher for years and was in a unique position to interpret Rachelle's behavior in the summer and fall of 2004.

"Based on your relationship with Rachelle, based on your training with psychology and child development as a teacher, did you see anything in the years 2003 and 2004 before Lauri's death to suggest that Rachelle was anything other than an ordinary teenager?" asked Wells.

"No," said Don Pierce, "I didn't."

"Did you see anything other than ordinary teenager angst that she displayed?"

"No."

"Did she seem particularly angry or hostile or hateful?"

"No more than my kids," he said.

Wells tried the same line of inquiry with the next witness, Trooper Bob Claus, who traced the course of the investigation from the day he first saw the burned van and concluded that the murder had to have involved Rachelle, Jason, and Brian. But he acknowledged under cross-examination the weaknesses in the case.

"You're not going to have any of Rachelle's DNA on the flashlight that was used to kill Lauri Waterman, are you?" asked Wells.

"No, sir," said Claus.

"You're not going to have anybody that can walk in and say, 'I saw Rachelle Waterman buy this bottle of wine to force her mom to drink,' are you?"

"No, sir."

"You're not going to have anybody that can say, 'I saw Rachelle Waterman buy duct tape and towels to bind Lauri Waterman,' are you?"

"No, sir."

"All you're going to have is the word of Jason Arrant saying, 'Rachelle Waterman told me to do it,' right?"

Claus refused to concede this point. "No, sir," he said.

"Aside from Rachelle Waterman's statements, that's all you have, right?"

"No," repeated Claus, "I believe that the totality of the evidence from Mr. Radel, from Mr. Arrant, from all of the physical evidence we collected, from Rachelle's statements to us, all of those things lead to that conclusion—not just Jason's statement."

"So you wound up ultimately taking the word of some-body you don't really know, who happens to be the son of a dispatcher, over somebody you've known for twelve years. Is that a fair statement?"

West objected but was overruled by Judge Collins.

"It wasn't a matter of taking a word of any individual," said Claus, exasperation in his voice. "It was the totality of the evidence collected, from the time I went to the van through the last interviews, that led all of us together, with our collec-tive experience to that [conclusion]. No, I didn't take Jason Arrant's word for this as the sole basis for anything."

Claus would be the prickliest of witnesses for the de-fense. When Wells asked the same question he had earlier posed to the Pierces—"Did you see anything before Lauri Waterman's death that indicated that Rachelle was anything other than just a regular teenage girl?"—the trooper would not concede.

"I knew that she was, through what my children told me and through what my direct observations, that she was more rebellious than most, and that it caused difficulties in the house," he said.

"But teenagers can be rebellious?" pressed Wells.

"Yes, sir," agreed Claus.

"And certainly as trooper you were never called to inves-tigate any crimes that were committed by Rachelle, where you?"

"No, sir."

The prosecution called more law enforcement witnesses—Craig police chief See; Fire Marshal John Bond; the state's coroner, medical examiner Frank Fallico; crime scene tech-nician Dale Bivens—to set the scene for the first critical wit-ness of the trial.

Brian Radel, hulking in a jail jumpsuit, rattled up to the witness stand in handcuffs and leg irons on Friday, January 27. His attorney monitored the proceedings over the phone but said nothing during the questioning.

Brian began, for the record, confirming that he was a bulk

of a man: six feet five inches, 277 pounds, the same weight this day as he was in 2004.

For the first half of 2004, he considered himself to be in a relationship with Rachelle Waterman; she was fifteen to his twenty-five. They had sex, he said, even though she may have been also dating Ian Lendrum at the time.

"I don't really know," Brian said. The relationship ended in June 2004 when he opened the Dark Wolf Computer Design store, the gathering place for his Dungeons & Dragons group until it closed later that summer. As with many of her friends, Rachelle spoke to Brian about her mother abusing her.

"What did she tell you?" asked Woot.

"Mostly that she was hit, mentioned being hit with a baseball bat," Brian said.

"She ever mention anything about knife?"

"Not sure."

"She mention anything about her selling her into prostitution?"

"Yes."

"How about her mother trying to throw her down [the] stairs?"

"Not sure."

"Did you do anything to try to get her to report this?"

"No."

Instead, he said, a plan emerged to kill Lauri Waterman. Prosecutor West fast-forwarded through the months during which various schemes were discussed and abandoned, and brought Brian to the night of the murder, giving the jury— and the public—the first detailed account of how Rachelle's mother died.

It began with a shopping trip to Craig and Klawock, Brian said.

"What did you buy the rubber gloves for?" asked West.

"So that I wouldn't leave fingerprints at the scene," he said.

"What did you buy the duct tape for?"

"To bind Lauri Waterman."

"And what did you buy the towels for?"

"So that there wouldn't be any marks left from the duct tape."

"How were you going to use the towels?"

"I was going to wrap those first and then put the duct tape over them."

"And why was that?"

"So that there wouldn't be any marks left by the duct tape."

"And why were you afraid to leave those marks from the duct tape?"

"Basically because it was supposed to look like a car accident."

"What was your plan?"

"Find Lauri, tie her up, have her drink the wine, stick her in her van, and drive out to wherever Jason was."

"And then what were you going to do?"

"Go out to where there was a steep drop-off from the road that we found, and I was going to kill Lauri, break her neck, try to make it look like whiplash, and drive the van, or push the van over the edge."

In eerie detail, the tension heightened by Brian's calm, unemotional voice, he retraced his steps after Jason dropped him off near the Waterman house.

Wearing a black polar fleece jacket, black knit hat, black jeans, Xtratuf rubber boots, and two sets of socks, Brian stood next to a power pole at around midnight, casing the neighborhood. It was cold and blustery. He crossed a ditch and through a yard to the side of the Watermans' house and checked a window to see if it was unlocked.

Looking around for any witnesses, he peered through the window into the garage, realizing he was on the other side of a workbench covered in tools. He jimmied the window open and lugged himself inside onto the workbench, then reached back out for his backpack containing the duct tape, towels, rope, and wine bottle.

In the darkened garage, he looked for keys to the house but didn't find them. He could make out the two vehicles parked there, a blue truck and a minivan. He checked the door to the house; it was locked. He had no idea where anything was. He had asked Jason for a plan but didn't get it. "I basically was going in blind," he said.

With a butter knife, he tried to unlock the dead bolt—TV style—but couldn't get it to move. That's when he got the idea to break in through the cat door, removing the flap and reaching his arm through and up to undo the lock. He opened the door and entered the downstairs. Making his way up to the kitchen, he found the wine in the refrigerator and set his own bottle on the counter, then went up the stairs again to what he assumed was Lauri's room, the door ajar, but when he got near he heard her open it. He ran around the corner to hide.

"I thought she'd seen me," he said. "I figured she was probably calling the cops."

Had she dialed 911, the night would have been over and Lauri Waterman would be alive today. Instead, "I didn't hear any sirens," he said. "I stood there for an hour debating going into the room. . . . I finally decided to go in, and so I opened the door and I rushed in. Lauri was laying facedown on the bed."

He subdued her and she started to cry. The first thing he told her was to stop crying, which she did after a time. He bound her hands behind her back, gagged her with a dishtowel and duct tape, and untied her long enough for her to get dressed in sweat pants, bra, socks, T-shirt, and sweater.

"Originally I got jeans, but apparently they were broken," he said. "She was gagged. She motioned that the zipper was broken, so I got sweat pants then."

Also, he said, "for some reason, she wanted a different bra, so I got a different bra."

"How was she reacting to all this?" asked West.

"I don't know," said Brian. "It could have been anything. Terror or whatever. She was doing it."

She didn't cry and followed his every direction, said Brian.

"I asked her if the tennis shoes next to door were hers," said he. "She nodded her head. I gave her the shoes to put on and she put them on."

He said he got her to the kitchen, where she downed the rest of the wine, then led her into the van. He returned to the house to wipe away any fingerprints, retrieved the wine bottle he had brought with him but didn't need, wiped down the glass and put in the sink, got her purse, then returned to the car. He removed Lauri's gag so she could tell him where the garage door opener was, and headed to the rendezvous spot.

Driving out of Klawock, he saw Jason's pickup and flashed his headlights, and they pulled alongside each other to discuss their next move. Brian led Jason to the gravel pit, where they stopped again. "He got out, I got out," said Brian. "He came up, asked me if I had her. I said, 'Yes.' We said a few other things and then we both got back in our vehicles and headed out."

Brian said that after they arrived at the turnout, he wiped down the van with a paper towel or rag.

"I was getting pretty nervous by that time," he told the jury. "I had seen several cars pass us."

In the turnout, either Brian or Jason got out a garbage bag from the van—"I don't know if it was him or me," he said—to cover the wet and muddied ground, then Brian got the limp Lauri from the back of the van. Her hands and feet were still bound, though she was ungagged. She said nothing. Brian assumed she was still drunk.

"I had her kneel," said Brian. "I attempted to break her neck back backwards."

"How'd you do that?" the prosecutor asked.

"By yanking up on the chin, forcing it back."

"How far back did you pull her chin up?"

"A ways, but—"

Brian's testimony was interrupted. At the defense table, Rachelle put her hand to her face and broke into tears.

"Judge, could we take a break please?" Wells said urgently. "I'm sorry, we need to take a break."

Judge Collins called for a recess as Rachelle fled the courtroom.

The trial resumed twenty minutes later, with Rachelle back at the counsel table and Brian back on the witness stand.

"You testified that she's on the ground," said West, picking up Brian's testimony exactly where he had left off. "How is she on the ground? Is she standing or what?"

"Kneeling," said Brian.

"And are you having to hold her up? Or is she able to kneel by herself?"

"At that point, before I tried to break her neck, she was kneeling on her own."

"Then the first time you tried to break her neck, were you standing behind her or in front of her or on the side?"

"Behind her."

"And where on her head were your hands?"

"One at the back of her neck, one on her head."

"And then when you said you pulled her head back, did you jerk it back or were you pulling it steadily?"

"I tried to jerk but I don't think I— Nothing happened."

"So what did you do then?"

"I tried to break her neck sideways."

"And what do you mean by 'sideways'?"

"Pulling, pushing on the chin. Basically trying to use brute strength."

"How far were able to get her head around that way?"

"Uh," Brian said, then sighed. It was the first time in his testimony he paused or showed anything other than straightforward narration. "Somewhere in this area," he said, tilting his own head to demonstrate.

"At least 90 degrees over?" asked West.

"I think a little bit over," said Brian. "She was fighting by that time."

"She was still restrained?"

"Yes."

"How many times did you do that?"

"It was drawn out."

"How long of a time?"

"Couple of minutes."

"What did you do then?"

"Laid her down on the ground," Brian said. "Jason held her down for me, I karate chopped her in the throat."

"With what?"

"The side of my hand."

"Which hand?"

"I think it was my left hand."

"How many times did you try to karate chop her?"

"Couple of times."

"What effect did it have?"

"I couldn't tell anymore at that point. I wasn't sure. I mean, I wasn't really sure how you were supposed to do that if you're going to kill somebody that way."

"What did you do then?"

"Jason had a flashlight. He handed it to me. I think I might have asked for it."

"What kind of flashlight was it?"

"It was one of the cheap ones you buy in the store. I don't know what the name of it is. It's a disposable flashlight."

"And you got the flashlight—how did you hold it?"

"I was holding it the way you would normally hold it, and I used the bottom of it, and I struck her repeatedly in the throat."

"Where was she at when this was going on?"

"She was on the ground."

"She was on her back or her side?"

"Back."

"And was she struggling or doing anything at this time when you hit her?"

"I really—"

"You didn't look?"

"I was doing my best not to look."

"How many times did you strike her in the throat with the flashlight?"

"At least a half dozen."

"How hard were you hitting her?"

"As hard as I could."

"What happened then?"

"She didn't die."

Lauri continued to breathe, Brian said. Whether her eyes were still open or closed, he didn't know. Brian had stopped looking at her. But he could hear her.

"She did say something," said Brian.

"Could you make it out?" asked West.

"She said, 'Can I ask a question?' But I think she was too delirious by that time to realize that I would let her ask the question."

"Did you answer?"

"I said, 'What is it?' but she kept repeating, 'Can I ask a question?'"

"So you didn't say anything else?"

"No, Jason said something, but I didn't say anything."

"Do you remember what he said?"

"He got down in front of her. By that time she was kind of on her side, and he crouched down in front of her and said something along the lines of 'You won't ever effing hurt Rachelle again.'"

Even in the midst of describing such a horrible act, Brian refused to use the actual profanity.

"And what did you do then?" asked West.

"Me and Jason attempted to suffocate her," said Brian.

"And how'd you do that?"

"By placing our hands over her mouth."

"Who placed their hands on her?"

"I did. I think Jason did. I'm not too sure on that. I wasn't paying attention. I had to let go at one point to check her pulse."

"And what part of her face did you cover?"

"The mouth and nose at one point, both at one point, and just the nose at one point."

"And how long did you do that for?"

"Jason timed it. I think it was four minutes."

"After four minutes, what did you do?"

"It was taking a long time, so we took her—and she was still alive because I could hear her breathing—and stuck her in the van. . . . She was rasping in the back of the van," said Brian. "Eventually I heard her stop breathing."

After he put her back in the van, he drove toward the logging road, arriving at the turnout about forty-five minutes later. With Jason behind him in his four-wheel-drive truck,

Brian labored to get the van as far up the steep and rocky road as he could. It was pitch-black and raining.

"I put it in park, got around to the other side, opened the door, and checked Lauri's pulse," he said. "Jason had mentioned he had some medical training or something, so he checked her pulse too. There wasn't any pulse that either one of us could notice at that point."

Brian doused the van and Lauri's body with gasoline from Jason's truck, then set the van on fire with a torch made from a burning roll of paper towels, and they sped away from the scene in Jason's truck, seeing a "reasonably big" fire in the rearview mirror. By now it was about five thirty a.m., with dawn approaching. Jason got him to Lee Edwards's house in Hollis well before eight a.m. with a quick stop along the way to burn cotton rags, garbage bags, ropes, socks, "whatever was left." Brian lay down and went to sleep.

Two days later the first troopers interviewed him, and he denied knowing anything about the murder. By the end of the week he had confessed his role in it, but didn't tell all.

"When you were talking with the troopers, you described this as a 'cold-blooded.' Is that still your view?" asked West.

"It was murder," Brian said. "At that time, at the same time, I was trying to take the blame. I was trying to look as bad as possible."

"So you don't think it was cold-blooded now?"

"It was murder," he said again. "I mean, I didn't want to do it, but I don't know. The perception that I was trying to get across at that point was someone who would be willing to go out and do it on their own without anyone else's input."

"But in your interview, you did talk about how Jason was involved," said West.

"I still didn't tell everything," said Brian. "I was in between."

The only thing he told investigators initially was that Jason had planted the seed for the murder plot in late August of 2004 by relating Rachelle's tales of abuse. What he left out was how insistent Jason was that it be carried through.

"He pretty much just kept bringing it up [but] I told him I

wouldn't kill somebody unless somebody's life was in jeopardy. He just would bring up that he felt that it was better off if Lauri was dead."

"What was the reason he gave for asking you to kill her?" asked West.

"He felt that Lauri was a threat to Rachelle."

"Did you agree with him?"

"At that time I didn't think she was that much of a threat," said Brian.

Finally, Brian reluctantly agreed to commit the murder, and the pair cooked up a number of plans. Jason suggested "injecting Lauri with bleach," he said. Brian wanted to encase Lauri's feet in cement and throw her off the boat owned by Jason's police dispatcher mother and her husband. But Jason nixed that idea.

"Jason said that he didn't think that would work because he didn't normally go fishing, and he didn't think he could come up with an excuse to borrow his parents' skiff," said Brian. "So I said, 'What about a lake?' He thought that was a great idea. So it was decided to go with that. And we started trying to find a lake."

"Were you able to locate a lake?" asked West.

"No," said Brian.

They talked about using explosives, but that idea was scotched too. "So I listed every possible thing I could think of," said Brian, "everything I'd see on TV, anything possible. And let him pick one." At one point they planned to go into the house and kill Lauri.

"It turned out there were volleyball girls over, and I wasn't interested in having anybody else hurt," said Brian. "When I found out the volleyball girls were there, I said no."

Another time, Jason wanted to kill Lauri after Rachelle was grounded from using the computer. "Jason was freaking out because he couldn't get ahold of her," said Brian. "He was saying, 'What if Lauri killed Rachelle?' or 'What if Rachelle couldn't take it anymore and killed Lauri and killed herself?'"

They called the Waterman house from a pay phone at the

Black Bear Market in Klawock. When Lauri answered the phone, they hung up and drove to the house.

"As I was getting out of vehicle he had a large knife," recalled Brian. "He told me that if I didn't see anything to go in and kill Lauri. I went down and standing in front of the house, I didn't see anything, but I just wasn't ready to kill anybody yet. After a few minutes, I went back up and got back in the vehicle."

The murder plan went into higher gear in September when Jason got a phone call from Rachelle at his parents' house while Brian was there on the computer. Whatever Rachelle told him sent him into a fury.

"He went back through the hallway to his room, and I heard the sound of a rifle being loaded," recalled Brian. "I went back and he was in his room loading a rifle, and I was concerned that if I told him that I wasn't going to let him do it, he'd shoot me."

Brian said nothing to him at first. Jason settled down enough to tell him what Rachelle had said.

"Lauri again threatened Rachelle's life, that Rachelle was afraid to go home, and that he was going to go up to the Craig school and shoot Lauri Waterman," said Brian. "And I tried to talk him out of it. I brought up that despite the fact that he had hid the relationship, that I felt a lot of people knew he had being going out with Rachelle. If he shot Lauri, he would be the next person they'd look at. I wasn't convincing him."

Brian finally got Jason to put down the rifle by telling him to wait a week while Brian came up with a new plan—"something that wouldn't involve going to jail," he said. "And I couldn't come up with something. So I finally decided just to go ahead with shooting Lauri."

That's how he decided to hide in the bushes across from the school and gun Lauri down with his 30-30 Model 94 lever-action Winchester after she dropped off Rachelle at volleyball practice. He noted that even as he was debating whether to go through with it, he realized he had left a piece of the gun at home and had to abandon the assassination.

"When did you come up with the idea for the DWI plan?"

"Originally what I had come up with was simply a car accident. Jason suggested getting her drunk and decided that he wanted it outside of town, so we end up going out until we found a location that satisfied him."

"Why did you pick the weekend of November 13 and 14?"

"Because Doc Waterman was going to be out of town, and Rachelle Waterman was going to be at a tournament."

"How did you know that?"

"Jason told me."

"Did he tell you how he found out that information?"

"He said that Rachelle had told him. He had at one point in the past, probably from the very beginning, he had mentioned that if Rachelle went to the tournament that he thought that would be the best time to kill Lauri."

Even after Brian was told that Lauri would be home alone that weekend, he insisted, "I had been rather forceful to see if we could wait until December at least." Brian expected to be receiving $3,000 to $10,000 from a business venture and thought that could help fund alternative ways to help Rachelle than murder.

"Why did you go along with it?"

"I don't really know," said Brian. "He pushed real hard. Jason even brought up to me that if I didn't do something, and something happened to Rachelle, I was responsible for that. If she got hurt, if she got killed that it would be my fault. So I decided to go along with it."

Asked by the prosecutor why he went along with plan from the beginning, why he had ever listened to Jason, he said, "I am someone who I count my loyalty very, very important. And as I showed, I ended up doing literally anything for someone. It was the fact that I felt Jason was lying that made it where I was not willing any longer to just say it was me."

He protected Jason as much as he could. But after he was arrested, and was shown what Jason had said about him—and about Rachelle—he changed his mind, realizing, as he wrote to his parents, that Jason had the backbone of a jellyfish.

Prosecutor West asked, "Is that still your view?"

"I agree with the whole backbone-of-a-jellyfish bit," said Brian. "He doesn't want to take responsibility for his part."

"But do you still love Rachelle?"

"I assume so," he said. "I still care."

"Do you still feel that your life is a small price to pay to protect her?"

Brian sighed. "If it was under different circumstances, yes," he said. "This was not one of them."

West noted that the letter to his parents concluded with this thought: "I'm not saying what I did was right or wrong. I haven't come to a decision on that."

West asked, "Have you come to a conclusion yet?"

"Yes, for me that was more a question of why did I regret being in jail? Did I regret it because I was in jail or did I regret it because I had killed somebody?" he said. "I came to the conclusion—it took me about five or six months—but I came to the conclusion it was because I killed somebody. I can do the jail time. I've been in worse places. But killing someone is not something to be taken lightly."

After a brief break, defense attorney Steven Wells cross-examined Brian, and immediately established who did the dirty work.

"Mr. Radel, did Rachelle ever ask you to kill her mother?" asked Wells.

"No," said Brian.

"Did Rachelle Waterman ever tell you: 'I want my mom dead'?"

"No."

"Did Rachelle Waterman ever come to you and [say] 'Let's figure out plans to get rid of my mom'?"

"No."

"You killed Lauri Waterman?"

"Yes," said Brian.

The murder, Brian told the jury, stemmed from his close friendship with Jason. After breaking up with Rachelle, Brian was instrumental in getting Rachelle together with Jason.

"I basically defended Jason's honor, that he was good guy, but I wasn't directly trying to get them together," he said. "I trusted Jason and felt confident he would treat her right if he got with her."

Friends with Jason since they were both sixteen, Brian considered him a "blood brother."

"I was raised: an oath is an oath. You keep it," Brian said. "To me that meant anything that was mine was his. He could ask for the shirt off my back, my money, my boat—and sometimes he did ask for stuff like that. If he asked for something, I would be there for him."

That's why Brian listened to Jason when he insisted that Lauri Waterman must die. The stories of parental abuse of Rachelle resonated with Brian. He grew up in a home that was "very religious" with "lots of discipline" enforced by "switches, berry bushes, cedar branches, thin, whippy pieces of wood, one-by-fours, one-by-twos, broom handles, rubber hoses, hands. Not too many fists, mainly open hand."

"Basically, my parents believed in the verses that say 'Spare the road, spoil the child,' " he said. "You didn't stick children in corners."

"Big difference between a wooden spoon and a rubber hose?" said Wells.

"I thought that," said Brian, "but at the same time I grew up in that. I thought it was wrong, and I tried to express it, but I usually just—there had been wooden spoons at one point. I graduated to a metal spoon eventually, after the wooden one broke."

So when Rachelle told him she had been hurt by her mother—and later Jason said that abuse was continuing—Brian knew he had to take action.

"I have a major problem with people who abuse their children," he said. "It's just something that I don't like, and I was [remembering] what it was like for me. I thought about what it would be like in her situation. . . . I felt it was that bad for me, how much worse could it be for her."

Still, Brian reiterated he didn't think murder was the answer—that there were other alternatives—and, looking back, Brian now knew he should have been skeptical. Jason's behavior in the summer of 2004 showed signs of paranoia. In addition to asking Brian to kill Lauri, he also asked him to kill Rachelle's former boyfriend Ian Lendrum.

"He said he'd had a dream where Ian forced Rachelle to commit ritual suicide," recalled Brian, "and he knew that I believed in psychics, and I believed in prophesy and things like that, and he brought it up to me. And I told him that I didn't care how much I believed in that stuff, I wasn't going to kill somebody over a dream."

Instead, Brian stormed into the pizza shop where Ian worked and told him to leave Rachelle alone.

As summer ended and Jason saw less of Rachelle, Jason's pressure on Brian to murder Lauri grew stronger. The idea seemed "harebrained" to Brian, who thought that Jason was being "overly protective" of Rachelle. By September and October he was bringing up the murder plot constantly. He insisted that Rachelle approved of it, but from what Brian knew of her, it didn't sound like her.

"She didn't like war, she didn't like killing," he said. "When he told me she said yes, it flabbergasted me. She just had always seemed to dislike violence." Brian recalled a day at the T-shirt shop where she worked when he and another man "basically got into a macho contest talking about how tough we were," and Rachelle got "very upset with me afterwards."

"I happen to be someone who's conservative, and I may be a little more warlike than some, and we had a difference of opinion on those issues," he said. "So I just didn't think she was someone who would be that way."

It had crossed his mind that Rachelle might have been exaggerating her troubles. But she had complained about things an old boyfriend had done—Brian didn't specify what to the jury—and those claims turned out to be true.

"I felt, if she hadn't lied to me about that, I didn't feel that she had lied to me about the other," he said. "I still was a little uncomfortable about it, but Jason ended up informing me at one point that Rachelle had had her Web cam on—

because he and her had chatted—and he had seen Lauri hitting Rachelle with a baseball bat. That was kind of the final confirmation for me. To me it was independent confirmation that it was happening."

It never occurred to Brian that this time Jason was lying. A week or so later, when Jason asked Brian to kill Lauri, "I said, 'I guess so,' which basically counted as saying yes."

He now wished he hadn't said that, he told jurors.

"I regret most of it," Brian said. "I regret helping Jason get with her in the first place. There's a lot of things I wish I had done and hadn't done. Even at the end, I could have gone down there and talked to [Rachelle] and asked her, 'What's up? Is this really true?' But I just didn't think Jason would lie."

By October, Jason openly worried about losing Rachelle. She was apparently telling Jason she wanted to wait until she was eighteen before having a relationship with him so that her parents wouldn't be so upset. Jason said that if he waited that long, Rachelle might no longer love him. He wanted Lauri taken care of—now. They kicked around some ideas, none of which seemed good enough.

"I told him that if I couldn't come up with anything else, I'd do it myself," he said. "I thought I was expendable. I'd been having suicidal thoughts at that point. I was looking to get sued. I still owe $60,000 or so [on the failed store]. Contracts came due and I couldn't pay them, couldn't pay for my shop, getting sued for not paying rent. Basically I was living on a boat with no money. My power bill was already late. I didn't have food. I felt my life wasn't worth very much, and if he was going to go ahead and do it, I'd rather I did it. I wasn't going to report him to the cops. I'd rather I went down for it than he would go down for it."

Wells asked, "If you had listened to your instincts, would we be here today?" asked Wells.

Brian laughed. "No," he said. "Bottom line is: What we did, shouldn't have happened. I look at it: We killed a forty-eight-year-old woman. She could have had twenty, thirty years of life left. That's just—on top of it, it's a woman. I guess a guy isn't better. But for me, that makes the crime worse. The only thing worse would be killing a kid."

"Did Lauri's death accomplish what you had been told it would accomplish?" asked Wells.

"No. It's very obvious that it hasn't," he said. "It didn't help Rachelle. It didn't help anybody else for that matter. It hurt a lot of people."

CHAPTER SIXTEEN

The trial was drawing a crowd. One TV camera in the courtroom fed several news organizations, and seats were at a premium. Government employees walked across the street from the State Office Building to catch the action. Locals welcomed a hometown hero, NBC's John Larson, originally of Anchorage, whom *Dateline* sent to the trial. Larson's career took him through Juneau, and he told the *Juneau Enterprise* he was happy to be back. "I think I had my first beer when I was right out of college in Alaska at the Baranof Hotel."

Harriet Ryan traveled from Los Angeles to cover the case for Court TV, and her Alaskan hosts were eager to know what she thought of Craig. "Our experience in Prince of Wales was just great," Ryan told the *Juneau Enterprise*. "Those people are so nice and so welcoming, and it seemed like a wonderful place to live. I want to go back fishing in the summer." A few days in Alaska and she had already gone native, buying a pair of Xtratuf neoprene boots.

The activity caused only a few hiccups. The state's coroner and two investigators got into trouble when they wandered into the overflow room. As witnesses, they were barred from being in the trial at any time other than during their testimony. When it was discovered, Rachelle's attorney, steven Wells, called for a mistrial. The judge considered the potential damage and found none. "Essentially, there's no testimony to change or shave, given these witnesses," Collins said.

The mood in the courtroom also had been largely low-key, despite the horrific nature of the crime. Defense attorney Wells played Brian Radel mostly as his own witness, since he readily admitted committing the murder and had no idea what role, if any, Rachelle played in her conversations with Jason. For the first week of the trial, few facts were in dispute, save for the level of animosity between Rachelle and her mother. Prosecutor West called Rachelle's friends Stephanie Claus, Amanda Vosloh, and Katrina Nelson to show that Rachelle had complained about her mother's physical abuse, but none of the girls believed Rachelle and saw the arguments as normal mother-daughter conflict.

The tone changed, however, on Monday, January 30, when Rachelle's former boyfriend, Ian Lendrum, strode to the witness stand exuding hostility. Still protective of Rachelle sitting just a few feet away, Ian bristled at being put in the position of providing evidence against her.

When West asked if he ever saw bruises on Rachelle, Ian reluctantly confirmed it, but snapped, "There's no sign on any of the bruises that said 'Made by Lauri Waterman' or 'Made in China,'" he said.

Asked if he witnessed problems between Lauri and Rachelle, he acknowledged, "I remember there was tension. They fought. Yelled at each other. Sometimes she'd be grounded. I never found out why exactly."

"Did you ever tell [anybody] that she had told you that she hated her mother?"

Lendrum sneered, "I don't recall."

The tension heightened the next day, Tuesday, when guards led another big man into the courtroom. A figure who loomed large throughout the case, it was the first time the jury saw Jason. He screamed prisoner: handcuffs, leg irons and yellow jail jumpsuit. He, too, had a lawyer on the phone—bad weather had stranded his attorney in Sitka—but his lawyer also would say nothing.

After taking the oath to tell the truth, Jason gave an outline of his life story: raised on Prince of Wales Island, his failed stint in the Marines, his acquaintance with Sergeant Mark Habib through his police dispatcher mother, the day he ran into Brian Radel at a Bible camp in Ketchikan, and, in February 2004, how he met the then fifteen-year-old Rachelle Waterman.

Like Brian, Jason was a big man with a small voice who spoke calmly and quietly. He told the jury that he and Rachelle began dating in the summer of 2004 and that the relationship soon became sexual, with Rachelle sending him nude photos of herself.

"I actually requested them," he said "I filled out text documents just kind of detailing some poses I'd like to see. She obliged."

Asked by prosecutor West when their relationship ended, Jason said, "It was going on pretty much up to the point of the arrest. I'd say that's what stopped it."

Early in their relationship, Rachelle confided in him how her mother had hurt her, trying to throw her down the stairs, hitting her with a baseball bat, Jason said. The bruises he saw on Rachelle when they had sex confirmed her stories. He wanted to help her, and they discussed emancipation and running away, but she dismissed those ideas.

Finally, she told him, "It would be better if my mother weren't around."

"Did you ask her what she meant by that?" asked West.

"Well, yes," said Jason.

"And what was her response?"

"That she thought it would be better if her mother was dead."

"And what was your response?"

"I was obviously trepidatious about it, but I loved her and I already told her I would do anything for her. So at that point, I decided that I needed to enlist some help."

"Did she offer you anything to help her in doing this?"

"No."

"Did she offer you any money?"

"No."

"Drugs?"

"No."

"Sex?"

"No."

It was love, he said, nothing more, that drove him to re-cruit Brian Radel to concoct murder plans that ranged from the cement shoes to a rigged car accident. Rachelle knew about some of the plans, including the one to gun down her mother outside the school.

"Had you talked to Rachelle Waterman about this?" West asked.

"Yes, she called me on the phone," said Jason. "And I relayed to her that that's what the plan was going to be."

"What was her response?"

"She wasn't too into that plan," he said. "She wanted something a little more concrete. She asked us to abort. But by then it was already too late to contact Radel."

"What was the reason she gave you for calling it off?"

"She didn't like the plan because it was—there was too many ifs. If Radel had stood up and shot her there, there was too much chance of being caught. She was too close to the situation."

He said he sent Rachelle an e-mail later in the evening—the "hunting trip" message—and conversed by instant mes-saging in an effort to come up with another plan of which she'd approve.

"How often would the conversation talk about the plans to kill her mother?" asked West.

"That only came up probably one in every five phone calls. We tried to keep that sort of thing to a minimum."

"And why's that?"

"Just because we were both getting a little paranoid about things by then."

"Who's 'we'?"

"Well, myself, and I know Miss Waterman was probably getting a little antsy about it."

In November, Rachelle provided the details that would set the final murder plan in motion.

"How did it come up?" asked West.

"We were always sort of planning or plotting if you will, different scenarios. I don't even remember if it was on the phone or online or what. She mentioned that a good window of opportunity would be coming up when she would be going up north for volleyball and when her dad would also be gone from home."

Jason said Rachelle told him how to get into her house through the garage window, telling him it was how she had snuck out at night in the incidents that led to her groundings. He didn't ask for a detailed map of the house but "basic layout," and she "kind of described what she could" but didn't put anything to paper.

From the very beginning Jason was nervous about the murder plan, and when it came to fruition, he reacted much differently than Brian.

The actual perpetration of the murder began when Jason dropped off Brian near the house on the wet and windy night, then drove to their rendezvous spot at the gravel pit. He described his anxious hours chain-smoking and waiting, until he finally began driving back and forth looking for Brian. When the minivan headlights came into view, they drove back to the gravel pit, where he saw Lauri tied up in the backseat.

"What happened then?" asked West.

"We both climbed back into our respective vehicles and drove out the point where we were going to kill her," said Jason.

They pulled into a wide spot in the road—Jason wasn't sure exactly where they were—and Brian opened up the side door of the van. Jason stood ten feet behind the van watching the scene in the light of his truck headlights. A garbage bag got placed on the wet ground; Jason couldn't remember if he did it or Brian. Limp and apparently dazed, Lauri was placed on the plastic.

"She was so inebriated at that time that she wasn't really capable of moving on her own," said Jason. "She just was very loose. She couldn't even hold her own head up."

"What did he do next?" asked West.

"[Brian] held her up on her knees, stood behind her, and then made the first attempts to break her neck."

"What did he do then?"

"He put his hands on her shoulders and tried to whip her head back and forth to break her neck."

"How many times did he do that?"

"Half a dozen."

"Did that work?"

"No."

"So, what did he do then?"

"Then he went for the movie approach, which was just to grab the back of her head and chin and twist."

"How far back did he get her head?"

"Easily 180 degrees."

"That break her neck or not?"

"I can't speculate whether the bones broke. I know she was still alive at that point."

"Then what did he do?"

"Then he laid her out on the ground, because she was already so muddy at this point that it didn't really matter anymore if she got any more [dirty]. And he took one of the flashlights and started to strike her in the throat to collapse the windpipe."

"How many times did he hit her with that?"

"Easily a dozen."

"And where did he hit her?"

"Right in the throat."

"And she was lying on the ground at this point?"

"Yes, on her side."

"On her side? And where was he at?"

"He was standing behind her."

"Was she doing anything when he was hitting her?"

"Aside from some various noises I would care to forget, not really, no. I think she was beyond struggle at that point."

"What were you doing during this time?"

"At first I was watching, but after about the third blow I couldn't. I turned around."

"Then what did you do?"

"I threw up."

The surreal and violent scene had become "kind of a blur at this point," with Jason reeling against the sickening sound of Brian pummeling Lauri with the little flashlight they had purchased hours earlier at the Black Bear Market.

"Then what happened?" asked West.

"Well, she was still alive at that point," said Jason. "She was still breathing. And so then he just put his hands over mouth and nose to cut off her air and waited."

"Waited for what?"

"Waited for her to die."

"And she did?"

"Yes."

"How long did he have her hands over her mouth and nose?"

"Easily four or five minutes."

"Did she struggle or was she just lying there?"

"I couldn't tell if it was struggles or just nerve response. She did move."

"After he removed his hands from her nose and mouth, what happened then?"

"He checked for a pulse. I did as well."

"Were you able to detect one?"

"No."

They then drove to the logging road and set fire to the van—and Lauri's body. Jason dropped Brian off at home and returned to his own bed early Sunday morning. Jason got a call at his house in the afternoon. It was Rachelle, back from the volleyball tournament in Anchorage.

"She said she noticed her mother was gone and the mini-van as well. And I said, 'Well, yeah, we did it. It's done,' " recalled Jason. "And she asked what happened to the minivan. I said that it had been burned; it was completely destroyed. She expressed disappointment that she wouldn't be inheriting it."

"And what else do you remember about the conversation?" asked West.

"I asked her to do a last minute wipe-down, go over the

railing on the stairs, doorknobs, anything that might have been missed."

"Did she say that she would do it?"

"Yeah."

They talked maybe ten minutes. He didn't describe in detail what happened to her mother and she didn't ask. But he sent her a letter, which he read to the jury:

"I'm sorry to hear about your mom turning up missing, baby. I'm sure she'll turn up all right though it'll be OK. And if heaven forbid you guys end up forming a search party or something then let me know. I'll want to help out for you if nothing else."

Jason explained to the jury that the letter was "just basic damage control in case anyone read it." They were in touch the next night over instant messaging, making "mostly small talk," he testified, before the conversation came around to her mother.

"She was curious exactly how things had happened," said Jason. "I told her I didn't feel all that comfortable discussing it. I would just as soon forget all about it. She said that was fine."

The next time they spoke was over the phone when she called him from school like she usually did. They didn't discuss her mother. But later in the day she called him again. "She was just in tears, asking me to come down," he said. "I was worried something had gone wrong."

This was the afternoon that Jason arrived at the school at the same time as Rachelle's neighbor Don Pierce.

"They showed me into the office," Jason said. "She was with the principal, I think; she was just destroyed, in tears. I was a little curious about what was going on, obviously. We did have a conversation. I kind of played my supportive role for the benefit of the principal that was there. He left and gave us a few minutes alone. The crying switched off like a light. She just wanted to see me. We spoke for a few minutes. I recall her saying, 'I told you I was a good actress.'"

After Don Pierce took Rachelle home, Jason headed there, too, with a stop at the police station.

"I knew something was going on," he said. "They must have found something. So I went down to the police station where my mother worked to try to find out what I could about what they knew. She told me that they discovered the vehicle and that it was obvious the body was in it, but she hadn't been identified yet."

Over the next few days, as troopers spoke to him, he at first was "still pretending that I had no knowledge of it, trying to salvage what I could." He said he was "kind of throwing things out on the fly that I hoped would placate them," giving investigators a half-baked alibi that he was with Brian in Hollis and had gone to Craig to buy munchies.

By that Wednesday, however, when Jason went to the trooper station to give another statement, he realized he couldn't keep lying.

"It's kind of hard to describe what I was thinking at that point," he said. "One part of me just wanted to be done with it, and another part of me still wanted to salvage it. I kind of ended up somewhere in the middle."

That's when he got the idea to stage being attacked at the school, nicking himself on the throat with a serrated knife and dropping garbage bags on the side of the building where he would say he was assaulted by the unknown assailant. When Claus and McPherron arrived, he cooked up a description—"big guy, dark clothes, could have been anybody"—and the phony story.

"The implication was it was somebody involved in the murder," he said. But by the next day, Thursday, Jason knew that story wasn't going to hold up, either, so he gave a half-truth of what he knew about the murder.

"I was still trying to salvage what was rapidly becoming the rest of my life," he said. "The half-truth was that I had no prior knowledge and that Rachelle had no prior knowledge, but that Brian kind of pulled me into it at the last moment."

Jason said he then admitted what the investigators already knew—that he had made up the assault report—and agreed to wear a wire to get Brian to confess. When he met Brian in Hollis, Brian was "jumpy" and told him "he had been seeing cops and that he believed the home was being monitored"—which of course it was, in a way. Sergeant Habib in full tactical gear had encountered Brian with his flashlight just minutes before.

The next day, after Jason was arrested, he implicated Rachelle during the talk with Habib.

"Did he plant the idea?" asked West.

"I already knew she was involved," said Jason. "I can't say that he planted it."

"What was the reason that you and Mr. Radel killed Lauri Waterman?"

"It was to protect Rachelle."

"From?"

"From her mother."

"From?"

"From physical and mental abuse."

"And this was the abuse that Rachelle described to you?"

"Yes."

As the only witness to point the finger at Rachelle, Jason got the fiercest cross-examination of the trial.

"Tell me something," began defense attorney Steven Wells, "when you make up your lies, are they all on the fly or do you think about some of them ahead of time?"

"Most of them were on the fly."

"So you do think about some of them ahead of time?"

"I suppose so."

"Do you think about lies you were going to tell when you were going to—how did you put it?—'salvage what would remain of the rest of my life'?"

"Some of them, yes."

"You thought about lies to tell as you thought about how to salvage your life?"

"Yes."

Wells suggested that the biggest lies came when Jason wanted to get a plea deal, selling out Rachelle and "getting a pretty good deal" that could result in parole when he's forty-two years old

"At forty-two you might even still be young enough that

you could still pick up teenage girls, couldn't you?" asked Wells.

Jason didn't flinch. But West objected, and the judge sustained it.

"At forty-two," Wells asked, "you would be young enough that the difference in age between you and a teenage girl might be overcome by giving them booze and marijuana and cigarettes, right?"

Again Jason's face showed no reaction.

"I don't think that's where I want to go with my life," he said.

"You were the first to squeal in this case, weren't you?" asked Wells.

"Yes."

"You just sacrificed her so you could salvage the rest of your life?"

Again the judge sustained a prosecution objection.

"Did you not have the guts to go ahead and really dig the blade in to make the story seem real?" asked Wells.

"No, I guess not," said Jason.

"Just like you didn't have the guts to kill Lauri Waterman yourself? You had to get Brian to do it, right?"

"I can't kill anybody, no."

Wells brought Jason through several lies he had told police, from his initial concocted alibi to the fake assault at the school. He noted that Jason had even told the investigators during one of his interviews that he knew he had credibility problems because of his previous lies.

"Are you going to tell this jury: 'I know that destroys my credibility but I'm not lying now'?"

"I'm not," said Jason. "I would like to point out this is the first time I've been under oath."

"So it makes a difference? You don't feel the need to tell the truth when you're not under oath?"

"I felt the need, but I didn't. I am now. I don't know how many more times I can make that clear to you."

For two days Wells pounded at Jason. The defense lawyer

repeatedly threw Jason's own words at him about "trying to salvage what was rapidly becoming the rest of my life."

Finally, on the second day of cross-examination, Jason snapped at the lawyer.

"I'm glad you have such a fun phrase to play with," he said.

Wells did not let up. He had Jason read his love letters to Rachelle, including one suggesting Jason worried the relationship would end. Each letter had a more desperate, pleading tone, his obsession with Rachelle growing as he was unable to see her. He read the letter about sneaking to her house in the middle of the night and looking in her window. And he read the letter in which he urged her to share her sexual fantasies.

When they got to one letter, the lawyer asked, "Could you read it out loud?" but Jason balked.

"I would prefer not to," he said. "You're certainly welcome to read it, but I would prefer not to."

The attorney looked to Judge Collins, who nodded to Jason. He had no choice. He was under oath and his deal with the prosecutors hinged on testifying openly about everything. His lawyer, on the phone line, did not raise an objection.

Jason sighed and read.

"'And yet your present sits just a couple of feet from me tucked away and it smells so good, and admittedly tastes incredible. Just that little taste on the tip of my tongue made me shiver like a crackhead, and your pictures are so sexy, I would love to get my tongue in between your thighs right now.'"

Under questioning from Wells, Jason said that he was writing about a pair of underwear she had sent him.

On it went. He read more letters; some, he explained, were written while he was stoned on marijuana, including the letter telling Rachelle that he almost starting cutting again.

He explained in court, "When I was an adolescent I was a cutter." At the defense attorney's instruction, Jason showed the jury his arm covered in scars.

CHAPTER SEVENTEEN

Jason Arrant was led back to prison and a parade of law enforcement witnesses took the stand, including two more troopers and trooper computer expert Christopher Thompson, who had found the nude photos of Rachelle. The defense wanted to bar the pictures from evidence, with Wells saying they served only to "titillate" jurors and "embarrass Miss Waterman." Prosecutor West argued the photos showed the nature of the relationship Rachelle had with Jason. In the end, the judge did not allow the pictures to be shown but did allow witnesses to talk about them, which Thompson did, in somber, dispassionate tones. Judge Patricia Collins instructed the jury to consider the photos only in terms of explaining the nature of the relationship between Rachelle and the two confessed killers, and not to "prove that Ms. Waterman is either a person of bad character or has a tendency to commit bad acts."

The final police witness was the lead investigator, Sergeant Randy McPherron, who related some details of the case but was mainly called to introduce the centerpiece of the case: Rachelle's interrogation. The detective set the scene and the video was played, the black-and-white images of Rachelle tearfully acknowledging she was involved in the murder plot and then lied about it to investigators. Her wails filled the courtroom and when it was over the mood was bleak.

The video carried an extra punch because it was the last evidence presented to jurors before a long weekend. They would have three days to let it sink in, without any answer from the defense, and the judge delivered a longer and stronger-than-usual warning.

"During this long break, get lots of rest," she told them. "Please remember the admonition that you could probably recite in your sleep by now. Of course it's important over this three-day break that you avoid any contact with reports that might be generated about the case either in the paper or on the radio or television or the Internet, that you not conduct any independent investigation, that if you're inadvertently exposed in any way, or if someone attempts to influence you or contact you in any way, that you notify me immediately. And of course, sometimes inadvertently, people tend to just want to start a conversation, and you'll just have to be incredibly careful about that. No experiments outside the courtroom. Remember, you haven't heard all the evidence, so it's important to continue to keep an open mind. Have no contact with the parties, the witnesses or others. We will see you Monday morning at 8:30."

After the jury left, the judge asked if there was anything else to talk about. West said that the prosecution's case was nearly over. Wells said that on Monday he planned to call psychologist Marty Beyer and Rachelle's father, Doc Waterman.

He added, "I can tell the court that the other witness that we would potentially have would be Ms. Waterman, but the decision about whether she's going to testify has not been made yet. So obviously we have to deal with that issue separately."

The following Monday, it was Sergeant Randy McPherron's turn in the hot seat. Defense attorney Steven Wells elicited that McPherron's army experience included battle simulation training in which McPherron played the enemy. As he led McPherron through the last interrogation of Rachelle, the lawyer sought to show that he was still the enemy.

McPherron acknowledged he employed a number of interrogation techniques, starting with getting Rachelle from her house to the cramped room at the police station to create a "psychological sense of being isolated and alone," along with getting her to a place where they had a video camera so there would be no issues later on about what they did.

"You didn't wait for Doc, did you?" asked Wells.

"Well, no," said McPherron.

"You wanted to get Rachelle alone—I think 'isolated' was the word that you used—to talk with her?"

"Yes, but I don't need Doc's permission. I didn't have to wait for his permission."

"She's sixteen years old, right?"

"At the time, yes."

"She's sixteen years old," repeated Wells. "Actually if a doctor is going to operate on her, the doctor needs—"

West objected, saying it was irrelevant what a doctor does. The judge overruled him.

"The doctor needs," Wells continued, "absent an emergency right then and there, the doctor needs her dad's permission?"

"I believe so. I'm not absolutely certain on that. But I think so, yes."

"And under the law, at being just barely sixteen, she can't sign a contract, can she?"

"I don't know much about contract law."

"She can't buy a car, can she?"

"I don't believe so, no."

"She can't buy cigarettes?"

"No."

"She can't buy a gun?"

"No."

"She can't get married without her dad's permission?"

"That's correct."

"She can't even sign for a cell phone by herself, can she?"

"I guess so, yes, I wouldn't know."

"But that's all right—you just wanted to isolate her?"

"Legally, I do not have to get her father's permission to

speak to her," said McPherron. "He wasn't there. He'd given permission earlier to speak to her. He hadn't withdrawn it. He hadn't told me 'No, don't ever talk to her again, no, don't talk to her without me being there.' I didn't have to wait, time was of the essence, since both codefendants had been arrested. Things were falling into place quickly. I felt if we waited much longer it could have been detrimental to the case. I asked her. She agreed to come, and we went to the police station."

"When you say, 'If we had waited much longer things could have been detrimental to the case,' you mean that if Doc had known that you were going to take her down and sweat her, he might have said no, right?"

"Well, first of all I didn't sweat her. I don't even know what that term means. I went down and interrogated her. Doc's permission or withdrawing his permission wasn't material to me. Didn't matter."

After Rachelle agreed to speak with them by herself, McPherron and Habib then used another interrogation technique.

McPherron acknowledged that in their questions to Rachelle they repeatedly overstated the strength of the case and in some instances made up things. McPherron told Rachelle that both Jason and Brian had sold her out, when in fact only Jason implicated her in the murder plot: Brian said he never had direct contact with her and worked only off of what Jason said about her wishes. The detectives told her they had incriminating evidence off the computers of Rachelle, Jason, and Brian when in fact they only had a single e-mail, given to them by Rachelle's father, in which Jason spoke about the "hunting trip."

McPherron even waved an envelope full of papers at Rachelle implying that was the evidence, but in court he admitted it was just a "prop."

McPherron had told her detectives found "evidence at the scene" that pointed toward her, when in fact they never collected physical evidence implicating her in either the plot or the actual murder. McPherron knew she wasn't in Craig at the time and that her alibi was unshakable. Even telling her that they were her "friends" was a lie: McPherron had considered Rachelle a suspect from early on and was seeking to get her to confess.

Yet, even as they lied to her, the detectives accused Rachelle of lying to them at least two dozen times.

"I wanted her to tell me the truth about what happened," McPherron told the jury. "Obviously when dealing with a juvenile, you have to be extra cautious," he added, noting that a detective has to take into account the suspect's age, maturity, and education. He also said there had been debate among researchers about whether such interrogation techniques risk generating a false confession from younger suspects. "There's a lot of opinion on both sides of issue," he said.

Among the techniques he said he doesn't do—and didn't do in this case—was promise leniency if she cooperated. Although a staple of cop shows, the tactic of "Work with me and I'll cut you slack with the DA" is considered both improper and legally risky: it could lead to a court finding the confession coerced. Interrogation subjects are not allowed to be lured into giving up their constitutional rights against self-incrimination with false assurances of leniency. "I don't make any deals with the people I interview," McPherron said

But Wells suggested that both McPherron and Habib attempted to do just that. When Habib was alone with Rachelle after they took a break, lecturing her about telling the truth and showing respect, McPherron was actually secretly watching the exchange over a video monitor. But McPherron denied this was cutting her a deal.

"I'm trying to appeal to her sense of maturity," he said. "I'm just basically telling her, 'Listen, you know, you're going to be judged, it's your life, you're going to have to figure out what you want to do with it.'"

"With the evidence," Wells said, "that you had exaggerated?"

"In the interview that I had exaggerated."

After a few follow-up questions by the prosecution—McPherron said he followed all the legal procedures, reading Rachelle her rights, telling her she could have her father there, and telling her she could leave anytime—the detective left the stand. Prosecutor West had an announcement.

"Your Honor," he said, "the state rests."

CHAPTER EIGHTEEN

After a morning break, the defense called its first witness—psychologist Dr. Marty Beyer—to give a scaled-down version of her report from the pretrial hearing. The judge had found that some of her findings about Rachelle's mind-set were inadmissible—unless Rachelle herself testified. For now, Steven Wells was not revealing whether his client would take the stand.

Called to explain why Rachelle had made the statements she had during the interrogation, Dr. Beyer said research had found that teenage brains are not fully developed. Specifically, the frontal cortex—responsible for judgment and impulse control—is still forming throughout the adolescent years, leaving teens to rely upon more primitive centers of the brain.

"They can't think like an adult because they don't have an adult brain," Dr. Beyer said.

In Rachelle's case, this immature thinking was exacerbated by such traumas as low self-esteem from her early maturing body and by being raped by a stranger at age thirteen.

"That had a major impact on her, not only because it was frightening, but it was her first sexual experience," said Dr. Beyer. "She also was traumatized by her mother's disapproval of her grades, her clothes, her weight, and her friends. This consistent disapproval was very painful for her."

By age fifteen, even though Rachelle had a summer job,

got good grades, and led an active life, "she remained more needy" and was wracked by depression. "It's not surprising that she would be flattered by attention by older guys."

Alone, leery of her mother, her brain too immature to see the consequences of her actions, "she thought that crying on Jason's shoulder about her mother was nothing more than venting," said Dr. Beyer. "She didn't see the dangers of hanging around with creepy older guys. She dismissed Jason's planning as being stupid fantasies, as she called it."

It never seriously occurred to her that Jason would follow through with the murder, and by the time the police interrogated her, Rachelle was so filled with grief and confusion that she fell prey to the detectives' aggressive questioning.

Defense attorney Wells asked, "In interviews in which there is a tremendous amount of psychological pressure, such as this with juveniles, can they come to believe things that are told to them?"

"Yes," said Dr. Beyer, "there are examples that have been written about in the literature."

Under cross-examination, Dr. Beyer acknowledged that she relied on Rachelle for all of her information, including the account of the rape, for which there were no witnesses, police report, or physical evidence. The therapist also said that in forming her opinion that Rachelle had low self-esteem about her body, she hadn't known that Rachelle sent explicit nude photos of herself to Jason.

Beyer also said that while a person's brain is not fully developed until the mid-twenties, teenagers are still capable of making important decisions with serious consequences. And she agreed that by law they are allowed to vote, join the military, and get abortions—all at age eighteen.

The defense next called Rachelle's father for his second round of testimony, this time to give the jury a glimpse at what he lost when Lauri was killed.

"What was your relationship like with Lauri?" asked Wells.

"I think that we were probably as close as most couples and hopefully closer than most," he said. "Over the years, she learned to tolerate me very well."

"Did you all have plans for essentially a long future together?"

"Yes, we had just recently been discussing what we would do when I retired."

He had purchased property near Hollis on which he planned to build a retirement home.

"Did you ever have those conversation around Rachelle?"

"Yes, occasionally, we would just be sitting there talking and the kids would be around."

Doc said again that Rachelle never said anything about Lauri hurting her, but he could surmise why Rachelle may have told people her mother wanted to sell her into slavery.

Wells asked, "Growing up, did Lauri ever have a phrase: 'Selling somebody to the Gypsies'?"

"That was an old childhood phrase of hers," Doc said. "I'm not sure that it had any real in-depth meaning. It was a teasing or a taunting."

And Doc also sought to show that Rachelle couldn't have tipped off Jason and Brian about how to break into the house. Doc noted that when Rachelle snuck out of the house, she returned through a different window from the one Brian used. Also, Rachelle could have simply given them a key to the house.

"Each child had a key," said Doc, who found Rachelle's key after she was arrested. "It was in a dish on her dresser."

After a short cross-examination, all eyes were on Wells and whether he would call Rachelle to the stand. Although Wells wasn't revealing his trial strategy, his decision-making process is similar in all cases. Decisions on what motions to file and what other witnesses to call are always his, in consultation with the client. The client decides whether to go to trial or take a plea agreement, whether the trial will be conducted before a judge alone or a jury, whether to appeal a verdict, and finally whether to testify on his or her own behalf.

After Doc Waterman walked off the stand, Wells announced Rachelle's decision.

"Your Honor, at this time the defense would rest," he said.

The drama of the moment was marred by the fact that

Wells committed a procedural blunder, and the judge, in a rare flash of anger, quickly dismissed the jury with a warning that the case wasn't over just yet and jumped all over him.

"Mr. Wells, I specifically asked you—directed—that you advise me before the defense rests because as you know the law requires that I address the defendant before the defense rests about their right to testify," Judge Collins scolded him. "Is there some reason you didn't do this?"

"I'm sorry," said Wells. "No, I'm sorry, Your Honor, I just got flustered, for lack of a better word. I'm sorry."

Judge Collins made clear that she wasn't going to have this held against her if the case was appealed—that the fault was all Wells's. "I consider it invited error to the extent that there is any error that is ever alleged," she said.

Then, with the jury still out, the judge had a courtroom heart-to-heart with Rachelle.

"Let me turn to Miss Waterman," Judge Collins said, "because, Miss Waterman, as I just instructed, this case is by no means over at this point, and you have a very important decision that you must make at this point."

Rachelle locked eyes with the judge and nodded.

"While the advice of your lawyer or your father or others might be of assistance to you, the ultimate decision about whether to testify or not testify in this case is yours and yours alone to make," the judge said. "If you choose not to testify, I will instruct the jury that they cannot hold that fact against you. But the decision as to whether or not to testify is a very important one, and it's so important that the law requires that I address you personally about whether or not it's your choice whether or not to testify."

The judge lowered her voice to a near whisper.

"When I talk about your choice, it's a choice freely made without being influenced unfairly by your lawyer or anybody else," said the judge. "Is it your choice not to testify in this trial?"

Rachelle said, "Yes, Your Honor."

Just minutes after Rachelle's lawyer called a witness

saying her seventeen-year-old brain wasn't developed enough for fully mature judgments, Rachelle was now making the biggest decision of her life.

"Do you have any question about the right you are giving up?" the judge asked.

"No, Your Honor," said Rachelle.

The jury was released, and closing arguments were scheduled for the next day.

CHAPTER NINETEEN

Ketchikan district attorney Stephen West brought the jury back to where he began, showing a photo of Lauri Waterman.

"This case," he said, "is about Lauri Waterman. Unfortunately, it's about the cold-blooded execution of Lauri Waterman. I use the word 'execution' because that's exactly what it was. It was planned, they decided to kill her, and they went out and executed her."

The conspirators, he said, were Jason Arrant, Brian Radel, and Rachelle Waterman. Two had already pleaded guilty and were facing long prison terms, the third's fate would soon be in the hands of the jury.

If ever a case relied on effective summations, this one was it. West needed to convince the panel that Rachelle set in motion and cooperated with a plot to commit a crime that occurred while she was hundreds of miles away. It was a chain-reaction conspiracy, he said, triggered and nurtured by Rachelle and carried out by Jason Arrant and Brian Radel.

"They did it because they believed they were trying to protect Miss Waterman," said West. "Miss Waterman did it because she was wanting to get out from under control of her mother."

It was an argument that appealed to jurors' reason and their ability to grasp the nuances of conspiracy law. West, relying on an outline of his presentation on a legal pad, delivered a businesslike presentation, detailed and carefully reasoned, illustrated by images projected on a courtroom screen, but lacking soaring rhetoric. He spoke in the same low-key Texas-flavored drawl as he had throughout the case.

The emotion came from Rachelle. West replayed portions of her 2004 police interrogation video, including the most incriminating exchanges when she tearfully acknowledged that she first told Jason in August 2004 that she wanted to get rid of her mother. The jury watched again as Rachelle admitted that she knew first about the plan to shoot her mother, though urged Jason to call it off, and then telling Jason that if they wanted to try again, the weekend she and her father were out of town "would be the opportune time."

Proof that Rachelle was in on the scheme could be found in Jason's e-mail and Rachelle's letter talking about the "hunting trip," which West said "everyone agreed" referred to the plot. After her mother disappeared, Rachelle betrayed her knowledge of what happened by telling people her mother probably died in a DUI accident, even though police had not yet revealed that the burned van had been found. And when police talked to Rachelle, she admitted to lying about talking to Jason on the phone the night of the killing.

"She's trying to give him an alibi so he can get away with the murder of her mother," West said.

But after initial resistance, Jason told detectives everything, including Rachelle's involvement, West said, arguing that Jason should be believed because everything he said about the killing was corroborated by the evidence that he showed Trooper Claus during their drive around the island. Jason, the prosecutor said, had cooperated long before he was ever offered a plea deal.

"If it hadn't been for Mr. Arrant telling the police that Mr. Radel had killed Lauri Waterman, and wearing the wire, this would probably be an unsolved homicide," he said.

As for the thorniest part of the case—Rachelle's young age at the time of the alleged conspiracy—West insisted that she was not a passive figure. Under the law, simply knowing about a conspiracy and not doing anything to stop it is not in and of itself a crime. A person needs to know that conspiracy exists and agree to be part of it, even if they don't know all the details of the plot.

"She wasn't just sitting around and heard Mr. Arrant and Mr. Radel talking about this," he said. "She actually was communicating with them about the murder. She was actually talking with them about what the plans were."

Under the law, he said, that makes her as guilty as if she had suffocated her mother herself—guilty of all the crimes alleged, including first-degree murder, kidnapping, second-degree murder, theft, and tampering with evidence due to the burning of the van.

"Some people will say they would have difficulty convicting someone of that age in this case and that she really shouldn't be involved in this case at all," West acknowledged. "First of all, the law says that somebody who is sixteen, seventeen years old and commits or is an accessory to murder is treated the same as an adult. Their age makes no difference. Once you get to be sixteen or seventeen and you kill somebody or you are involved in killing somebody, you're getting involved in adult activities."

West implored jurors to "determine the facts" and make a decision "relying solely on the evidence, not governed by sentiment, prejudice, public feeling." Even if they had sympathy for Lauri Waterman, "your job is to be judges and take it on fair consideration of evidence in this case."

West wrapped up the first part of his summation—he would be allowed a rebuttal after the defense's closing argument—by using a word that so far had not been spoken in the courtroom, but which had permeated the case.

"Unfortunately, children do kill their fathers and their mothers. It occurs. It is rare. But it occurs. And that is what occurred in this situation," he said. "Miss Waterman was involved. She asked Mr. Arrant to kill her mother, she was involved in discussing plans with them, she even called one of the plans off, she told them about being alone, that being a weekend that they could do it. She was involved in this case. She was involved in the murder of her mother. She committed what's called matricide."

After a break, defense attorney Steven Wells rose before the jury.

"Did Rachelle Waterman want her mom to die?" he asked. "That's the question in this case. Did she want her mom to die? Did this teenage girl want her mom to die?"

He said, "No. No, she did not want her mom to die. We know that from who she is. We know that from what she said. We know that from how she's acted. We know that from what other people have said and the other evidence. The fact of the matter is, ladies and gentleman, this is not a case of whether Rachelle Waterman is not guilty. This is a case where Rachelle Waterman is innocent."

In stark contrast to the prosecution's reason-based approach, Wells delivered an impassioned defense of his young client, taking a chance by telling jurors from the onset that he wasn't going to merely poke holes in the state's case to show reasonable doubt. He wanted Rachelle exonerated.

The issue of who Rachelle is, Wells argued, loomed large: she was a mere teenage girl, plunged "in denial" about her mother's horrific fate and feeling guilt—"not legal guilt, human guilt.

"Was Rachelle Waterman giving an alibi for Jason Arrant?" asked Wells. "No, Rachelle Waterman was saying: 'You know, I don't want to accept that my mom is dead. I don't want to accept that Jason did this. I don't want to accept that I didn't see the signs'."

The detectives then pounced on this emotionally fragile girl using "interrogation techniques that border between offensive and abusive," said Wells, "and they break down Rachelle." By the end she would tell them anything they wanted to hear, just to make it stop, he said, but even then she never fully and completely confessed.

"What is it they get?" he asked, his voice rising. "They get them saying [to Rachelle]: 'You knew and did nothing about it.' Now if you assume that that is true, the law requires you find Rachelle not guilty."

Shouting and pounding the podium, Wells said, "Knowing

is not enough! Not doing anything is not enough! That's not enough!"

While the detectives refused to believe Rachelle, they clung to every final word against her by Jason Arrant, whose letters showed him to be a "deranged, stalking, manipulative, child predator," said Wells. When examined closely, the only thing incriminating in this communication between Jason and Rachelle—the reference to the "hunting trip"—was perfectly innocent. " 'Hunting trip' is smoking and drinking," he said—not murder.

The driving force in the plot, Wells argued, was not Rachelle but Jason, his obsession with his teen object of sexual desire manifesting itself as a twisted homicidal urge against her mother, whom he blamed for keeping them apart. As evidence, he said, Jason went "nuts" when Rachelle was grounded and stripped of her computer privileges. Rachelle, in contrast, was "getting along better" with her mother by late fall 2004.

"I ask you, which is more likely: that Rachelle Waterman said, 'Get rid of my mom because she's a little hard on me'?" said Wells. "Or Jason said: 'I'm getting rid of Lauri because I can't have access to Rachelle and I'm not having sex with a sixteen-year-old girl anymore'? Jason had a motive."

If Rachelle had been involved in the final murder plot, Wells argued, she would have handed over her house key, or at least told Jason about the key her father hung near the garage door, and she would have provided a floor plan to her house.

"It never happens. Why? Because Jason's not talking to her about killing her mom," said Wells. "Jason is not talking to her because Jason knows that she does not want her mom dead. It isn't that she wants her mom dead. It's that Jason wants Rachelle."

After the killing, detectives refused to accept Rachelle's denials but believed her coerced admissions while seizing upon Jason's self-serving statements that Rachelle was involved. He urged the jury not to make the same mistake police did.

"Unless you are convinced that Jason Aarrant is telling only the truth from that stand, if you have questions about what Jason Arrant said, you have to find Rachelle Waterman not guilty," said Wells. "And let's face it: Jason Arrant was a lying sack of snitch."

Jason, Wells went on, "is absolutely, completely unbelievable when he talks about Rachelle" and is "out to save his own hide" in an effort to score a plea deal.

"I don't know about anybody else but right now you can smell that brimstone from the depths of hell because the state made a deal with the devil," said Wells. "That devil is Jason Arrant. They bought his testimony to implicate a sixteen-year-old girl. . . . I know that you will find that Rachelle, like teenagers, just made stupid mistakes, that she didn't want her mom dead."

Drawing his two-hour summation to a close, Wells read a letter that Doc Waterman found on Rachelle's nightstand in November 2004 after her arrest.

"My dearest daughter, I'm sorry that things between us are tense right now. Please don't feel like I think you're a bad person because you're not. I know I worry way too much about you, but that's what moms do when they love their daughters as much as I love you."

Speaking so softly only the jury could hear him, Wells asked, "Why would she keep this. Why would this be on her nightstand? Why? It's because she loved her mom. It's because she did not want her mom to die.

"This has gone on long enough," the lawyer said. "It's time to put this to rest. We can't bring back Lauri Waterman. But you can reunite Rachelle with her dad. I ask you to do that."

The quiet of the courtroom was broken only by the sounds of crying. Doc Waterman shed his first public tears since the days after his wife's death. Sniffles came from the audience section. Three women jurors wept.

It was a different scene at the prosecution table. Throughout the summation, West had been scribbling in his notepad and whispering so loudly to Trooper Bob Claus that the jury sent a note to the judge asking her to tell them to be quiet. At 12:42 p.m., when West gave his final remarks, he shed the business-as-usual tone.

Anger crept into his voice.

"Mr. Wells gave a very dramatic closing," the prosecutor acknowledged—and he told the jury why: the defense was trying to blind the jury with emotion.

"Quite a bit of [time] was spent on Mr. Arrant, calling him a child molester, stalker. Why is he using these phrases?" asked West. "To build up an emotion in you about it. Now, why does he want to do it? Because he wants you to have a lower opinion of Mr. Arrant so you won't believe what he has to say."

He noted that Wells didn't use the same terms for Brian Radel, who also admitted to a sexual relationship with Rachelle, "because when Mr. Radel testified, he gave testimony favorable to the defendant."

Jason was no stalker, West insisted, and as a criminal defense attorney Wells knew it. All the e-mails, letters, and testimony showed that the contact between Jason and Rachelle was consensual. "His argument is based on emotion, being dramatic is what he's trying to do," West said.

On one point West said he agreed with the defense.

"I don't doubt for a second that Miss Waterman would not be able to kill somebody," he said. "That's why she contacted Mr. Arrant. Mr. Arrant couldn't kill anyone, that's why he contacted Mr. Radel. Unfortunately for all of us, Mr. Radel could kill people. He had it in him to kill somebody. The other two, they could get involved in it but couldn't actually do the actual killing with their own hands."

Which brought West back to the concept of a conspiracy. He told the jury again that the law didn't require that Rachelle kill her mother with her own hands, that it was enough that she was a participant in the plot.

"Look at all the evidence," West said. "All of this shows that Miss Waterman was involved in the conspiracy to kill her mother, and that conspiracy went to its finale with her death and her being murdered. And that makes Miss Waterman as much responsible as Mr. Arrant and Mr. Radel."

West went back to his seat, having expressed as much prosecutorial indignation as this amiable Texan could muster. But would it be enough?

CHAPTER TWENTY

Bob Claus saw the jurors crying but remained confident of what he saw as the strength of the prosecution case and of the evidence he and the other investigators had collected. Before trial, the state's team had decided to proceed with a straightforward, no-nonsense presentation of evidence, what he later called a "logical, piece by piece building of the case." As Steve Wells gave his stirring summation, Claus and prosecutor West conferred by whisper and felt they could counter his key points with facts and logic and, most of all, the law, as read to the jurors by the judge. Rachelle's age didn't matter; the law said so in black and white.

But the jury had deliberated for six hours on Wednesday, February 8, when it became clear that Wells had struck a nerve. The judge got a note from the jury asking for the legal definition of the word "intended." She instructed them that the word meant the panel had to find a "conscious objective" that led to the result, in this case murder. The jury next wanted to know if it had to find every legal element of each offense to reach a verdict; the judge said they did. Then the panel wanted to hear the recordings of the actual police interviews with Jason and Brian, which—except for Jason's jailhouse interview discussion with Sergeant Habib—were referenced in court but not played for the jury. The judge said no, but invited the jury to rehear any testimony from the trial. The judge also turned down the jury's request to see an exhibit put together by Rachelle's attorney, a timeline of key events in the case. The judge said that was Wells's interpretation and not evidence.

The panel retired for the night, returned the next morning, and deliberated all day Thursday and all day Friday without reaching a verdict, apparently hung up on the very question that Wells had asked them: Did Rachelle want her mother dead? This was a good sign for the defense and cause for worry for the prosecution team.

After a weekend break, the jury returned Monday for another day of deliberations, and still no decision. On Tuesday morning, ninety minutes into the fifth day of deliberations, the jury finally sent the judge a note: they could not reach a unanimous verdict. Attorneys assembled for a hearing and Judge Collins declared a mistrial.

It was a momentarily confusing scene. After more than two years of investigation, litigation, and incarceration, Rachelle was neither guilty nor innocent. Wells announced there was a "good chance" the state would try her again, and the judge set a later court date to reconsider bail. Rachelle was still as much a prisoner today as she was the night she was arrested. She burst into tears as she was led back to the women's jail. Her father, overcome with emotion, was comforted by Wells. "You know she's not guilty," the attorney said.

When they later spoke to reporters, the jurors said that early on they came to an important agreement: that Jason was most responsible for the murder of Lauri Waterman. They agreed that he wanted Lauri out of the way so that he could be with Rachelle. They also agreed that Rachelle had invented her stories of abuse by her mother. They didn't doubt that Rachelle had wanted her mother gone, but the panelists agreed that it was likely the exaggerated complaints of a teenage girl. One juror said her own sister had expressed similar sentiments about their mother. Where they hung was on the question of Rachelle's involvement in the murder plot. The two voting for conviction were swayed by her statements during the interrogation. "Clinched it," juror Curtis Blackwell later told NBC's *Dateline*. "What can I say? She admitted it." But the ten other jurors found cause for reasonable doubt. Although many were not comfortable with letting Rachelle get off scot-free, they decided that the investigators coerced the confession.

"For a fifteen-year-old who's scared out of her mind, they're professionals," juror Andrea Jones told *Dateline*. "They know how to get people to talk. And I mean if she said, 'Yes, I did it,' I don't even know if I would put a lot of weight on it just because through the whole thing she stuck with 'no.'"

It was just as Bob Claus had feared.

"All of us failed to realize the power of what we saw as irrational arguments," Claus said later. "Wells was either emphasizing things that hadn't been emphasized in testimony or talking about things as fact that weren't proved."

The defense had branded Jason as a lying, stalking pervert and portrayed Rachelle as a naïve girl who got in over her head. Claus saw both much differently, particularly Rachelle, whom he believed had played investigators just as effectively as she had Jason and Brian. The trooper had wondered if the prosecution shouldn't have tried to introduce more evidence of Rachelle's mind games with Jason and Brian. "The sexual material pretty graphically showed this isn't Miss Sweet Sixteen," Claus said. "The jury never got to see that."

Three weeks later Rachelle returned to court, seeking to have her bail reduced so she could be free while awaiting word on whether she would face another trial. Judge Collins took the bench and the two lawyers—prosecutor Stephen West and defense attorney Steven Wells—announced their presence over the courtroom speakers. West remained in Ketchikan and Wells was in Anchorage for what they thought would be a standard bail hearing. When the prosecution wrapped up its case, Wells made the defense's usual request for a directed verdict of acquittal on the grounds the state didn't meet its burden of proving guilt beyond a reasonable doubt. As usual, the judge denied the request.

But what the lawyers didn't know at the time was that as

Judge Collins watched Rachelle's interrogation video again and heard the testimony of investigators, particularly Sergeant Randy McPherron, something stirred. This former criminal defense lawyer started having second thoughts about the prosecution's case, and at the hearing on Tuesday, March 7, she aired them for the first time.

Several aspects of the interrogation bothered the judge. She didn't think the investigators were being straight with the jury about their efforts to contact Rachelle's father before taking Rachelle to the police station. She didn't think that Rachelle fully understood her right to have her father present during questioning. She didn't like that the investigators lied to Rachelle when they told her that what she said would be confidential when they knew they were going to use it against her. In all, Judge Collins said, the prosecution had a heavy legal burden to prove that a juvenile's statements to police were not coerced, and in her mind, having now considered the "totality of the circumstances," she now, upon reflection, didn't think the prosecution had met that burden.

Judge Collins dismissed the indictment against Rachelle.

In the courtroom, Doc Waterman gasped. Tears came to Rachelle's eyes. Both lawyers were momentarily stunned—Wells at his good fortune, West at what he saw as a blindsiding by the court. "You've really caught the state by surprise, Your Honor," said West. Pressed for an explanation, the judge said, "I have reconsidered. That was the order I entered today."

The prosecution was given two weeks to decide whether to file new charges, and since there was still a good chance the state would do so, Judge Collins ordered bail for Rachelle. But instead of $150,000, it would be only $50,000, payable by a bond that would cost $5,000 in cash.

Doc Waterman said he could raise the money the next day—the banks by now had already closed—and so Rachelle was led crying out of the courtroom for what would be her last night in jail. When Doc left the courthouse, he was hugged by several jurors.

"This is a good thing," he told reporters. "At least I get my daughter back."

The next day Rachelle walked out of the Lemon Creek Correctional Facility after spending a year and two months in a cell. A small group of reporters gathered outside the jail, but neither Doc nor Rachelle had anything to say to them. The last image of Rachelle was a glimpse of her in the backseat of a car, reading the newspaper as her father drove off.

Where they went from there, nobody really knew. She didn't go back to Craig, which was to be expected. The judge herself had suggested Rachelle stay away from her hometown, where nerves were still raw and the chatter in the coffee shops and bookstore, on the docks and in the schools, still ran strongly against Rachelle. Craig had lost more than Lauri Waterman. People locked their doors at night for the first time, eyed outsiders with more suspicion, and wondered whom or what to blame. Jason and Brian? Rachelle? Her parents? Life on an isolated island? Or even the Internet?

As months and then years passed, Rachelle never returned to the place she once branded as "Hell, Alaska," this tiny community that served as the setting for her crappy life. But this spruce-scented strip of land in the sea left her with her happiest memories, from her best Christmas ever to a T-shirt store job that gave her the first taste of adult responsibility and rewards, to a sports triumph that had the citizens parading in the streets.

Doc came back, still sold real estate, still advertised in the local paper. Many still didn't know what to make of this man oddly calm in the face of crisis, whether to hate him for raising a demon child or sympathize with a man who had done the best he could with one tough teenager, only to suffer an unimaginable loss. Doc was still spotted around town every day. He'd wave to people at the bank, even people like Bob Claus and Mark Habib, who all thought—and still think—his daughter got away with murder.

Rachelle had disappeared. The Internet's most infamous

blogger never blogged again, at least not under her own name, and her whereabouts became a favorite game of speculation. Doc would be asked many times, and usually he refused to say. Once he said she was in Florida getting a college degree. Her lawyer, Steven Wells, also refused to say where she was—for her own safety, he said. It seemed that Rachelle Waterman, even as she entered her twenties, was still a girl who was being protected.

In time, as life returned to normal on Prince of Wales Island, those same people who cheered at Rachelle's volleyball games remained divided on whether she was a tragically misguided teen or, as Sergeant Habib had called her, an up-and-coming black widow. Even after so much had happened and so many secrets were revealed, many still asked who Rachelle really was. It was a question she often explored herself as she tapped away on her brand-new computer in her warm bedroom on cold and rainy nights. "I live in Alaska," she once wrote, "a very small town which I'm sure most of you have never heard of. And no, I don't live in an igloo. I'm involved in a little bit of everything and am usually kept pretty busy."

AFTERWORD

The day after Rachelle left jail, Brian Radel and Jason Arrant were formally sentenced in a Ketchikan court. The prison terms had long since been negotiated, and both men made good on their deals by testifying. But the hearing on Thursday, March 9, offered both men a chance to explain themselves, to try to come to terms, and to seek, if not forgiveness, then some semblance of understanding.

Anchorage psychologist Susan LaGrande, who spent a day conducting tests on Jason, came away with the same impression that the investigators had: Jason was a moody, socially isolated man-child whose "paranoia scale was off the charts" and who had retreated into a world of video games and fantasy. His parents testified that Jason was a sad and lonely child.

Jason spoke for himself, telling Judge Collins, "I can never say how sorry I am. What I did was a horrible thing. I won't dispute that by pretending to be innocent." His was a crime born out of trusting too much in a girl. Rachelle told him stories of mental and physical abuse by her mother, told him she was in danger, "and I bought it hook, line, and sinker," Jason said, "because I loved her with all my heart."

Jason turned to Doc Waterman, who sat in the audience section, and said, "You have every right to hate me. Instead, I can only offer my deepest apologies and regrets, for whatever that may be worth." He also offered a message to the woman he watched die on a rainy Alaskan night: "To Lauri Waterman, if you're listening, I can never tell you enough how sorry I am, no matter how many prayers I offer up. Rest in paradise."

Judge Collins sentenced Jason to the agreed-upon fifty years in prison, with the possibility of parole in thirty, and suggested he serve his time in a facility with mental health treatment available.

As for Brian, his public defender, Marvin Hamilton, portrayed his client as a man who committed a bad act "for a noble reason," a product of parental abuse who empathized with Rachelle and "wanted to prove he could act selflessly." The attorney bolstered his argument by reading from Clarence Darrow's *Attorney for the Damned* and *Adventures of Huckleberry Finn*.

After hearing from Brian, who said, "I wish Lauri were alive today," the judge saw not a Mark Twain character but a "cold-blooded killer," and sentenced him to the already negotiated ninety-nine years in prison, with the possibility of release in forty-six years.

In an interview later with NBC's *Dateline*, Brian said he thought about Lauri's murder every night and had come to believe that Rachelle never faced any real danger from her mom. Asked if, despite his change of heart, he still loved Rachelle, Brian said, "I still do," and said she was not to be blamed for everybody's pain. "I personally think she's a good person," he said. "I don't think she wanted her mom killed."

In the same program, Lauri's brother Don Martelli Jr. had a different view: "I'm pretty bitter about it and I don't know if I can forgive her."

Two days after the sentencing of Jason and Brian, Rachelle's attorney Steven Wells made a career change. He announced it on his Alaska Blawg, in what he called "one of the saddest and yet most exciting posts I have written." After months of soul-searching about his future, he decided to leave the Office of the Public Advocate and hang his shingle in private practice. He was burned out by the travel and the workload. He would continue to represent Rachelle while exploring new areas of criminal defense. "The Waterman case has provided me unprecedented publicity," he wrote, "which means that this is a good time to make this move."

He wasn't the only one to feel this way. Disillusioned by law enforcement because of the Waterman case, Bob Claus retired from the state troopers and took a job with the Southeast Alaska Conservation Council, an environmental group to protect the forests. Those years of lamenting the damage to his beloved island by clear-cutting prompted him to finally do something about it. When he's not traveling to Washington to lobby lawmakers, he works out of a little office in Klawock not far from the trooper post. He enjoys the new work but remains bitter about how his last big investigation ended.

"I thought this case was a vindication of the way that I think police work ought to be done. I lived with those people I worked for, I did the job the best way I could. When I saw what happened, I knew that we had to talk to Jason Arrant and Brian Radel right away. I knew who did it and I knew why they did it," he said. "In three days, we had three people in jail. That's as good as it gets. And it didn't fucking matter a bit."

Chief Jim See also retired, and Sergeant Mark Habib was promoted to his old job, though, in time, he, too, was eyeing a retirement, in Las Vegas.

The case did stay in the news, though not making the headlines it had before. After Judge Collins refused to reconsider her decision to throw out the charges against Rachelle, the state of Alaska asked the Alaska Court of Appeals in April 2006 to grant a new trial. It would take more than two years before the three-judge appellate panel heard oral arguments. Assistant Attorney General Diane Wendlandt minced no words, saying that if the state lost the appeal and the interrogation was ruled inadmissible, "you'll be letting a murderer off the hook." Rachelle didn't attend the hearing, but her father did.

The panel finally ruled in December 2008. It was a mixed decision. The reviewing court agreed with prosecutors that

Rachelle was a bright girl who knowingly and willingly went to the police station and spoke without her father present, and for a time everything about her interrogation was legal and admissible. The appeals court said that a jury may watch as Rachelle admitted to talking to Jason by phone from Anchorage and imploring him to call off any murder plot he might have been considering.

But the appeals court was troubled by the second part of the interrogation. When McPherron got heavy-handed, telling Rachelle that this was a serious offense, that she would be tried as an adult, that she was playing in the big leagues, the appeals court felt, "arguably, this speech constitutes a prohibited threat, a threat of harsher treatment if Waterman declined to cooperate." By law, this can be construed as coercion, but the court said that Rachelle withstood the pressure and didn't change her statement.

"It thus seems clear that Waterman's will to resist was not overcome," the appeals court found.

But when Sergeant McPherron left the room and Sergeant. Habib launched into his speech about being straight with the detective, the interrogation had entered improper territory, the appeals court ruled. The justices took particular issue with Habib telling Rachelle that if she was straight with McPherron, "I will stand up, he will stand up, and the DA will stand up and say she cooperated."

"Sergeant Habib threatened Waterman with harsher consequences for not cooperating with the investigation," the appeals court wrote. "In our view, Sergeant Habib's statements constitute an impermissible threat. . . . Waterman's statements following this threat no longer rebut the presumption of involuntariness."

Everything she said that followed, including her admissions that she knew about the murder plot and did virtually nothing to stop it, would be barred at a new trial.

Despite the setback, Ketchikan district attorney Stephen West obtained a new grand jury indictment against Rachelle, charging her with first- and second-degree murder and a lesser charge of criminally negligent homicide. In March

2006, Rachelle posted $50,000 bond and remained out of sight for the next five years until her second trial began.

It was a twenty-two-year-old Rachelle who entered the courtroom on Monday, January 24, 2011, for the start of her trial. In the nearly seven years since her mother's murder, she had changed little physically: she was still fair-skinned and rosy-cheeked despite having made her new home, it was confirmed, in Florida—as far away from Craig, Alaska, as she could get while still being in the continental United States. Her reddish-brown hair was long and dark and held in a ponytail.

The case was to have been tried in Ketchikan, but passions still burned even five years after the first trial ended in a hung jury. Half of the would-be jurors filling out questionnaires said they felt Rachelle was "probably guilty." That left just eighty-four people who had not heard of the case or who had no opinion. The new judge on the case, William Carey, feared that the remaining pool was too small from which to pick an unbiased jury, and with a trial date now finally bearing down and set in stone after years of delays, he didn't want to risk a false start. The judge contacted the presiding judge in Anchorage and a decision was made. The case moved north.

The Nesbett Courthouse, guarded by a pair of twelve-and-a-half-foot tall totem poles of a raven and an eagle carved out of cedar, was in the city's downtown section near gift shops and restaurants. It was not far from the Marriott, from which Rachelle had spoken on the phone to Jason Arrant one night seven years earlier. The courthouse was big and modern, the staff accustomed to high-profile trials. In 2007, an Olympia, Washington, housewife and mother named Mechele Linehan was convicted in the 1996 shooting murder of her fiancé, fisherman Kent Leppink, in a sensational case that exposed Linehan's secret past as a stripper in a club south of Anchorage. Her conviction was overturned on appeal and she is awaiting a new trial.

For Rachelle, the retrial came with more than a new judge and a new courtroom. A shift in attitudes about juvenile crime that had begun even before her first trial now gained momentum. In 2005, while Rachelle was awaiting the start of her first trial, the U.S. Supreme Court outlawed the death penalty for defendants under age eighteen, citing some of the reasons that her defense had raised at the first trial: younger people's characters still being shaped, their maturity still developing, their decision making more influenced by peer pressure than adults' decision making is. With youth crime declining in recent years, states began taking a more critical look at the wave of laws calling for the prosecutions of younger teens as adults.

Rachelle's second trial unfolded in cold and icy January and February—winters are more severe in Anchorage than in Craig, the days even shorter—with no significant new evidence. Not only did the prosecution lack the interview statements ruled inadmissible by the appeals court, but one key witness also didn't appear. Risking his plea deal with a possible contempt charge, Jason Arrant refused to testify. Instead, the prosecution played a recording of his testimony from the first trial. (Brian Radel did appear, giving the same unemotional account of kidnapping and killing Lauri Waterman.)

Rachelle again waived her right to testify in her own defense, and on Thursday, February 17, the jury announced its verdict. Rachelle was acquitted of the most serious charge against her—murder—but the jury did come to a guilty verdict on criminally negligent homicide. The panel found that the seventeen-year-old Rachelle was so outrageously negligent, had deviated so far from what a reasonable person would have done, that she had caused her mother's murder.

It was not what prosecutors and many of the investigators had wanted originally, but they said they were satisified. Prosecutor Stephen West, who tried the second case with the help with another DA, Jean Seaton from the Sitka office, told reporters he was "glad" a jury finally found that Rachelle was "responsible in some way" for Lauri's murder. The charge carried felony weight: the possible sentence ranged from two to ten years in prison.

Rachelle's attorney, Steve Wells, who also returned for the retrial, expressed relief that she was at least not convicted of murder, but said he planned to appeal. Rachelle's father, Carl, told the Associated Press, "One of my strongest emotions right now is anger." He said his daughter never should have been charged with anything.

As for Rachelle, the woman whose teenage words formed the foundation of a murder case had nothing to say this time.